MUSIC

IN THE ELEMENTARY SCHOOL

AN ACTIVITIES APPROACH TO
MUSIC METHODS AND MATERIALS

MUSIC

IN THE ELEMENTARY SCHOOL

ROBERT EVANS NYE

School of Music, University of Oregon

VERNICE TROUSDALE NYE

School of Education, University of Oregon

PRENTICE - HALL, INC.

Englewood Cliffs, N. J.

LIBRARY OF CONGRESS
CATALOG CARD NO.: 57-9391

First printing .... April, 1957
Second printing .... September, 1957
Third printing .... January, 1958
Fourth printing .... July, 1958

PRINTED IN THE UNITED STATES OF AMERICA

60815

To the authors of basal music series,
who have made a major contribution to music education

Preface

Elementary teacher preparation should include a clear concept of the place occupied by music activities in the classroom. In college classes, a workshop-type organization helps to develop this concept, for it provides the student the opportunity to plan, execute, and evaluate the various activities with his instructor and his classmates. Often he assumes the role of either an elementary school child or a teacher in charge of a group of children. Chapter One of *Music in the Elementary School* outlines a background for this approach, and subsequent chapters offer suggestions for its development in classes for students of both elementary education and music education.

Some college classes begin with emphasis on singing (Chapter Four). Others stress instrument playing (Chapter Three) or listening (Chapter Five). Whatever his preference, the instructor will find the organization of this book flexible enough to fit into his program. The authors find the sequence of activities given here most suitable for them, particularly when working with students who have a limited musical background. Concentrating upon rhythmic responses and the playing of instruments, Chapters Two and Three review music fundamentals and prepare the way for the section on singing in Chapter Four.

The Music Series Reference Guides make possible the use of music series books as subsidiary texts. The student thus becomes familiar with the specific titles he will find in his student teaching and professional teaching situations. In some colleges, the elementary education major may purchase the series book of a certain grade level; in other schools, sets of these books are provided for students' use in the library and in the classroom. Access to these sets of books is a necessity for the music major. Certain states have adopted one basal music series; others have made multiple adoptions. *Music in the Elementary School* is useful in either instance. The songs (page

vii

numbers) listed in the Guides should be regarded as music to be evaluated, not as material listed selectively.

Basic equipment for an activities class includes recordings, phonograph, piano, Autoharps, keyboard instruments of the "bells" type, and a variety of percussion instruments. The student should own some easy-to-play instrument, such as the Song Flute, Flutophone, or Tonette. Movable classroom furniture is also necessary, and a reference shelf containing all current methods books in the elementary music education area is recommended.

Basic Music for Classroom Teachers by Robert E. Nye and Bjornar Bergethon (Prentice-Hall, 1954) has as its purpose the learning of music fundamentals in a manner which introduces some methodology, but *Music in the Elementary School* emphasizes the learning of methods and materials. Although either book may be used independently, it is the authors' intention that they be used in sequence for the music preparation of the education major.

The education and teaching experience of one of the authors has been predominantly within the field of music; that of the other has been predominantly within the field of education. They hope that their collaboration in this volume will reinforce the position of music as an essential part of elementary education.

ROBERT EVANS NYE

VERNICE TROUSDALE NYE

Contents

Music in the Elementary Classroom

One

There exist in the elementary schools of the United States three general groupings of music teachers. One is composed of classroom teachers who are expected to know how to teach every aspect of the total educational program. It is assumed by most educators that these teachers can know the individual child very well, can include music at whatever point it is needed during the school day, and can achieve interrelatedness of music and other subjects. A second group is composed of specialized music teachers who are responsible solely for teaching music. Most educators consider the teachers in this group capable of the most creditable work in the subject-matter skills of the music area and best able to organize a logical sequence of music activities throughout a school. The third group is composed of both classroom teachers and music teachers. The classroom teachers in this group, like those in the first group, bear the basic responsibility for the teaching of music, but they have the aid of specially trained music teachers who work with them on a *cooperative* basis. This latter group should be able to combine the advantages of the other groups. The trend of the times favors this plan as one that can eventually make possible for children a superior learning situation.

Any specially trained music teacher who has the duties of elementary music consultant (coordinator or helper) needs to be aware of the background and training of the classroom teachers with whom he may work. We shall therefore proceed from the point of view of the elementary classroom teacher, for whom this book is written.

1

WHAT CONSTITUTES A GOOD LEARNING ENVIRONMENT FOR CHILDREN?

The four major factors constituting the learning environment for children are the teacher, the physical environment, the social environment, and the curriculum.

The teacher

The most important influence in the development of a good environment for learning is the teacher. He understands the characteristics of a good school for children, and he knows what qualities are needed by the teacher in this kind of school. He is sensitive to the needs of *each* child. Whatever he teaches, such a person shows enthusiasm and interest based on the confidence that what he is doing is significant to the physical, social, emotional, aesthetic, and intellectual development of children. He is happy, well-adjusted, and really wants to teach. He understands the total school program and works cooperatively with his fellow teachers. He is professionally qualified; therefore, he knows and practices the Teachers' Code of Ethics (see Appendix A). He continues to grow personally and professionally. He understands the problems of the community, realizes the influence of the community on the curriculum of the school, and appreciates the value of working closely with parents.

The physical environment

The educational philosophy of the teacher is reflected in the physical environment of the classroom. Since the physical environment is of great importance in the development of children both as individuals and as members of groups, it is a matter of prime consideration for the good teacher. The classroom should be a healthful place for children to live; therefore, the teacher is conscious of the effect of temperature, ventilation, lighting, cleanliness, furniture arrangement, and color schemes on the pupils' physical and emotional health.

The good classroom is spacious and has moveable furniture that is adjustable to the physical and social needs of the individuals comprising the group. Essential to a good classroom is a variety of instructional materials. There are many attractive books appropriate for the varied interests and abilities of children; these should include a basal music series book for each child and supplementary music books.

The various art media are present: paints, brushes, easels, chalk, metal, wood, paper, looms, and clay. Chalkboards, bulletin boards, and flannel boards are present in ample numbers. The teaching of music becomes simplified and more attractive through use of such equipment as the following: record player and recordings, metal xylophones, percussion instruments (both pupil-constructed and commercially made), piano (used in new ways), flannel board, Auto-harp or Harmolin, recorder-type and flute-type instruments, staff liner and tape recorder. Equipment made available to the classroom when needed includes projectors (slide and strip, motion-picture and opaque), motion-picture films and film strips, slides and duplicating equipment. Available in the primary-grade classroom are blocks, toys, and games for creative play.

A contemporary trend in classroom arrangement is establishing a *center of interest.* For example, a science center may be constructed on table, shelf, or counter space where specimens of plants, animals, and minerals are assembled, together with references (bulletins, books, pictures) and materials for experimentation and examination, such as batteries, magnets, thermometers, and chemicals. Other possible centers of interest are those in reading, social studies, arithmetic, art, and music. The music center has often been called the "music corner." Here may be pitch-producing materials of wood, metal, glass, and stone with which children may experiment, pointing toward later experiments with pitches produced by water glasses and bottles and by wooden strips which may be arranged to form a xylophone. There may be a metal "xylophone" and music to play on it. Pictures of musicians and musical instruments, and appropriate books, articles, and news clippings about music can be centered here. The children should feel free to use such centers of interest during the part of the school day set aside for special interests or at other times, such as before and after school and after satisfactorily completing assigned work.

Every school needs an acoustically-treated auditorium. The stage of this auditorium should be large enough to accommodate large groups, and it should be easily accessible to the classroom.

The social environment

The center-of-interest concept is in keeping with the present-day philosophy that children need a social environment where opportunities are provided for each child to make progress according to his individual capacities, needs, and interests. In a good school, provision is made for pupils to participate in the planning, directing, and evaluating of school and classroom activities. Through such *group action,* they learn to respect the opinions of others and to work well with others. They feel free to discuss and to share their ideas and to study and examine issues in the light of all available facts. They are given guidance in the solution of problems in terms of their own thinking and study. In a good school, children gain an intelligent and realistic understanding of present-day society and of their own problems of living in relation to the problems of all social groups on community, state, national, and worldwide levels.

In order for children to be happy in a classroom, certain basic human needs must be satisfied. Each child needs affection, security, success, and a feeling of belonging. A good teacher provides a classroom environment in which these needs are met. This necessitates a proper pupil-teacher relationship. Such a relationship, when it is achieved, is the best foundation for good learning conditions and good discipline. Twelve helpful suggestions for building rapport with children are given by Burr, Harding, and Jacobs:[1]

1. Be friendly but not familiar. Your own childishness should be past. Children prefer you to be a sympathetic, kindly adult.
2. Know not only the children's names but also much about their personal backgrounds which affect their personal relationships in the classroom.
3. Recognize sensitively children's individual differences. Build constructively upon these differences rather than expect every child to fit into an identical pattern.
4. Take into account the maturation level of the group and proceed to get better acquainted and to establish rapport in the light of these observable growth gradients.
5. Be as consistent a personality in dealing with the children as is humanly feasible. Do not be too strict one day and too lax the next.
6. Face each day's work realistically and cheerfully with the children. Even when you do not feel cheerful, you must remember the negative effect upon children if you reflect your problems and anxieties.
7. Create a permissive atmosphere in which every child is, first of all, free to be himself and free to let you see him be himself.
8. Plan with and in consideration for children in such democratic

ways that your guidance is prized by the other members of the group.

9. Participate actively and naturally with children in what they enjoy doing—in their work and their play.

10. Take time to listen to children's questions, problems, joys, dilemmas, and treat their confidences clinically and confidentially.

11. Demonstrate to the children that you believe in them and in their potentialities.

12. Encourage every child in the cultivation of self-confidence, self-expression, independence, and social effectiveness.

The curriculum

The curriculum includes all the experiences made available to boys and girls in the classroom, in the school, and in the community. A well-rounded school program provides for the appropriate inter-relatedness of the following areas:[2]

Areas[3] of Work	*Time Allotment*
I. *Daily Living Activities.* Mid-morning and noon lunch, rest (which can include listening to appropriate music), toileting, washing hands, and housekeeping duties.	1/6 of the day
II. *Social Living Program.* Group socializing experiences which emphasize problem solving in history, geography, science and health and which involve such activities as planning and discussing, reading and research; trips, observations, experiments; learning appropriate songs, poems, and dances; using audio-visual aids; and creative work—writing poems and songs, creating rhythms and chants, and designing costumes in connection with a unit of work.	1/3 or more of the day
III. *Skills.* Small-group or individual instruction in reading, writing, spelling, listening, speaking, music, and arithmetic skills.	1/4 to 1/3 of the day
IV. *Recreational and Creative Activities.* Art, music, poetry, story-telling, dramatics, rhythms, literature, and play activities. (Time *scheduled* for music is in this area.)	1/4 or less of the day

[2] Adapted from the 1950 *Alabama Course of Study and Guide for Teachers* (Montgomery: State Department of Education).

[3] The term *area* should not be confused with the term *class period.*

V. *Special Interests.* Individual projects, reading, research, and experiments in any worthy area of special interest; special group interests such as band, orchestra, and chorus.   less than 1/6 of the day

The above allotment varies from day to day. The daily program must be flexible in order to provide for the children's varying interests and needs. The different stages in the development of an experience require different lengths of time. The amount of flexibility varies in accordance with the age of the children, the size of the class, and the personal needs of the group.

In order for music to function properly in the lives of boys and girls, it must be an integral and vital part of this program. It belongs logically and naturally *in each of the above areas,* and the good teacher sees opportunities for its use and employs it at appropriate times throughout the school day as is shown in the following paragraphs.

Daily living activities. All phases of a well-balanced school program are closely related in order to provide the balance of activities needed for the children's normal development. Properly organized daily routine activities establish an environment conducive to a feeling of security and freedom. Physical needs must be met before learning in music or in any other activity becomes satisfying and worthwhile. Daily living needs are taken care of by both the children and the teacher so that work in all areas of learning will be more attractive and effective throughout the entire day. *Music is frequently employed in connection with resting in primary grades and with relieving fatigue by providing variety in all grades.*

Social living program. In this area, experiences center around the personal and social problems of living. Pupils use many fields of knowledge; therefore, a large block of time is essential for carrying out these activities. The subject matter incorporated in this program includes history, geography, health, and science, with language arts, art, and music also included whenever they add to the solution of a problem. In most states, the social living program for grades one and two concerns problems of living in the immediate community—home, school, and neighborhood. Children in grades three and four are generally concerned with the community and its relationship to other communities. In grades five and six the major emphases are on problems of the community, state, and nation, and their relationship to the problems of other countries. Since the areas of study for the various grades have been chosen by educators according to the needs, interests, and past experiences of the particular age groups, it follows that combining music with these areas is one of the surest ways to make music meaningful and purposeful. In turn, *music has the power to "illuminate" subject matter, thereby adding interest, understanding, satisfaction, and enjoyment to learning. It motivates learning because it appeals to children's imagination, emotions, and moods.*

Skills. This area provides for the teaching of reading, speaking, listening, writing and spelling, scientific thinking, computation, work-study skills, music skills, and social skills. The need for work on these and other skills grows out of the social-living program, thus making the activity more meaningful to the children. Ideally, the most effective time for teaching them is when the need arises—no matter in which area. But, since all children do not need the same amount of guidance, a special skills program is necessary. Special assistance in music is thus given to individuals and groups in the class, just as it is given in developing any of the other skills. Activities designed to teach skills can comprise one of the most interesting and satisfying areas of the daily program when the children understand the application of these skills in terms of everyday needs in solving problems.

Recreational and creative activities. This is the part of the day in which provision is made for the special scheduling of art, music, literature, and physical education. During the time thus provided, interests and abilities in music can be developed. Pupils are encouraged to sing, to experiment with and play various simple instruments, to listen to appropriate radio programs and recordings, to write songs and words for songs, and to participate in rhythms and create rhythmic responses. Experiences in the social-living program often motivate experimentation in the recreational and creative activities area. However, activities in art, music, literature, and physical education must not necessarily be related to other activities of the day; they may be enjoyed for their own value and interest to children. Wholesome learning implies *satisfying* experiences with what is to be learned. During this time, the pupils should feel free to express themselves through many media. *Music can be an important means whereby children experience success, belonging, and satisfaction.*

Special interests. Although individual interests are considered in recreational and creative activities and in the social-living program, some children cannot be satisfactorily dealt with in these areas. Therefore, time is provided for children to pursue their special interests in science experiments, in music groups such as band, orchestra, and chorus, in art projects, and in individual research in connection with various subjects (including reading about music and musicians). Special-interest groups seldom meet more than once or twice a week. In order for these activities to be of real value in developing genuine special interests, careful planning with individuals and small groups is essential. It is in this area that the children who possess superior interest and ability in music have an opportunity to develop beyond the point ordinarily possible in activities that include the entire class.

Any classroom teacher who understands the characteristics, needs, and interests of his group, and who has a thorough understanding of how children learn, will plan, first in advance and then with the children, worthwhile activities to pursue in each area. If this is done, discipline problems seldom arise. Of course, today we would like to eliminate the traditional meaning of the word "discipline" since it implies dictatorial control of the children by the teacher. The traditional meaning of "discipline" contradicts the philosophy expressed in this chapter. A curriculum that is purposefully and democratically planned is more conducive to the development of self-direction (self-discipline) than one imposed by the teacher.

HOW CHILDREN GROW AND LEARN

In order to be effective, the teacher must consistently enlarge his understanding of how children grow and learn. The child learns in any situation as a complete personality. He is a product of everything that has happened to him in the past and of everything that is happening to him now. All experiences of the child would have to be analyzed before one could have a complete understanding of his total behavior.

How children learn

Understanding some of the opinions concerning the learning process stimulates teachers to seek better ways of organizing the experiences of children. Some of these beliefs are as follows:

1. The child learns best in a rich and stimulating environment.
2. Learning takes place best in real-life situations in which the

learner participates and sees a need for learning.

3. Learning is more effective when the activities selected relate to the past experiences and the maturation level of the learner.

4. Wholesome learning implies satisfying experiences with what is to be learned.

5. Learning takes place best when the learner's daily living needs are being met adequately and when he is in good health.

6. Effective learning involves continuous participation by the learner in self and group evaluation.

The characteristics of children and implications for the teaching of music

To be able to teach children skillfully, it is vital that the teacher know each one of them and perceive how he interacts with people. In order to understand a child, the teacher needs to know the general characteristics of children. It should be recognized, however, that no one list of general characteristics will apply to all children at any age, since there are several maturation levels within an individual child and marked variations within groups of children.

Lists of characteristics and needs of children may be found in many professional education books. A portion of one such list, "A Chart of Normal Development," which concerns children aged six through eleven (commonly grades one through six) is reproduced below. Opposite this the authors have listed implications for the teaching of music.

A Chart of Normal Development[4]	Implications for Teaching Music
AT SIX	
Physical Development	
Growth proceeding more slowly; a lengthening out.	Suitable furniture and seating arrangements. Begin singing with little calls and phrases. Small repertory of simple songs well learned and frequently repeated.
Large muscles better developed than small ones.	Stress fundamental and free rhythmic movements; finger plays develop small muscles.
Eyes not yet mature; tendency toward far-sightedness.	Rote singing; rote playing of simple melodies on Song Bells; incidental use of large-sized notation.

[4] From *These Are Your Children* by Jenkins, Shacter, and Bauer (Chicago: Scott, Foresman, and Company, 1949). Copyright, 1949, by Scott, Foresman, and Company, and used with their permission.

A Chart of Normal Development[5]	Implications for Teaching Music
Permanent teeth begin to appear.	
Heart is in period of rapid growth.	Time allotted to strenuous rhythmic activity should be brief.
Characteristic Reactions	
Eager to learn, exuberant, restless, overactive and easily fatigued.	Music employed both for physical action and for rest; music used to relieve tensions.
Self-assertive; aggressive; wants to be first; less cooperative than at five; keen competition and much boasting.	Group activities in music needed to teach cooperation; individual activities in music encouraged; the child enjoys songs about himself, what he does and likes.
Whole body is involved in whatever is done.	Listening to music in terms of bodily response; "doing what the music tells him to do."
Learning best through active participation.	Listening experiences through individual and group experimenting with tones produced by wood, metal, glass, skin, stone.
Inconsistency in level of maturity evidenced—regression when tired; often maturity level lower at home than with outsiders.	
Inept at activities using small muscles.	Action songs and singing games using large muscles.
Relatively short periods of interest.	Music activities brief; 20 minutes of varied activities is sufficient.
Difficulty in making decisions.	Children need opportunities to choose songs and to suggest interpretations and dramatization.
Group activities popular; boys' and girls' interests beginning to differ.	Action songs, singing games and percussion instruments as group activities.
Much spontaneous dramatization.	Creative dramatization of music; spontaneous song-creating.
Special Needs	
Encouragement, ample praise, warmth, and great patience from adults.	Patience required of teacher since children learn slowly; much help needed in learning to hear pitch differences and in tone matching.

[5] From *These Are Your Children* by Jenkins, Shacter, and Bauer (Chicago: Scott, Foresman, and Company, 1949). Copyright, 1949, by Scott, Foresman, and Company, and used with their permission.

A Chart of Normal Development[6]	Implications for Teaching Music
Ample opportunity for activity of many kinds, especially for use of large muscles.	Accommodate individual differences through a varied program of music activities including rhythmic responses, listening, singing, playing instruments, and creative responses of all types.
Wise supervision with a minimum of interference.	Allow sufficient freedom for creativity despite necessary direct guidance.
Concrete learning situations and active, direct participation.	Exploring Song Bells and piano and learning to play very simple melodies on them; using percussion instruments with music; songs concerning the known and the immediate: things, animals, people, activities.
Some responsibilities; though without pressure, and without his being required to make decisions and choices or achieve set standards.	Freedom for the child to make suggestions in music activities.

AT SEVEN

Physical Development

Growth slow and steady.	Larger repertory of longer songs.
Losing teeth; most sevens have their six-year molars.	
Better eye-hand coordination. Better use of small muscles.	More skillful employment of percussion instruments, Song Bells, and piano in simple ways; action songs and singing games of more complexity; more fundamental movements.
Eyes not yet ready for much near work.	Emphasis on rote singing continues even though music books are often in the hands of children by the second semester; recognition of scale (step) patterns and chord (skip) patterns in the notation of familiar songs.

Characteristic Reactions

Sensitive to feelings and attitudes of both peers and adults; especially dependent on approval of adults.	Children who take private music lessons may be invited to play for the class upon occasion.
Interests of boys and girls diverging; less play together.	Need for types of music activities that unite the group.

[6] From *These Are Your Children* by Jenkins, Shacter, and Bauer (Chicago: Scott, Foresman, and Company, 1949). Copyright, 1949, by Scott, Foresman, and Company, and used with their permission.

A Chart of Normal Development[7]	Implications for Teaching Music
Full of energy but easily tired; restless and fidgety; often dreamy and absorbed.	Provide for variety throughout the daily program with action songs and singing games to release energy normal for this age.
Very little abstract thinking yet; seven learns best in concrete terms and where he can be active while learning.	Continued emphasis on active listening; growth in listening to detect mood, rhythm, instruments, and melodies, and in recognition of distinctive types of music such as Indian and Spanish; numerals used to explain pitch relationships.
Cautious and self-critical; anxious to do things well; likes to use hands.	Employ percussion instruments, Song Bells, piano, and simple conductor's beats.
Talkative, exaggerates; may fight with words instead of blows; highly competitive.	Use of songs with nonsense words; creating new words to songs.
Enjoys songs, rhythms, fairy tales, myths, nature stories, comics, radio, movies.	Learning and creating songs and more complicated rhythmic responses; entering more fully into discussions about song interpretations; guidance and discussion concerning selection of movies, radio and TV programs that include music; songs that express the everyday experiences, interests, and feelings of children.
Rudimentary understanding of time and money values.	Comprehension of simple note values through identification with rhythmic responses involving the entire body.

Special Needs

The right combination of independence and encouraging support.	Plan music activities in terms of individual differences; continued helpful attention to children who have difficulty in singing.
Chances for active participation in learning situations with concrete objects.	Use of Song Bells, piano, and percussion instruments.
Must make adjustments to rougher ways of playground; needs adult help to do this without becoming too crude or rough.	

[7] From *These Are Your Children* by Jenkins, Shacter, and Bauer (Chicago: Scott, Foresman, and Company, 1949). Copyright, 1949, by Scott, Foresman, and Company, and used with their permission.

A Chart of Normal Development[8]	Implications for Teaching Music
Warm, encouraging, friendly relationship with adults.	An atmosphere of friendliness which is conducive to security and to free participation in music activities of all types; encouraging singing independently of teacher's voice or recording; encouraging creation of original rhythmic responses, melodies on instruments, songs and song interpretations, listening responses, dramatizations and percussion instrument scores.

AT EIGHT

Physical Development

Growth still slow and steady; arms lengthening, hands growing larger.	Larger repertory of longer songs; some children can easily play recorder-type instruments.
Eyes ready for both near and far vision; near-sightedness may develop this year.	Rote and note singing; use of notation in playing instruments and singing; creating and reading percussion instrument scores.
Permanent teeth continuing to appear.	
Large muscles still developing, small muscles better developed too.	Playing of recorder-type instruments en masse possible although nine-year-olds are better able to do this.
Poor posture may develop during this year.	Action songs interspersed throughout the day relieve fatigue and thus can aid posture.

Characteristic Reactions

Often careless, noisy, argumentative, but alert, friendly, interested in people.	
More dependent on Mother again, less so on teacher; sensitive to criticism.	
New awareness of individual differences.	Plan music activities in terms of individual differences; children who are ready sing rounds and descants, chord on Autoharp and piano; tone-matching activities continue for children not able to sing in tune.

[8] From *These Are Your Children* by Jenkins, Shacter, and Bauer (Chicago: Scott, Foresman, and Company, 1949). Copyright, 1949, by Scott, Foresman, and Company, and used with their permission.

A Chart of Normal Development[9]	Implications for Teaching Music
Eager, more enthusiasm than wisdom; higher accident rate.	Emphasis on learning new facts about music notation; longer attention span; songs emphasizing safety.
Gangs beginning; best friends of same sex.	Group music activities as a socializing influence.
Allegiance to peer group instead of to the adult in case of conflict.	Child interest in peer group and individual music performance; increasing teacher-pupil planning; use of tape recorder for improving individual and class music performance.
Greater capacity for self-evaluation.	Improved tone quality in singing; more critical listening; developing more musical discrimination and taste.
Much spontaneous dramatization; also ready for simple classroom dramatics.	A variety of experiences in dramatizing and creating music.
Understanding of time and use of money.	Learning the meaning of meter signatures.
Responsive to group activities; both spontaneous and adult-supervised.	Simple dances, play party games and dramatizations; sharing of creative ideas in all types of music activity; teacher guidance in self-evaluation of child's musical expression and his evaluation of the musical expression of his classmates, leading to respect for and appreciation of the accomplishments of others.
Fond of team games, comics, radio, adventure stories, collections of all kinds.	Further guidance in selection and evaluation of motion pictures, radio and TV programs; adventure songs.
Special Needs	
Much praise and encouragement from adults.	Child needs self-confidence and emotional release through participation in music activities.
Must still be reminded of his responsibilities.	
Wise guidance and channeling of his interests and enthusiasms, rather than domination or overcritical standards.	Freedom to experiment with creative activities in rhythm, singing, playing instruments and dramatization, both as individual and as member of the group.

[9] From *These Are Your Children* by Jenkins, Shacter, and Bauer (Chicago: Scott, Foresman, and Company, 1949). Copyright, 1949, by Scott, Foresman, and Company, and used with their permission.

A Chart of Normal Development[10]	Implications for Teaching Music
A best friend.	
Experience of "belonging" to peer group; opportunity to identify with others of same age and sex.	Use of songs about Scout and other groups.
Adult-supervised groups also; planned after-school activities.	Class piano; some children ready for class violin instruction.
Exercise of both large and small muscles.	Mastery of basic fundamental movements.

AT NINE

Physical Development

Slow, steady growth continues; girls forge ahead, some children reach the plateau preceding the growth spurt of pre-adolescence.	
Lungs and digestive and circulatory systems almost mature; heart especially subject to strain.	Instruction on some band and orchestra instruments may begin for the more physically mature child; strenuous physical activity should be engaged in only briefly.
Teeth may need straightening; first and second bicuspids appearing.	
Eye-hand coordination good; hands ready for crafts and shop work.	An emphasis on playing melody instruments (recorder-type and Song Bells) and harmony instruments (Autoharp and piano chording) in conjunction with singing; use of keyboard experience to see, feel, and hear music technicalities; classroom orchestra activities.
Eyes almost adult size; ready for near work with less strain.	Some sight singing of music notation; use of notation in playing melody instruments; some rote singing continued; writing of music notation to record selected original songs.

Characteristic Reactions

Decisive, responsible, dependable, strong sense of right and wrong.	
Individual differences distinct and clear; abilities apparent.	Provision for individual differences through a program of varied music activities; special provision for advanced and slow readers of music notation; tone-matching activities if necessary.

[10] From *These Are Your Children* by Jenkins, Shacter, and Bauer (Chicago: Scott, Foresman, and Company, 1949). Copyright, 1949, by Scott, Foresman, and Company, and used with their permission.

A Chart of Normal Development[11]	Implications for Teaching Music
Capable of prolonged interest; often makes plans and goes ahead on his own.	Music activities may be of 30-minute duration; rounds stressed; simple part singing introduced; more analytical listening to recordings of instrumental music; understanding simple song forms; discriminating use of percussion instruments for song accompaniments, increased emphasis on quality of musical performance, especially tone quality in singing; recognition of instruments in listening experiences; identification of common dance rhythms through listening; creative experiences in all music activities; child brings favorite recordings from home, explaining reasons for his interest in them.
Gangs strong and of one sex only, of short duration and changing membership.	Songs in which boys sing one part or verse and girls sing another (dialogue songs).
Perfectionist; wants to do well, but loses interest if discouraged or pressured.	A learning environment that provides time to experiment and to develop skills in music activities; teacher encourages growth of self-confidence through successful participation, both as individual and as member of the group.
Interested less in fairy tales and fantasy, more interested in his community and country and in other countries and peoples.	Songs related to the realities of life— in such areas as social living and language arts.
Loyalty to his country and pride in it.	Patriotic songs emphasized; songs dealing with heroes; association of composers with hero concept, and the resulting study of some of them and their music.
Much time spent in talk and discussion; often outspoken and critical of adults.	Pupil participation in discussion and planning of music activities.
Much arguing over fairness in games.	
Wide discrepancies in reading ability.	Emphasis on reading and pronouncing the words of songs.

[11] From *These Are Your Children* by Jenkins, Shacter, and Bauer (Chicago: Scott, Foresman, and Company, 1949). Copyright, 1949, by Scott, Foresman, and Company, and used with their permission.

A Chart of Normal Development[12]	Implications for Teaching Music

Special Needs

Active rough-and-tumble play.	Action songs and active rhythms; stressing folk dancing.
Friends and membership in a group.	Band, orchestra, class piano groups.
Training in skills, but without pressure.	Stepping the note values of selected songs to learn note values through this type of rhythmic response.
Reasonable explanations; no talking down to him; definite responsibility.	Simple, clear explanations of technical aspects of music as these occur in the various music activities (meter signatures, key signatures, simple chromatics, dotted notes).
Frank answers to questions about the coming physiological changes.	

IN PREADOLESCENCE

(AT TEN AND ELEVEN)

Enlarge upon the activities listed for the nines with the following additions:

Physical Development

A "resting period" followed by a period of rapid growth in height and then growth in weight; this usually starts somewhere between nine and 13; boys may mature as much as two years later than girls.	Activities such as the grand march and floor patterns aid in overcoming awkwardness; rhythmic activities planned to improve coordination; study, appreciation and skill in the basic steps of the polka, schottische, and the square dance; social dance steps for the 11's.
Secondary sex characteristics beginning to develop.	Increasing richness of voice quality but rarely any true change of voice before 12.

Rapid muscular growth.
Uneven growth of different parts of the body.
Enormous but often capricious appetite.

Characteristic Reactions

Wide range of individual differences in maturity level among this age group.

Gangs continue, though loyalty to the gang stronger in boys than in girls.

---

[12] From *These Are Your Children* by Jenkins, Shacter, and Bauer (Chicago: Scott, Foresman, and Company, 1949). Copyright, 1949, by Scott, Foresman, and Company, and used with their permission.

A Chart of Normal Development[13]	Implications for Teaching Music
Interest in team games, pets, radio, comics; marked interest difference between boys and girls.	Discussion and evaluation of radio and TV programs concerning music.
Much teasing and antagonism between boy and girl groups.	Emphasis on coeducational music activities to foster a healthy boy-girl relationship.
Awkwardness, restlessness, and laziness common as result of rapid and uneven growth.	
Child approaching adolescence often becomes overcritical, changeable, rebellious, uncooperative.	Music activities selected in which each child can succeed; select children to assume leadership roles; praise for work well done.
Interested in activities to earn money.	

Special Needs

Knowledge and understanding of the physical and emotional changes about to come.	Study of classifications of the adult voice; knowledge and understanding of the voice change coming when 12 to 14.
Skillfully planned program to meet needs of those who are approaching puberty as well as those who are not.	
Warm affection and sense of humor in adults; no nagging or condemnation or talking down to him.	
Sense of belonging and acceptance by peer group; increasing opportunities for independence.	Band, orchestra, and chorus groups; two-part singing for tens and three-part singing for 11's; creating harmony parts to songs; study of some composers and the unusual instruments of the orchestra; experimentation in music activities; continued creation of original songs, melodies, accompaniments, and dances; constantly increasing amount of teacher-pupil planning; creation of song stories; increasing emphasis on music skills in purposeful activity; increasing comprehension of national characteristics in music; listening experiences with longer composition; addition of the Melody Flute and strings to classroom orchestra activities; independent sight singing.

[13] From *These Are Your Children* by Jenkins, Shacter, and Bauer (Chigago: Scott, Foresman, and Company, 1949). Copyright, 1949, by Scott, Foresman, and Company, and used with their permission.

In order for a classroom teacher to give proper guidance to music activities it is necessary that he have practical experience in the skills mentioned in this chapter and emphasized in the succeeding chapters. The material presented is so organized that it aids both the teacher-in-training and the teacher-in-service in applying these skills to the specific music books, recordings, and instruments available to elementary classrooms today.

The responsibility of the American public schools for the teaching of music is well expressed in the following pronouncement of the Music Educators National Conference:

The Child's Bill of Rights in Music[14]

I

Every child has the right to full and free opportunity to explore and develop his capacities in the field of music in such ways as may bring him happiness and a sense of well-being; stimulate his imagination and stir his creative activities; and make him so responsive that he will cherish and seek to renew the fine feelings induced by music.

II

As his right, every child shall have the opportunity to experience music with other people so that his own enjoyment shall be heightened and he shall be led into greater appreciation of the feelings and aspirations of others.

III

As his right, every child shall have the opportunity to make music through being guided and instructed in singing, in playing at least one instrument both alone and with others, and, so far as his powers and interests permit, in composing music.

IV

As his right, every child shall have opportunity to grow in musical appreciation, knowledge, and skill, through instruction equal to that given in any other subject in all the free public educational programs that may be offered to children and youths.

V

As his right, every child shall be given the opportunity to have his interest and power in music explored and developed to the end that unusual talent may be utilized for the enrichment of the individual and society.

VI

Every child has the right to such teaching as will sensitize, refine, elevate, and enlarge not only his appreciation of music, but also his

[14] *The Child's Bill of Rights in Music* (Chicago: Music Educators National Conference, 1950). Quoted by permission.

whole affective nature, to the end that the high part such developed feeling may play in raising the stature of mankind may be revealed to him.

REFERENCES

Adams, Fay, *Educating America's Children* (2d ed.) chap. 13. New York: The Ronald Press, 1954. An excellent overview of music education in the elementary school.

Association for Supervision and Curriculum Development of the National Education Association, *Fostering Mental Health in Our Schools,* 1950 Yearbook. Washington, D.C.

———, *Organizing the Elementary School for Living and Learning,* 1947 Yearbook. Washington, D.C.

Burr, James B., Lowry W. Harding, Leland B. Jacobs, *Student Teaching in the Elementary School.* New York: Appleton-Century-Crofts, Inc., 1950.

Child Study Association, *Our Children Today.* New York: The Viking Press, 1952.

Cole, Natalie R., *The Arts in the Classroom.* New York: John Day Company, 1940.

Cunningham, Ruth, *Understanding Group Behavior of Boys and Girls.* New York: Columbia Bureau of Publications, 1951.

Educational Policies Commission, *Moral and Spiritual Values in the Public Schools.* Washington: National Education Association, 1948.

Gesell, Arnold L., *The Child From Five to Ten.* New York: Harper and Brothers, 1946.

Hymes, James L., *Understanding Your Child.* New York: Prentice-Hall, Inc., 1951.

———, *Teacher Listen: The Children Speak.* New York: Committee on Mental Health, State Charities Aid Association, 1949.

Jenkins, Gladys G., Helen Shacter, and William W. Bauer, *These Are Your Children.* Chicago: Scott, Foresman, and Company, 1949.

Lee, J. Murray, and Doris May Lee, *The Child and His Curriculum* (rev. ed.). New York: Appleton-Century-Crofts, Inc., 1950.

Macomber, Freeman S., *Guiding Child Development in the Elementary School.* New York: American Book Company, 1948.

Millard, Cecil V., *Child Growth and Development.* Boston: D. C. Heath and Company, 1951.

Morgan, Hazel N., ed., *Music in American Education.* Chicago: Music Educators National Conference, 1955.

Mursell, James L., *Education for Musical Growth.* New York: Ginn and Company, 1948.

———, *Music and the Classroom Teacher,* chaps. I, II. New York: Silver Burdett Company, 1951.

Prescott, Daniel, *Helping Teachers Understand Children.* Washington: American Council on Education, 1945.

Witty, Paul, ed., *The Gifted Child.* Boston: D. C. Heath and Company, 1951. The American Council on Education.

Teaching
Responses
to Rhythm

Two

Response to rhythm is an integral part of both music education and physical education. An understanding of the values of rhythmic experience in the natural growth of boys and girls, and of how to teach these values, is an essential part of any elementary teacher's professional equipment. This chapter presents material not only for students in college but also for teachers in service. Thus, there follows more material than can be utilized in a college class without taking time away from the other aspects of music. How much stress should be given to this area depends in part upon how much some of these activities are emphasized in college physical education classes.[1] The busy classroom teacher needs to know how to find and use suitable music materials in connection with responses to rhythm.

Of primary concern is listening to music in order to respond to it with physical movement. Singing will be actively engaged in but will not be stressed here. In the authors' opinion there is good reason for this initial emphasis upon active listening, particularly in the primary grades. When children aged five, six, and seven begin their school year, a great many of them will not be able to match tones (i.e., sing in tune). Therefore there is logic in first listening to music, then responding physically to what is heard, and in the process becoming

[1] In the same vein, if simple percussion instruments can be made in arts and crafts classes, time may be saved which is needed for other aspects of music teaching in music education classes.

oriented to rhythm, pitch, and mood. This builds a background of experience for better singing a little later.

However, there are important values in rhythmic responses other than the building of a background for successful singing. Among these are the development of bodily control, imagination, willingness to experiment, emotional responsiveness, and concepts of fast and slow, heavy and light, long and short, in terms of bodily movement. Furthermore, rhythmic response is a necessity in carrying out a balanced daily program of activities for children. As stated in the preceding chapter, it is unnatural for boys and girls to sit quietly for long periods of time. There is evidence to show that teachers who guide their pupils in appropriate rhythmic responses, and who know the proper time to use them, can by so doing reduce pupil fatigue to a marked degree.

FUNDAMENTAL MOVEMENTS AND FREE RHYTHMIC PLAY

Music is not always required to initiate rhythmic response. For example, appropriate words[2] for walking can be chanted, then clapped, then walked, and finally appropriate music can be added in time to the children's walking. Walking, running, skipping, and other fundamental movements can be introduced by the teacher's drum beat and learned by the children through clapping before they move to them with their whole bodies; the music can be brought in after the rhythm is learned.

In primary grades further understanding of fundamental movements can be gained by using songs that suggest impersonation (imitative play). Children who are five and six years of age tend strongly to *be* what they impersonate, such as the horses that gallop and the rabbits that hop. The teaching of fundamental rhythms can continue also from the point of view of free rhythmic play. The teacher may tap a drum, play the piano, or use a recording, and ask the children what it "makes them feel like doing." From their own experience should come the suggestions which will eventually include movements such as clapping, walking, running, skipping, galloping, sliding, hopping, leaping and jumping. Through the freedom of children to respond to the rhythms of music they can discover other bodily movements which may include swinging, pushing, bouncing, pulling, bending, stretching, twisting, shaking, dodging, and striking. Through all of this the teacher controls and guides the learning situ-

[2] Such words may be found in *The American Singer Book One,* pp. 110-111.

ation by helping the children relate familiar physical responses to the music to which they listen. The teacher, while guiding the children, should do so in such a manner that each child feels he has made his personal contribution.

Occasionally teachers take a rhythm from something a child is doing, or from nature or machines outside the classroom, and repeat this on a percussion instrument or on a piano. The children are then asked to move to this rhythm. Percussion instruments may be chosen to accompany or to represent these bodily movements. Children should not be asked to respond to rhythm until they have had the opportunity to listen carefully. Teachers frequently ask them to close their eyes while they listen. After that may come the question, "What did the music tell you to do?" There may follow a discussion, then the music will be repeated and the children will begin to contribute ideas to the group. Sometimes the teacher will help by asking other questions such as, "Does the music make you feel like walking or skipping or running? Is it happy, sad, fast or slow? High or low?" Free rhythmic responses grow most naturally from a previously learned background of fundamental movements.

Free rhythmic responses are so numerous that probably no listing of them can ever be complete, particularly since each of them can be varied almost endlessly. Some, in addition to those already mentioned, may be:

trotting	tapping	stroking	swaying
dipping	reaching	patting	rolling
tripping	grasping	creeping	hammering
stamping	banging	rocking	whirling
tossing	circling	crawling	tumbling
skating	beating	turning	sliding

Others are rising and falling in terms of crescendo (gradually louder) and decrescendo (gradually softer) and in terms of rising and falling pitch, bouncing a ball and jumping a rope.

Space is needed for freedom of movement and it must be acknowledged that some classrooms may be too small, have bolted-down seats or have unhappy proximities to other rooms. Any of these or other reasons may handicap some types of rhythm activities. Yet, a great amount of excellent work can be done despite such difficulties. First, rhythmic activities should never be boisterous or unruly. Second, activities requiring space may be arranged for in some larger room. However, this room should rarely be the size of a gymnasium because large rooms can destroy the intimate feeling of the classroom. Excellent work of certain types can be done on the playground. Third, should rhythm activities take place in a room that is not suitable, certain substitutions of responses may be made. Children seated at desks can "walk with their hands" in the air. Galloping and skipping rhythms are sometimes done with the hands also. When clapping is done, children may be taught quiet ways such as striking the tips of the fingers of both hands together rather than using the palms, or striking the fingertips of one hand on the wrist of the other hand. Fourth, part of a class may do an activity while the others watch; then students may be chosen in turn. Those who are watching may be singing, doing a quiet substitute for the activity, or both.

To sustain interest, variety is essential. For example, no child enjoys skipping to the same music over a long period of time. A variety of accompaniments is also recommended. The teacher may use recordings, the piano, various percussion instruments, and the chanting of the voice. Still more variety may be attained by changing the tempo of the music. When song material is used, more effective teaching often results when part of the group sings while part does the rhythmic response. Jumping ropes, bouncing balls, scarves, and balloons may be used to make appropriate activities more colorful and impressive. Scarves for this purpose are made of silk or lightweight nylon[3] which is in length double the height of the child. Such length permits many uses, including dramatization.

> *Walking* is commonly done to $\frac{4}{4}$ and $\frac{2}{4}$ meters. It is relaxed and swinging, never tense and jerky. Children may develop different types of walking by pretending they are different characters or animals. Marching is an outgrowth of walking.
>
> *Running* is done to $\frac{4}{4}$, $\frac{2}{4}$, and $\frac{6}{8}$ meters. Running on tiptoe is commonly stressed and the movement should be kept light.
>
> *Skipping* is generally done to $\frac{6}{8}$ meter. It is a step, hop, first on one foot, then on the other. Children enjoy a large, fast skip which gives them the feeling of moving high through the air.
>
> *Hopping* and *jumping* are done to $\frac{4}{4}$, $\frac{2}{4}$, or $\frac{6}{8}$ meters. Hopping is done on one foot while jumping is done with both feet together. Children can imagine jumping rope, kangaroos jumping, and frogs hopping. Overly-heavy movements are avoided.

[3] Some teachers report the use of nylon from old parachutes.

Galloping is ordinarily done to ⁶⁄₈ meter. One foot is kept ahead of the other throughout and the back foot is brought up to meet it. Heels never touch the floor. Children pretend they are ponies or horses.

Swinging, swaying, and *rowing* can relax the children after the stimulation of the more active movements. Swaying trees, branches or flowers are often imitated, as are swings, the pendulum of a clock, rocking a baby to sleep, and rowing a boat.

These and other fundamental movements are taken up in detail in physical education books.

Bodily response to note values

Term	Rhythmic Notation	Music Notation	Rests
Walking notes	— — — —	♩ ♩ ♩ ♩	𝄽 𝄽 𝄽 𝄽
Running notes	- - - - - - - -	♫♫♫♫	𝄾𝄾𝄾𝄾𝄾𝄾𝄾𝄾
Slow, long, standing or step–bend notes	—— ——	𝅗𝅥 𝅗𝅥	𝄼 𝄼
Holding notes	——————	𝅝	𝄻
Skipping note pattern	—- —- —- —-	♩♪ ♪♩ ♪♩ ♪♩ ♪	𝄾 𝄾 𝄾 𝄾 𝄾
Galloping note pattern	--- --- --- ---	♫ ♫ ♫ ♫	𝄾𝄾𝄾𝄾𝄾𝄾𝄾𝄾𝄾𝄾𝄾𝄾

(Speaking the words "galloping" or "merrily" is often used to explain this pattern.)

After boys and girls have associated fundamental movements with music notation, "stepping the melody rhythm" relates this knowledge to melodies of songs. Refer to the Music Series Reference Guide to Fundamental Rhythms, p. 26, and Things to Do, No. 5, p. 32, for examples of this activity.

In the first grade the term "walking note" makes sense to the child because it represents a bodily movement he knows. It is recommended that the conventional note names not be emphasized. Children in this grade do not know fractions, thus terms like "quarter" and "eighth" are usually meaningless.

When fundamental rhythms are properly taught they are invariably enjoyed by the children. It takes time to develop skill in rhythm activities, and the beginning teacher is likely to try too many things at the beginning and thus meet with some initial discouragement. As in so many other areas of education, we must "make haste slowly." Therefore, the teacher should strive for a simple and thorough approach. By the end of the first grade most children will have learned to walk, skip, run, gallop, and hop in time to music. During the second grade most children will have learned to slide, jump rope, and bounce a ball in rhythm. In third grade the ability to leap and to step-hop may be added.

The following page references are submitted for evaluation in terms of their value for imitative play, fundamental movements, and free rhythmic movements in the primary grades. The addition of "r" to a page number indicates that the song is recorded either in the albums that accompany the book of which the page is a part or in the RCA Victor Educational Albums. The addition of "a" indicates that the song is at the top of that page, "b" indicates that the song appears second on the page, and "c" third.

Music Series Reference Guide to Fundamental Rhythms

The American Singer, 2nd ed. (American Book Company)

BOOK ONE

Bending and stretching, 136, 137, 138, chants for, 136

Galloping, 127, 128, 129r, 153, chants for, 127

Hopping, 82, 125, 126r, 186a, chants for, 125

Jumping, 122, 123ar, 123b, 124r, chants for, 122

Multiple responses, 151r, 152r, 153r, 154

Running, 116, 117, 118, chants for, 116

Skipping, 130, 131r, 132r, chants for, 130

Sliding, 133r, 134a, 134b, 135, chants for, 133

Swinging and swaying, 139, 140, 141, 142a, 142b, 143, 144, 145, 174a, 179b, chants for, 139

Tiptoeing, 119, 120, 121, chants for, 118, 120, 121

Turning and twisting, 146, 147, 148ar, 149r, chants for, 136

Walking, 111r, 112ar, 112b, 113r, 114, 115, 185a, 186c, chants for, 110, 111

(See "Rhythmic Movements," 188)

BOOK TWO

Bouncing ball, 164

Marching, 106

Running, 61

Skating, 84r

Swaying, 162, 163r, 168r

Swinging, 47, 145r

Teeter-totter, 120

Walking, 57, 60, 66

(See "Rhythm Patterns in Rote, Rote-Note, and Note Songs," 189)

BOOK THREE

Bouncing ball, 58r
Hopping, 11
Marching, 44, 46, 127, 164, 174
Skating, 89r
Stepping melody-rhythm, 179r

Swinging, 50r, 58r
Walking, 76
(See "Rhythm Patterns in Songs,"
204)

New Music Horizons (Silver Burdett Company)
MUSIC FOR EARLY CHILDHOOD

Fundamental rhythms, 39, 43, 56, 65
Impersonation—see index, 132
Moving with music, 35-66 (eleven songs recorded)

EXPERIENCES IN MUSIC FOR FIRST GRADE CHILDREN

Galloping, 15b, 38, 98b
Hopping and jumping, 38, 65ab,
84a
Impersonation and pretending, 4a,
8a, 12ab, 15ab, 19, 24, 26ab,
27, 31a, 65ab, 84a, 100b
Marching, 16, 20a, 26a, 27, 53, 60,
64b, 105, 110br, 111ab

Running, 82b, 84a
Skating, 38, 99
Skipping, 37, 38, 99, 102a
Swaying, 6ab, 20b, 22b, 36b, 135
Swinging, 20b, 43, 72a
Trotting, 49b, 84a, 91
Walking, 20a, 64b, 71, 84a, 90a,
98ab, 99, 124ab

FIRST BOOK

Marching, 48
Rowing, 46

Swaying, 40
Trotting, 20r, 26r

SECOND BOOK

Bending, 67
Galloping, 36r, 80
Hopping, 27a, 75, 101, 116r
Riding a bicycle, 89r
Rowing, poling, 23, 93a, 95
Running—duple meter, 24r, triple
meter, 20r
Shuffling, 56, 85
Skipping, 3, 6b, 19, 53
Swaying and swinging, 2b, 5, 39,
54, 78b, 94b, 121, 122, 133r

Trotting, 42r, 82, 103
Walking—duple meter, 7r, 10a, 15r,
26, 27br, 29, 58, 64, 76, 79,
88, 118, 120r, 123r, 124b,
125, 127r, triple meter, 1,
45r, 106a, lilting walk, 3, 19,
30, 36r, 62, lumbering walk,
59, 74br, 87, waddling, 96r,
104r
Whirling, flying, 27a, 107, 115

THIRD BOOK

Galloping, 150
Loping, 131
Marching, 4r, 13, 17, 39, 54, 60,
70b, 74r, 79r, 86b
Riding bicycle, 76a
See-saw, 32

Skating, 62r
Skipping, 12
Swaying, 137
Trotting, 136
Walking backwards, 154b

FOURTH BOOK

(See 207, IV, A)

Our Singing World (Ginn and Company)

KINDERGARTEN BOOK

Free rhythmic play, 12ar, 12b, 13br, 14r, 15br, 16br, 17ab, 20abr

Galloping, 18r, 52ab, 53ab, 54a

Hopping, 19b, 22r, 98b

Imitative play, 10b, 11r, 12ar, 12b, 13br, 14r, 15br, 16a, 17ab, 18abr

Jumping, 19a

Running, 10br, 11r, 12ar, 12br

See-saw, 30r

Skating, 32

Skipping, 13ar, 14r, 15a, 15br, 16a, 17

Walking, 23r, 24, 25a, 25br, 26a, 26br, 27r, 28, 121r

FIRST GRADE BOOK

Balls, use of, 25a, 25br, 26a, 26b

Free rhythmic play, 14br, 12ar, 20br, 21a, 27br, 30br

Galloping, 22a, 22br, 24ar, 24br

Hopping, 18b, 19ar, 19br

Imitative play, 18r, 22br, 30br, 32b, 33r, 35a, 35b

Running, 11br, 12ar, 12br, 13ar, 14ar, 14br, 15a

Skipping, 18ar

See-saw, 27ar, 27br

Skating, 28ar, 28br, 29

Swinging, swaying, 30ar, 30br, 31a, 31b

Trotting, 23ar, 23br

Walking, marching, 9, 15b, 36a, 36br, 37, 38ar, 39, 40r, 41

SINGING AS WE PLAY

Contains many fundamental movements

SINGING ON OUR WAY

Free rhythmic play, 41, 112b

Fundamental movements, 17b, 18r, 19r, 41, 112b

Gallop, trot, 132b

Galloping, 29, 118

Imitative play, 22ar, 23r, 25a, 105a, 119b

Marching, 28, 158a

Skating, 22b, 24b

Skipping, 20, 24a, 63r, 68a, 113a, 116a, 136a, 137

Stepping melody rhythm, 101r

Swinging, 26r, 27a

Trotting, 55a

Walk, trot, gallop, 133

SINGING AND RHYMING

Galloping, 149

Imitative play, 60r, 160, 161r

Marching, 27ab, 64b, 164

Marching, running, 20ar

Running, walking, 20b

Skipping, 16ar

Stepping melody rhythm, 19a, 53b, 147, 150

Swaying, 61

Swinging, 9r, 23

Walking, 49ar, 51a, 82b

Walking, skipping, 21b

Walking, skipping, galloping, 21a

A Singing School (C. C. Birchard and Company)

OUR FIRST MUSIC

Free rhythmic response, 117-120

Fundamental movements, 75c,

103a, 104a, 108a, 108b, 114, 204r, 246br, 333ab

OUR SONGS

Galloping, 19, 64r, 90, 98r, 108r, 152

Running, trotting, 5r, 18, 20, 47, 53, 71, 94

Skipping and hopping, 31r, 40, 84, 108r, 112r, 141, 158

Stepping melody rhythm, 36ab, 37ab, 39, 40, 55r, 58r, 78, 79b, 84, 87r, 82r, 115, 148, 149r

Swaying, 8r, 34, 38r, 57, 62a, 63, 81, 89r, 106r, 107r, 114

Walking, 10r, 43, 83, 92r, 94, 110br, 124, 132ab, 150r

(See Teachers Manual, 12-15)

MERRY MUSIC

Hopping, 31, 86r, 88r, 92r, 104, 105, 106, 154, 158

Marching, 14, 27, 35, 39, 84, 93, 96r, 102r, 154, 155r

Running, 19b, 20, 25r, 55, 75, 104, 112r, 144

Skipping, 16, 24, 28, 76r, 78r, 83, 89r, 147, 166

Stepping melody rhythm, 8r, 10, 21r, 33, 41, 54r, 56, 63, 80, 82, 150

Swaying, 9, 12r, 17, 29, 46r, 51r, 64r, 79r, 81r, 90br

Walking, 37ar, 50, 58r, 61, 85, 99, 110r, 120b, 124, 159

Together We Sing (Follett Publishing Company)

TOGETHER WE SING, Enlarged Edition

Free rhythmic dramatization and fundamental movements, 1r, 5ar, 6r, 13r, 15b, 16ar, 16b, 23r, 24r, 27r, 30ar, 30br, 32br, 37a, 38ar, 47, 49r, 51, 57r, 61r, 69br, 241br

MUSIC 'ROUND THE CLOCK

Rhythmic dramatization and fundamental movements, 15-19, 47-56

MUSIC 'ROUND THE TOWN

Galloping, 63r, 110r

Jumping rope, 45

Rowing, 41r

Running, 24r, 42r

Skipping, 104r

Swinging, 44, 66

Walking, 13r, 22, 40r

MUSIC THROUGH THE YEAR

Refer "To Teachers and Parents," Responding to Rhythm, 170-173

MUSIC ACROSS OUR COUNTRY

Refer "Songs for Stepping of Notes," 191

Music For Living (Silver Burdett Company)

MUSIC THROUGH THE DAY (including children's books I LIKE THE COUNTRY and I LIKE THE CITY)

"Free Rhythms" and "Work Rhythms" indexes, 152

Recorded songs index, ii

"Rhythm" index, 149-150

"Rhythmic Movement," 146

MUSIC IN OUR TOWN

Fundamental movements, "Rhythms," 133

TM "Movement Helps Understanding" viii, "Rhythm," xi

ADDITIONAL REFERENCES

THINGS

TO

DO

1. When songs are introduced or reviewed, the teacher establishes the tempo and the pitch. The tempo may be established in a variety of ways—perhaps by singing or playing part of the song while the class listens, or by clapping, or by making an arm motion in proper rhythm. To be certain that everyone has sensed the tempo, the class may at times speak the words of the song "in rhythm," or respond by clapping, by walking, or by some other movement. Whenever a song is presented, the teacher should establish the tempo by one of these means. Practice starting the class in singing songs assigned by your teacher. For help in establishing the pitch, refer to Chapter Four, pp. 103-104.

2. Every meter contains natural accents as follows:

2/4, fast 6/8 ONE two ONE two ONE two etc.
3/4   ONE two three ONE two three etc.
4/4   ONE two *three* four ONE two *three* four etc.
6/8 (slow) ONE two three *four* five six etc.

It should be noticed that 4/4 and slow 6/8 meters have, besides the primary (heavy) accent on the first beat, a secondary (less heavy) accent on another beat. Play recordings of songs and ask the class to identify the meter. A question that frequently helps in identifying the meter is, "Does the music swing in two's or three's?"

3. Simple conducting is another rhythmic response. Be able to conduct familiar songs according to their meter signatures as follows:

   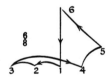

The above illustrations refer to right-handed conducting. Persons who are left-handed may wish to conduct with the left hand. To do so, conduct all left and right motions drawn above as right and left, respectively—just the reverse of the drawings. Should anyone conduct a very large group of children both arms may be used. Try conducting with the aid of a mirror to be certain your motions are those desired. (Remember to teach children the conductor's beats; this is an important rhythmic response.)

4. Prepare a demonstration and report on the value of scarves and balloons in rhythmic activities. See the *Our Singing World Guide and Teaching Suggestions for Kindergarten and Grades One, Two, and Three,* p. 86.

5. Try stepping word rhythms (melody rhythms) as mentioned on page 24, using familiar nursery rhymes as a beginning experience. After stepping these rhythms, write them in rhythmic notation, then in music notation. Try some of the following:
   a) Hot cross buns, hot cross buns,
   One a penny two a penny hot cross buns.
   b) Bah, bah, black sheep, have you any wool?
   Yes sir, yes sir, three bags full!
   c) Sing a song of sixpence a pocket full of rye,
   Four and twenty blackbirds baked in a pie!
   When the pie was opened, the birds began to sing,
   Wasn't that a dainty dish to set before the king?
   Now refer to the Reference Guide, p. 26, and step the melody rhythms of songs indicated for use in this activity in the music series books.

6. Explore the rhythm of names. Find classmates' names that sound like walking (Bob Smith), running (Ellen Dillon), like a walk and a run (Tom Adams), like a run and a walk (Susan Fry), like skipping notes (Marie McAnn) and like galloping notes (Gwendolyn Armitage). This activity is often done in the elementary classroom. The children in this way act out their names in rhythm and learn to identify them both by rhythm and by notation. Try this in your college class.

7. One way to learn certain songs is by unison reading of the words. This succeeds with songs having words that when spoken have the same rhythm as the song's note values. The rhythm of the words is learned first, then the melody is added. Find songs in the above Reference Guide that are suitable for this approach. (Since

words have rhythm, there is some value in the making up of new words for a familiar song.)

8. It is said that characteristics of rhythm include tempo, meter, rhythm of the melody, and accent. Using a song as an example, explain these terms.

9. Investigate the rhythmic chant. See the *Guide to the American Singer*, Second Edition, Grade Six, p. 8.

10. Play a guessing game by tapping or clapping the rhythm of the melody of familiar songs.

ACTION SONGS, SINGING GAMES, AND DANCES

Action songs are emphasized in the primary grades, singing games in the primary (but continuing into grades four and five), and dances in the fourth, fifth, and sixth grades. However, each type of activity is used to some extent in all grades.

Although many action songs can be taught without requiring a background of fundamental movements, this is not true of most singing games and dances. The title of this section is stated in an order that implies increasing complexity. Action songs are those to which children can add appropriate motions. Singing games are those that involve elements of game, chance, and sometimes dance. Dances are more formalized. The teacher will find that these terms are sometimes confused, and that the authors of the music books are themselves sometimes in doubt as to exact classification. Teachers and children who have imagination will find that they can transform some "ordinary" songs into action songs, singing games, and even dances of their own invention.

Most folk dances are easily taught in the intermediate grades. Some of them are taught to primary grade children in simplified versions. The easiest "dance" would be the Indian type in which first grade children do a thumping walk or hop. Occasionally a simplified waltz is taught in second and third grades. The polka step is sometimes introduced in those grades also. However, most dances are taught in the fourth and fifth grades. The words of certain songs direct the dancers. Often-enjoyed examples are "The Old Brass Wagon" (*Music Everywhere, American Singer Book Four, Music Across Our Country*), "Caller's Song" (*American Singer Book Four*), and "Red River Valley" (*Rhythmic Program for Elementary Schools*, Fielder).

When children sing and at the same time do extensive bodily movement, the result is usually detrimental to either good singing or good physical action or both. Consequently it is best to divide the children into two groups that alternate in singing and in doing the game or dance. The group that does the singing frequently adds hand clapping and percussion instruments to its accompaniment of the rhythmic activity.

Many singing games and dances contribute to organized play on the playground. The song forms the accompaniment. As previously implied, these activities whether indoors or out are valuable in relieving pent-up energies, in developing muscular control, in developing good citizenship habits and sportsmanship, and in releasing emotion by identifying the child with his group. When these activities take place indoors, the piano and recordings may provide variety.

One of the major values of certain singing games and folk dances is the contribution they can make to the social studies, for through them can come better understanding of peoples and customs.

In the following list, "TM" refers to the teacher's manual or guide that accompanies the book in question.

Music Series Reference Guide to Action Songs, Singing Games, Dances

The American Singer (2d ed.; American Book Company)

BOOK ONE
Action songs, 20a, 45, 71, 179b
Singing games, 93-102, 184c

BOOK TWO
Action songs, 9, 57, 92, 97r, 99r, 104, 109a, 164, 168, 172a
Singing games, 30, 31, 32, 100, 136, 137, 138r, 140, 141
Waltz (simplified), 125r
(See "Singing Games and Rhythms," 187)

BOOK THREE
Games and dances (American, with directions) 48, 52, 54, 56, 148, 150, 152, 158; (European) 126, 155
Waltz, simplified, with directions, 51 (TM 14), 156, rye waltz with directions, 152-154
(See "Rhythms, Games and Dances," 203)

BOOK FOUR
(See "Games and Dances," 204. Most include directions. See 62.)

BOOK FIVE
Action song, 107

Singing games, 2r, 50, 58, 86a, 88a (TM 35), 87, 89, 102 (TM 36), 109, 120r, 121br, 146, 155, 185
Waltz step, 38 (directions), 39r, 50, 75, 108 (directions), 156ar
Waltz walk, 26a, 26b, 31, 70
Wooden shoe waltz with directions, 166r

FIFTH BOOK

Folk dances with directions, 4, 19br, 43r, 92r, 148br, 154br, 162 (TM 43), 177r, 196a (TM 43)
Floor patterns, TM 45-46
Marching, 12, 38ar, 55, 60, 172b
Singing games, 38ar, 72, 84ar, TM 2
Social dances: English country dance, 126, 148a, 148br (directions), grand march with directions, 42, minuet, 57, TM 44, polka (see Fourth Book 97 for directions), 84b, 122b, 147a, 165a, TM directions 44, quadrille, 153b (TM 42), 175r, schottische, 38b (TM 43), 80b, 109, tarantella, 82 (TM 42 directions), Virginia reel, 20, 29r (directions), 128r, 129, waltz, 16, 59, 71b, 88a, 130 (TM directions 41), 154br

SIXTH BOOK

Floor patterns, creative, 21, TM 47
Social dances: gavotte, 98, longways, square and round dances with directions, 44, 88r, 191, marching, 1, 13, 29, 40, 168, mazurka, 31b, TM directions, 38, 47, minuet, 46, TM directions, 37, 46, polka, 20, 171, 172, polonaise with directions, 165, Virginia reel, 44, 88, 125, 126, waltz, 12, 19a, 52, 87r, 95, 116
Stepping-clapping, 2, 3, 6a, 10b, 11, 13, 16b, 41, 57b, 58b, etc.
Our Singing World (Ginn and Company)

KINDERGARTEN BOOK

Action songs, 9b, 21b, 30abr, 33abr, 36br, 37a, 49ab, 50abc, 51ar, 51b, 117b, 127abc, 134ab
Singing games, 37b, 38abr, 39a, 39br, 40a, 40br, 41ab, 42a, 43ab

FIRST GRADE BOOK

Action songs, 7ab, 21b, 34ab, 44br, 59a, 60ab, 78c, 105, 125ab, 132a, 159ar, 171ar
Singing games, 45, 46ab, 47ab, 48r, 49ab, 50ar, 50br, 51, 52ab

SINGING ON OUR WAY

Action songs, 26r, 42, 43, 45br, 54, 55b, 133, 153r
Singing games, 7r, 9r, 31r, 32r, 33ab, 34r, 35ab, 36r, 37r, 38ab, 39r, 44r

SINGING AND RHYMING

Action songs, 9r, 10r, 24r, 25r, 28r, 60r, 154, 161r, 165
Singing games, 11, 13r, 16r, 41r, 42r, 43r, 44 (TM directions 128), 45r, 46ar, 46br, 47, 48ar, 48br, 49ar, 49b, 51a, 51b

SINGING EVERY DAY

Action songs, 7r, 17r, 22br, 56
Dances, 12r, 54, 59 (polka)
Singing games, 45r, 46r, 47r, 49ar, 49b, 50a, 50br, 51r, 52r, 53, 57, 58b, 60, 61r, 158br, refer TM 6-28 for directions, use song index TM 29-31

SINGING TOGETHER

Dances, 31r (varsovienne directions), 33r (TM directions 113), 40r (polka)
Singing games with directions, 29r, 30r, 32r, 34r, 35r, 36, without directions, 186r

SINGING IN HARMONY

Action songs, 35, 38r
Dances, 37r (square, TM directions 239), 40r (TM directions 233), 41 (waltz)
Singing games, 39r, 44 (TM 241)

A Singing School (C. C. Birchard Company)

OUR FIRST MUSIC

Action songs, 31a, 54a, 75ab, 76, 77, 113, 116b, 192r, 199, 200, 201r, 202, 217, 255b, 264, 270b, 290ar
Dances, 126, 127, 131, 135r, 362
Singing games, 9ab, 29, 30, 42ab, 63ab, 125, 136, 152ab, 153ab, 246a

OUR SONGS

Action songs, 109, 158r
Dance, 95r (minuet)

MERRY MUSIC

Action songs, 83, 84r, 86
Dances, 88 (Morris), 89, 90ar, polka (TM directions 37), 139 (TM directions 48), 164 (minuet), 166 directions
Singing games 85r (TM directions 36)

WE SING

Action songs, 38a, 153
Dances, 81 (polka and waltz), 102r-120 (European national dances with directions), 126 (American with directions), 151 (Indian), 172
Singing games, 39, 77

OUR LAND OF SONG

Dances, 37, with directions: 53 (Morris), 128, 130, 132 (gavotte), 136 (minuet), 138, 140r, 142 (reel)
Singing games with directions, 126, 134r, 144, 146

MUSIC EVERYWHERE

Action song, 163
Dances, 88r (waltz) 105br (reel with directions), 142, South American with directions, 153, 154, 156r, 159r, original, 149, New Edition, 226, 230
Singing game with directions, 105a

Together We Sing (Follett Publishing Company)

TOGETHER WE SING, Enlarged Edition

Action songs, 15b, 16ar, 16b, 30ar, 33a, 37a, 243ar
Dance, 61 (polka)
Singing games, 38br, 39br, 45, 56ar, 66ar, 75r, 99r, 241br, 242br, 245r

MUSIC 'ROUND THE CLOCK

Singing games, 35-40

MUSIC 'ROUND THE TOWN

Action song, 106r

Singing games, 7r, 76r (directions 134), 46r, 95 (directions 135), 106r

MUSIC THROUGH THE YEAR

Dances and games, 15 (directions 174), 20r, 25, 35, 64r, 81, 105br, 133

MUSIC ACROSS OUR COUNTRY

Dances, 24ab (directions 182-183), 33br (directions 183), 48r (directions 184), 95, 105 (directions), 125r (directions 186), 139r (directions)

Refer, "Singing Games and Action Songs," 189

VOICES OF AMERICA

(See Classified Index* for dances and games)

VOICES OF THE WORLD

Dances and games, 222

Music for Living (Silver Burdett Company)

MUSIC THROUGH THE DAY (including children's books I LIKE THE COUNTRY and I LIKE THE CITY)

"Games" index, 151

TM index of recorded songs, ii

MUSIC IN OUR TOWN

"Games" index, 153

TM "Rhythmic Responses," vii, "Rhythmic Play," x, "Rhythm," xi, "Dances to Invent," xii

MUSIC NOW AND LONG AGO

"Games and Dances" index, 169

"Moving About," index, 170

TM "Rhythm," "Use of Bodily Movement," xi

TM "Pointing Up Rhythm," 133, "Work Rhythms," 134

MUSIC NEAR AND FAR

"Play—parties and dances," 184, "Songs for Acting Out," 183, "Work Rhythms," 185

TM "Clap and Tap," "Ethnic Dances," "Singing Games," xiii, "Activities," "Dances," 163, "Invitations to Dance," vii

MUSIC IN OUR COUNTRY

(See Classified Index* and Teachers Book)

MUSIC AROUND THE WORLD

(See Classified Index* and Teachers Book)

* Not available when this textbook was written.

THINGS

TO

DO

1. Learn how to teach the commonly-used dances by means of references in the above list and by the directions given in books such as those listed at the end of this chapter. Evaluate these directions in terms of teaching elementary school children.

2. Dances can be created from common rhythm patterns. Guide a group of class members in creating an Indian circle dance from the note patterns ♩♩ and ♩♩♩♩. (Suggestion: squaws form the inner circle and proceed ♩ ♩ or
step step
♩͜♩ ♩͜♩ . Braves form the outer circle
step slide step slide
and dance ♩ ♩ ♩ ♩ .) Next, create an
toe heel toe heel
Indian line dance with the pattern ♩ ♩
step step
♩ ♩ o . (Suggestion: count off. Even-
step step bow
numbered dancers may step while odd-numbered dancers may bow, and vice versa.) Other members may provide a percussion-instrument accompaniment for these dances.

   Invent a rhythm pattern, write it on the chalkboard in notation, and create a dance.

3. Examine state and city courses of study in physical education. Many of these have excellent lists of recordings of dances classified according to national origin.

4. Develop a repertoire of mixer dances in which the dancers are continually changing partners. These are useful when introducing dances and in situations where children may be reluctant to have only one partner throughout an entire dance.

THE USE OF PERCUSSION INSTRUMENTS

In the beginning this activity is of necessity teacher-directed. That is, it is the teacher who tells the children rather completely what they should do, and how to do it. As soon as possible the teacher directs the children's attention to what instrument or instruments sound most appropriate with the different types of music, and the building of a sense of musical discrimination is begun. This sense of discrimination develops until in the second grade the children should be able to make their own value-judgments of their sound effects, and as a group make their own selection of the instruments most appropriate to the mood and form of the music. For example, they have learned that the tinkling of the triangle can portray light and dainty music, while the heavier sound of the drum is best suited to a sturdy rhythm and heavier-sounding music.

Little children learn by having certain basic experiences in percussive sounds. In kindergarten and first grade they should be helped to experiment with the sound of tapping, shaking, and striking wood, metal, glass, and stone. A leading music educator once said that the purchase of commercial sets of rhythm instruments should be delayed until children have exhausted the surprising potentialities of scrap lumber, iron pipes, oatmeal boxes, gourds, ice cream cartons, and various other items found in homes, alleys, and junk piles.[4]

A suggested instrumentation for a primary grades classroom is as follows:

Wood	*Commercial*	*Homemade*
sticks	8-12 pair	doweling of small diameter cut in 12-inch length; hardwood is best
wood block	1	sections of old baseball bat
temple blocks	1 (not essential)	sections of old bowling pin
claves	1 pair (not essential)	paired resonant sticks; six-inch sections of old broomsticks
xylophone	1	redwood strips
coconut shells		split coconut shells; two paper cups struck together produce a softer sound
Metal		
triangles	2-4	horse shoes or large nails suspended
chimes	1 (not essential)	silver spoons of different sizes, suspended; resonant curtain rods
gong	1 (not essential)	length of iron pipe; old brake drums; use one cymbal
cymbals	1 pair	resonant metal covers; brass trays
jingle bells	1-2	
Rattles		
tambourines	2-4 (commercial ones are the best)	heavy cardboard pie plates with bottle caps, roofing disks, or sea shells attached near the rim; embroidery hoops may also be used

[4] An illustrated list of the almost limitless possibilities of homemade instruments is found in *Creative Rhythmic Movement for Children* by Gladys Andrews (Prentice-Hall, Inc.) pp. 109-118. Most state courses of study in music also have suggestions of this nature.

Wood	Commercial	Homemade
maracas (shakers or rattles)	2-4 pair	gourds with seeds or pebbles inside; various containers with chalk, gravel, peas inside, mounted on handles if desired; medicine bottles with rice; clam shells with shot; old light bulbs covered with papier mâché (when dry break glass)
jingle sticks (clogs)	4	jingling metal disks (disks used in roofing, bottle caps) fastened loosely on a stick
strip rattles		walnut shells and bottle caps suspended alternately on 3-4 inch cords suspended from a band; usually worn on the wrist or ankle in Indian dance

Drums

There should be at least two drums in the classroom: one of low pitch and one of high pitch. Many types of commercial drums are available including tom tom drums, tunable drums (tiny tympani), and bongo and conga drums. Homemade drums may be devised from chopping bowls, wooden kegs, lard cans, and waste baskets with calfskin or heavy rubber thumbtacked, nailed, or laced on. Smaller ones may be made from oatmeal boxes or other cardboard containers used as they are or with ends covered with a rubber sheet. Flowerpot drums may be made by stretching and taping wet heavy paper across the opening. (Paper tightens as it drys.) Ready-made drums of a certain quality are found in the extremely heavy cardboard round cartons used to ship chinaware, seed, and ice cream mix. If stood open-end-down on two books and pounded on the other end, they are quite resonant. The metal cover may be used as a gong. These drums come in several sizes and are often found standing in school corridors used as wastebaskets. Heads for drum beaters may be made of twine, cotton, or elastic wound on a stick. Color is an important element in constructing instruments because it makes them more attractive to children.

Percussion instruments are used in day-to-day classroom rhythm activities. Most public presentations should be outgrowths of this classroom work and not one made by a specialized "band" that in forced imitation of its elders has been made to rehearse especially for such a presentation. Rhythm bands or kiddie bands as organizations that perform regularly in public are contradictory to sound educational principles for this age group.

In the series books for kindergarten and first grade there are songs that introduce percussion instruments one or two at a time. When instruments are used with song material it is seldom that all children are playing at once. Some of the music books for primary grades listed at the end of this chapter include songs with good suggestions for using these instruments. Since the emphasis is on increasing originality and musical discrimination, fully-written scores for percussion instruments are used less frequently today than formerly.

In the third grade there is usually less emphasis on the mass use of these instruments. However, their use as an element contributing to songs continues through the intermediate grades and into junior high school. Sound effects heard on radio, television, and in the movies form a very real part of everyday living. Children in the intermediate grades enjoy the challenge of adding appropriate "sound effects" to songs. One or two drums can add an important element to an Indian song; a tambourine or two can increase the effectiveness of a gypsy song; a combination of tambourine, maracas, and drums can vitalize a Latin-American song. At times a characteristic rhythm played on percussion instruments can be both experimental and creative to the children who are led to discover it.[5] This experience can be of aid in teaching note values. The rhythm pattern may be written on the chalkboard or flannel board in notation, thus helping develop associations between playing the rhythm and visualizing it. Many of the songs listed in the Reference Guide to follow are of the type for which children create accompaniments. These percussion accompaniments may follow the rhythm of the meter, or a different pattern may be invented which is often combined with the meter rhythm. Contrasting rhythms may be played on two or more different instruments or groups of instruments; thus combinations of two or more patterns and the rhythm of the meter are possible in the intermediate grades.

It should be pointed out that the human body itself can produce sounds of rhythmic value. Hand clapping of various kinds (flat-palmed for loud, cupped-palmed for lower pitches, fingers only for soft) has an important place in rhythm activities. Even the sound made in pulling the tongue away from the roof of the mouth (to imitate a clock's ticking, or a "click") can be done in ways to produce high and low pitch. Snapping fingers and stamping feet also have their place.

[5] Example: *New Music Horizons*, Book Four, p. 100.

CARMEN, CARMELA

Mexican Folk Song
Singing in Harmony, p. 62

Possibilities:

Through use of percussion instruments a number of valuable concepts can be taught. Among them are:

1. Keeping time with music (basic rhythmic response)
2. Differences in dynamics (degrees of loud and soft; strong beats and weak beats)
3. Musical form (the phrase; contrasting sections)
4. Mood in music expressed in terms of percussion instruments
5. Awareness of notation and its use
6. Tempi (slow and fast)
7. Pitch (high and low)
8. Relation of rhythm patterns to appropriate instrumentation
9. The relatedness of tempo, dynamics, mood, melody, pitch, and instrumentation

10. Creative power on the child's level to invent and refine the percussion-instrument score and to invent "sound effects" to accompany songs.

Music Series Reference Guide for Using Percussion Instruments

The American Singer (2d ed.; American Book Company)

BOOK ONE

See pp. 156-169. Evaluate recorded songs, 143, 145, 162, 163, 164, 165, 169

BOOK TWO

Suggest use of songs in singing games and rhythms section of index, pp. 187-188

BOOK THREE

Suggest use of songs in rhythms, games, and dances section of index, pp. 203-204

BOOK FOUR

22, 23, 34r, 102, 139, 144ar, 161, 176

BOOK FIVE

37, 38, 102, 113, 157, 167, 172-176, 181r
Suggestions, 108-109 (claves, castanets and rattles)

BOOK SIX

12, 13, 16, 69, 72, 73, 82-84, 123, 132r, 162r
Evaluate songs listed in index 244-245 under headings Latin American, Czechoslovakia, Russia, Spain

New Music Horizons (Silver Burdett Company)

MUSIC FOR EARLY CHILDHOOD

68a, 68b, 69a, 69b, 72, 105b, 110

EXPERIENCES IN MUSIC FOR FIRST GRADE CHILDREN

34ar
(See index headings "Instrumental activities" and "Rhythm band" in index, 142)

FIRST BOOK

26r, 30r, 36r

SECOND BOOK

See IV "Music for the Rhythm Band" 1, 2, 3, p. 161. Recorded: 7, 86, 108, 120

THIRD BOOK

See IV "The Instrumental Program" 1 and 2, p. 184. Recorded: 15, 50, 65, 72, 85, 102, 108
See VI B "Rhythmic Discrimination" p. 185. Recorded: 4, 132

FOURTH BOOK

3, 10, 27, 79, 164. Recorded: 97, 100
See III A "Drum Music" 207

FIFTH BOOK

See III A "Drum Music" 229. Recorded: 38b, 84b, 92, 128, 148, 154b, 175, 177

SIXTH BOOK

Explore possibilities for use of percussion instruments in songs listed under
Czechoslovakia, Russia, Spain, Latin America, and others in index, 249

Our Singing World (Ginn and Company)

KINDERGARTEN BOOK

137r, 138abcdr, 138e, 139abr, 140abr

FIRST GRADE BOOK

134b, 173r, 174ab, 175, 176ab

SINGING ON OUR WAY

46b, 50r, 77, 78r, 101r, 103b, 155br

SINGING AND RHYMING

154ab, 155b, 156, 160, 164, 165, 168arb

SINGING EVERY DAY

43, 55, 170, 172ab

SINGING TOGETHER

45, 48, 58, 92, 138, 139, 188, 189

SINGING IN HARMONY

7, 9b, 38r, 40r, 43r, 52r, 53r, 56, 62r, 68, 146, 200r

A Singing School (C. C. Birchard and Company)

OUR FIRST MUSIC

Refer to Rhythm Band section in the units

OUR SONGS

19, 20r, 26, 46, 48r, 68r, 77r, 78, 79b, 94, 100ar, 106r, 108, 110a, 110br, 111a, 111b, 112r, 113, 114, 115

MERRY MUSIC

10, 12, 31, 37b, 51r, 68r, 82r, 86r, 90ar, 90b, 96r, 118. See pp. 83-91

WE SING

12, 15, 74br, 84
TM 41 suggests percussion instruments in study of $\frac{6}{8}$ meter 92-100

OUR LAND OF SONG

6, 79, 112a, 114r, 119, 151
Simple Latin American rhythm patterns, 150

MUSIC EVERYWHERE
Refer index 220 "Songs with Rhythmic Accompaniment" and "Latin-American Songs"
Recorded: 68, 79, 144, 145, 147
TM 174-178

Together We Sing (Follett Publishing Company)

MUSIC 'ROUND THE CLOCK
Coconut shells, 24, pounders, 17, cymbals, 55, sandblocks, 55, sticks, 7, 36, triangle, 55, woodblock, 7, 24, 48, 49, 55

MUSIC 'ROUND THE TOWN
36r, 53, 64r, 78r (see 135)

TOGETHER WE SING, Enlarged Edition
Recorded: 10, 24, 49, 56a, 108, 114, 133, 156, 234

MUSIC THROUGH THE YEAR
Cymbals, 71
Drum, 71, 118
Gong, 33r
Rhythm patterns, 11r, 35, 80b, 85, 118, 132, 143r
Sandblock, 40r
Sticks, 33r, 118
Triangle, 82, 126r
Woodblock, 40r

MUSIC ACROSS OUR COUNTRY
Claves, 39r
Drum, 25ar, 32r, 33br, 35r, 84r, 158
Gourd rattles, 31r, 38, 132b
Maracas, 39r
Tambourine, 25ar
Woodblock, 46r, 92

VOICES OF AMERICA
See Classified Index° for percussion instruments

VOICES OF THE WORLD
Percussion, classified, 223

Music for Living (Silver Burdett Company)

MUSIC THROUGH THE DAY (including children's books I LIKE THE COUNTRY and I LIKE THE CITY)
"Accentuation by Rhythm Instruments" index, 150
Index of recorded songs, ii
"Instruments" index, 151

MUSIC IN OUR TOWN
"Instruments," 154 (coconut shells, drum, cymbals, rhythm sticks, sandblocks, tambourine, triangle)
TM "Instruments," xi, "Instruments, rhythm," 133, "Instruments, use of," 133

° Not available when this textbook was written.

MUSIC NOW AND LONG AGO

"Instruments," 169 (castanets, tambourines, coconut shells, drums, finger cymbals, maracas, sandblocks, sticks)

TM "Instruments" rhythm, 132

MUSIC NEAR AND FAR

"For drum, other rhythm instruments," 184

TM "Instruments (rhythm, native, use of)," 163

TM "Drums, Scores for (and other rhythm instruments)," 164

MUSIC IN OUR COUNTRY

(See Classified Index and Teachers Book*)

MUSIC AROUND THE WORLD

(See Classified Index and Teachers Book*)

* Not available when this textbook was written.

ADDITIONAL REFERENCES

THINGS

TO

DO

1. Invent some rhythm patterns with hand clapping, percussion instruments, or piano. Write these patterns in notation on the chalkboard.

2. In every song there are ordinarily three distinct rhythms: the rhythm of the first beat of the measure (the primary accent), the rhythm of the meter, and the rhythm of the melody (or words). Try orchestrating a familiar song on this basis. Have the low-pitched heavy-sounding instruments play on the rhythm of the first beat and select others to play on the remaining two rhythms. Experiment by dividing the instruments into groups of like pitches, and also into groups of similar type. Find out which of these instruments are most appropriate to each rhythm.

3. Make some percussion instruments.

4. Investigate and play Latin American rhythms. Example: the rhythm played by the claves (klá ves), a pair of hardwood sticks. Place one on the left hand on the palm side, which is partly closed and rounded to make a resonating chamber. Tap it with one held in the right hand. A ¼ meter rhythm for claves may be expressed in eighth notes as follows: _1_ 2 3 _4_ 5 6 _7_ 8 (play on the italicized beats). Such a rhythm pattern is usually repeated unchanged throughout the song. Try it with a song. Make up rhythm patterns of your own. Experiment with maracas also.

5. Learn how to use the RCA Victor *Rhythm Band Album* of recordings or similar albums designed for percussion-instrument activities.

6. Sing Latin American songs from the series books and add percussion instruments.

7. Make up a story and use percussion instruments for sound effects. Example: The alarm clock (triangle) awakes us in the morning. The clock (gong) strikes eight. Mother calls, "Are You Sleeping?" (Sing the song to the accompaniment of the clock ticking—woodblocks, rhythm sticks). On the way to school we hear a train (sandblocks) and horses (coconut shells). Such a story is another way to teach the appropriateness of individual percussion instruments.

8. Practice some "drum talk."[6] In this activity, the drum plays the rhythm of words or names. One variant of this consists of the teacher playing on a drum the rhythm of the words of parts of a familiar song and the children answering by playing instruments or clapping the rhythm of answering words. Example for primary grades:

Teacher drums: "Mary had a little lamb

Children: Little lamb, little lamb

Teacher: Mary had a little lamb

Children: Its fleece was white as snow."

Example for intermediate grades:

Teacher drums: "Oh Buffalo gals won't you come out tonight?

Children: Won't you come out tonight, won't you come out tonight?

Teacher: Oh Buffalo gals won't you come out tonight?

Children: And dance by the light of the moon?"

9. Pretend you are in a classroom that contains no percussion instruments. Find what the potentialities of the materials around you may be. Examples: the sound of paper held in the air and tapped with a pencil, buckles or heavy costume jewelry, the radiator, and objects found in handbags. Use these in creating a rhythm score to a song.

10. Another kind of percussive rhythmic experience is one in which the teacher plays a rhythm pattern on a drum (or by clapping hands) while children listen, after which there is an immediate imitation by the children playing percussive instruments (or clapping). Experiment with this in your college class.

11. Play a recording of a march such as *National Emblem*. As a class project, create and notate a percussion score to play with the recording as children in intermediate grades might do it.

[6] A recording that introduces drum talk in primary grades is the Young People's Record, *Little Indian Drum*.

SOME ELEMENTS OF MUSIC STRUCTURE

Both in physical response to music and in the choice of appropriate percussion instruments to accompany music, comprehension of musical phrases and of contrasting musical ideas should gradually grow in the children's minds. Although in kindergarten and first grade much of this is done rather spontaneously and without emphasis, children in the second grade ordinarily are advanced enough to be able to understand that music "swings" in two's and three's, that it is put together in sections, and that these phrases, sections, or parts can be discerned if one listens carefully.

In making a simple analysis of songs from the standpoint of rhythm, one of the first questions is, "How does the music swing—in two's or in three's?" The children are taught to feel the *loud* beats (accents) and to respond to these strong accents with a downward motion of the arm. The arm then comes up on the beats that are not as strong. If in response to music the arm moves ↓ ↑ up down the music "swings in two's." If it moves ↓ ↑ up down up the music "swings in three's."

The question, "Is the music the same, or is it different now?" illustrates the basic principle underlying *form* in music. Children can be led to discover that in songs like "Au Clair de la Lune" (At Peirrot's Door), *New Music Horizons Book Five*, p. 15, that the first section of the song is repeated, a new melodic idea is brought in, then the original section is again repeated. It is therefore found that there are four phrases identifiable as A A B A. Other familiar songs that have similar contrasting phrases are "Blue Bells of Scotland," "Massa's in de Cold Cold Ground," "Long Long Ago" and "Oh Susanna." These form a good starting point for phrase analysis. Most of the songs in the series books for second and third grades are written phrase-wise with one phrase on each line. When songs are written otherwise, commas in the text or rests in the melody line often mark the length of the phrase.

Children in the second grade and above are sometimes guided to "act out" phrases in several ways, which include the following arm movements:

 *Moving the arm in a curved horizontal pattern for each phrase*

Moving the arm in a circular direction for each phrase

Moving both arms in a heart-shaped design

One method of teaching recognition of phrases or of contrasting sections of larger pieces of music is to have children *change direction* when they are moving to this music.[7]

Children do not always agree in their physical responses to the phrase, some feeling the phrase to be half the length that others may feel it to be. In certain songs it is interesting to note that adults are more apt to feel long phrases than are children, who often feel twice the number of phrases that the adults do. When this occurs, the children usually divide each long phrase into two shorter ones. In the opinion of the authors, this is not of particular importance, the real point being that children learn to sense that music is divided into logical sections. In view of individual differences in musical background, unanimity of response to phrase length cannot be expected. However, the simplicity of most of the songs found in music series books results in the phrase length being fairly obvious.

In some songs, and in free rhythmic response to recordings and piano selections such as those used for rhythm band, there are obviously contrasting sections of the music, each of which may be composed of a number of phrases. In rhythm-band work these contrasting sections call for differences in the percussion score.[8]

The child should gain certain definite benefits from his experiences with rhythm: sensitivity to rhythm as an element in music; bodily control and grace; an increased understanding of the world's peoples (through folk dances and games); and a growing concept of form in music. Important by-products of the above benefits are an understanding of note values (as they emerge from physical responses to music and from forms of rhythmic notation such as long and short

[7] No. 3 of Things to Do at the end of this section exemplifies this.

[8] Another application of the recognition of larger sections of music is found in the *New Music Horizons*, Book Five, reference to floor patterns, Rhythmic Activities F, p. 231.

dashes), and a knowledge of dance forms and rhythms, which can lead to a more enlightened understanding of these when they are found in the works of the great composers.

THINGS

TO

DO

1. Play a recording accompanying one of the series books that has several songs on it. As you listen, find out by your arm movements (p. 51) whether these songs "swing in two's or three's." Decide what the meter signature may be.

2. Find the phrases in songs in the music series books. Call the first phrase A, and its exact repetition A also. Should A appear in an altered form, call it A¹, A², and so on. When phrases appear that are different from A, the first of these would be called B, the second C, and so on. See how many different arrangements of phrases can be found. Which can be identified as two-part and three-part forms?

3. Class members may sing the familiar song "Row Row Row Your Boat," standing in rows as they sing. They may walk forward on the words "Row row row your boat, gently down the stream," then backward on the remaining words. This dramatizes the division of the song into two phrases. Another way of doing this is to have odd-numbered rows wait until the second phrase to begin their movement. Try this with other simple songs.

4. Do research on directional marching and floor patterns. For suggestions see the *New Music Horizons Teachers Manual for Intermediate Grades*. In this series, directional marching is suggested for fourth grade, floor patterns for fifth grade, and the inventing of floor patterns in sixth grade. These activities are based on the form of the music used.

5. Write a rhythm score to a song. How does the form of the song influence your score?

REFERENCES

Books

Andrews, Gladys, *Creative Rhythmic Movement for Children*. Englewood Cliffs, N.J.: Prentice-Hall, Inc., 1954.

Dykema, Peter, *Twice 55 Games with Music*. Boston: C. C. Birchard and Company.

Fielder, Grace, *The Rhythmic Program for Elementary Schools*. St. Louis: C. V. Mosby Company, 1952.

Geri, Frank H., *Illustrated Games and Rhythms for Children:* Primary Grades. Englewood Cliffs, N.J.: Prentice-Hall, Inc., 1955.

Harris, Jane, Anne Pittman, and Marlys Swenson, *Dance a While*. Minneapolis: Burgess Publishing Company, 1950.

Hood, Marguerite V., and E. J. Schultz, *Learning Music Through Rhythms*. New York: Ginn and Company, 1949.

LaSalle, Dorothy, *Rhythms and Dances for Elementary Schools*. Rev. ed.: New York: A. S. Barnes, 1951.

Murray, Ruth L., *Dance in Elementary Education*. New York: Harper & Brothers, 1953.

Myers, Louise, *Teaching Children Music in the Elementary School*, chap. 4. Englewood Cliffs, N.J.: Prentice-Hall, Inc., 1950.

Rohrbough, Lynn, *Play Party Book*. Delaware, Ohio: Cooperative Recreation Service.

Van Hagen, Winifred, Genevieve Dexter, and Jesse Williams, *Physical Education in the Elementary Schools*. Sacramento: California State Department of Education, 1951.

Recordings	Suggested R.P.M.	Grade Levels
American Book Company 351 East Ohio Street, Chicago 11, Ill.		
Listen and Do Series (stories and music to develop rhythmic coordination)	78	
Album 1. *Friendly Train; Ginger and Josh*		1-2
Album 2. *Handsome Scarecrow; Little Clown*		1-4
Album 3. *Panda Balloon; Dancing Monkey*		1-2
Album 4. *Work and Sing; Play and Sing; Shadow*		3-4
Album 23. *Traditional Singing Games*		K-1
Lets Dance Series	78	
Album SD-1. *Square Dances*		4-8
Album SD-2. *Longways Dances*		4-8
Album SD3. *Country Dances*		4-8
Album AS-25. *Calypso Music for Children*		4-6
Album AS-27. *Rhythm Band Patterns I*		1-3
Album AS-28. *Rhythm Band Patterns II*		1-3
Bowmar Records 4921 Santa Monica Blvd., Los Angeles 29, Cal.		
Album *Rhythm Is Fun*	78	K-3
Album 1. *Singing Games*		1-3
Album 2. *Singing Games*		2-3
Album 3. *Singing Games and Folk Dances*		3
Album 4. *Folk Dances of the World*		4-8
Album 5. *American Folk Dances*		5-8
Album 6. *Latin American Folk Dances*		6-8

Recordings	R.P.M.	Suggested Grade Levels
Album *Rhythm Time*		K-3
Album *Holiday Time*		1-5

Children's Record Guild and Young People's Records
The Greystone Corporation
100 Sixth Avenue, New York 13, N.Y.

	R.P.M.	Grade Levels
Sunday in the Park	45-78	K-2
Nothing to Do (fundamental movements)	78	K-2
My Playful Scarf (creative)	45-78	K-3
The Merry Toy Shop	45-78	K-3
I Am a Circus	78	K-2
When I Was Very Young	78	N-2
Do This, Do That!	78	K-1
Strike Up the Band (rhythm-band instruments)	45-78	K-3
Folk Songs for Singing and Dancing	78	2-5
Swing Your Partner (creating dances)	45-78	2-6
Little Indian Drum (drum talk)	45-78	K-2
Trains and Planes	78	N-1
Out of Doors	78	K-3
Slow Joe (fast and slow)	78	K-2
My Playmate the Wind (creative)	45-78	1-4
Visit to My Little Friend (fundamental movements)	45-78	K-3
Album EAD 2005. *Things to Do*	78	K-3
Album EAD 2006. *More Things to Do*	78	K-3
Album EAD 2017. *Let's Play Rhythms*	78	K-3
Album EAD 2027. *Rhythm, Fun, and Songs*	78	K-2

Columbia Recording Company
1473 Branum Avenue, Bridgeport, Conn.

Participation Records

	R.P.M.	Grade Levels
Put Your Finger in the Air and Join into the Game	45-78	1-3
Jum-A-Jingles (rope skipping and ball bouncing)	45-78	1-3
Lead a Little Orchestra (conducting)	45-78	1-3
Let's Have a Rhythm Band	45-78	1-3

Folkcraft Record Company
1159 Broad Street, Newark, New Jersey

	R.P.M.	
Collection of individual records, song plays, folk dances, play party games, square dances	78	

Follett Publishing Company
1010 West Washington Blvd., Chicago 7, Ill.

	R.P.M.	Grade Levels
Album RA 23 *Rhythmic Activities*	78	K-1

Phoebe James Records
Box 134, Pacific Palisades, Cal.   78

		Grade Levels
AED 1. *Animals*		K-3
AED 2. *Free Rhythms*		K-3

Recordings	*R.P.M.*	*Suggested Grade Levels*
AED 3. *Animals*		K-3
AED 4. *Garden Varieties*		K-3
AED 5. *Fundamental and Interpretive Rhythms*		K-3
AED 6. *Trains*		K-3
AED 7. *Boats and Harbor*		K-3
AED 8. *Branding Cattle* (creative, upper grades)		4-6
AED 9. *Dramatic Play* (Billygoats Gruff, Gingerbread Boy)		K-1
AED 10. *Indian Rhythm* (creative Indian dance, and the like)		1-6
AED 11. *Fire, Fire!*		K-3
AED 12. *Action Songs*		K-3
AED 13. *The Farm*		K-3
AED 14. *Santa Claus and Reindeer* (dramatic play)		K-3
AED 15. *Hallowe'en Rhythms*		K-3

Square Dance Associates
33 South Grove St., Freeport, New York

Albums 1, 2, 3, 4. a course in square dancing		4-12
Album 7. *Rhythms* (percussion instruments, fundamental movements)		K-3

Time Productions, Limited
260 Deansgate, Manchester 3, England

"Listen and Move" series of eight recordings:	1-4	K-2
	5-6	2-7
	7-8	4-8

R.C.A. Victor Educational Services
Dept. 390, Camden, New Jersey

Albums for Rhythmic Activity		
Six albums, one for each grade level	45-78	1-6
Album E 90. *Rhythm Bands*	45-78	1-3
Many selected folk dance records		

Ruth Evans Records
326 Forest Park Ave., Springfield, Mass.

Albums of Childhood Rhythms	78	
Vol. I (Fundamental, animal, toy, playland)		1-3
Vol. II (combinations, interpretative, balls)		1-3
Vol. V (animal, characters, play and dance)		1-3
Vol. VII (nursery rhymes and singing games)		1-3
Vol. III (response to basic musical meters)		4-6
Vol. IV (fundamental dance steps and formations)		4-6
Vol. VI (singing games and easy dances)		4-6
Vol. VII (singing games)		4-6
Vol. VIII (European folk dances)		4-6

Suggested
Grade Levels

Films

Coronet Instructional Films
65 E. South Water St., Chicago 1, Ill.

Rhythm in Music. From rhythm in life to rhythm   4-6
in music

Encyclopaedia Brittanica Films, Inc.
1150 Wilmette Ave., Wilmette, Ill.

Indian Dances   4-8
Rhythm Instruments and Movement (creating   1-3
rhythms)

Carl F. Mahnke Productions
215 E. Third St., Des Moines, Iowa

Rhythm Is Everywhere   1-4
Rhythm Instruments—Movement. How children   1-4
use percussion instruments to enrich their musical experiences.

Teaching Melody and Harmony Instruments

Three

One of the clearly evident trends in elementary music education has been the increasing importance of easy-to-play instruments. For some time it has been agreed that the elementary music program consists of four basic activities: rhythmic response, playing, singing, and listening. However, while the playing of percussion instruments has long been accepted, the value of other simple instruments to the children's musical development is not yet universally recognized—despite substantial gains in that direction. Making music by playing an instrument, regardless of how simple this instrument may be, is highly pleasurable to most human beings regardless of age. It follows that if teachers can learn to direct this natural enthusiasm properly, playing activities can be a source of important musical learning.

Water glasses and bottles

One of the first listening activities in primary grades is the experimenting with sounds made with metal, wood, glass, and stone. These early experiences lead to experiments with water glasses and bottles. By striking glasses and bottles when they are empty and when they contain water, the children can make certain scientific observations. They find that the pitch and tone quality are affected by the size and thickness of the glass or bottle. They may also discover that decreasing the amount of water raises the pitch and increasing the amount of water lowers the pitch—excepting some glasses or bottles that will not tune lower no matter how much water is added —and that striking glasses or bottles with soft objects (such as felt-covered mallets) produces soft tones.

After experimenting with glasses and bottles, children and teacher may decide that bottles are superior because if one can seal them, the pitch will remain stable. Water glasses spill easily and water can also be lost by evaporation, thus changing the pitch. Paint or paper strips can be placed on glasses and bottles to show to what level they should be filled to produce the desired pitch. Numeral names, note names, or syllable names can be painted on or written on paper stickers. Some teachers put vegetable dyes or other coloring in the water to add interest.

Interest in playing melodies on bottles may prompt the teacher or the children to make or obtain a rack from which to suspend the bottles. When this is done, each bottle is suspended by two loops of string, one on each side of the bottle neck, to help it to hang with more stability.

The first experience with playing songs on glasses or bottles is generally with only three pitches: 3-2-1 (mi-re-do). After this is understood, the next step is to use four- and five-tone melodies: 1-2-3-4-5 (do-re-mi-fa-sol). Favorite songs in the three-tone category are *Hot Cross Buns* and *Mary Had a Little Lamb* (slightly altered). Teachers usually devise their own three-, four-, and five-tone songs for this purpose and also encourage the children to compose them. After songs such as these are learned, the scale of glasses or bottles is completed, and melodies are played that can be sounded within the eight tones of the scale.[1] It is advantageous to transfer the skills acquired

---

[1] What is meant here is the *major* scale. Every major scale conforms to the following pattern:

    whole-step   whole-step   half-step

              whole-step

                    whole-step   whole-step   half-step

F major scale:

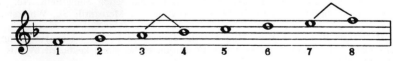

Notice that this scale consists of whole-steps with the exception of the intervals between 3 and 4, and 7 and 8, which are half-steps. One of the best ways to learn the major scale is to see it and play it on the keyboard. A major scale may begin on any note the player chooses, and its name is the same as that of the beginning note.

on glasses and bottles to wooden or metal xylophones. In this book the term "Song Bells"[2] will be used to denote the metal type of this keyboard instrument. These experiences soon lead to the piano keyboard.[3]

The song bells

Playing experience with the Song Bells often begins with songs in the key of C so that children are not confused by the black keys. However, with guidance, children in the first grade can play melodies or parts of melodies in keys such as F and G where one black key is used. The general procedure at first is to learn a song well by rote before attempting to play it (*listen, sing,* then *play*).

Before children understand music notation, teachers guide them to play by ear and by numeral notation.[4] The scale-tone numbers can be written on the white keys with black crayon. Numeral notation may appear as follows:

Hot Cross Buns		*Mary Had a Little Lamb*			
3 2 1 –	3 2 1 –	3 2 1 2	3 3 3 –	2 2 2 –	3 3 3 –
11112222	3 2 1 –	3 2 1 2	3 3 3 3	2 2 3 2	1 – – –

Use keys of F, G, or C Major to avoid black keys in the above songs. songs.

Are You Sleeping

1 2 3 1 | 1 2 3 1 | 3 4 5 – | 3 4 5 – | 56543 1 | 56543 1 | 1 5̄ 1 – | 1 5̄ 1 –

Use G or C Major to avoid black keys. Use F Major to introduce one black key (B♭).

Although children may begin playing the Song Bells with the aid of numerals, they are soon playing songs looking at notation that includes the numerals written beneath (or above) the note they represent. Later, the numerals appear only with the beginning note of each

[2] The specific instrument referred to here is the Perfection Song Bells, No. 1120 (two octaves, chromatic, G to G), Walberg & Auge, 31 Mercantile St., Worcester 8, Mass.

[3] *Hot Cross Buns* and *Mary Had a Little Lamb* can be played on the group of three black keys. Some teachers prefer to introduce the piano keyboard by this use of the black keys.

[4] A well-known book that introduces this practice in first grade is *Timothy's Tunes* by Adeline McCall (Boston Music Company). The *Psaltery Book* by Satis Coleman (John Day Company) is another. *Fun with the Melody-bells* by Rj Staples (Follett) further develops the use of numeral notation.

measure, then only with the beginning note of each phrase, and finally they are abandoned because the children have made the transition from numerals to the notes on the staff.

The "suggestions to the teacher" in one of the basic music series states that if children had free access to keyboard instruments, many of the problems in teaching understanding of pitch differences, of the interval relationship of tones, and of music notation generally would be greatly minimized. The reason is that the keyboard constitutes a highly significant *audio-visual* tool for learning. Children enjoy "picking out tunes" and in doing so on the Song Bells (or the piano) they *see* and *feel* and *hear* the interval relationship of tones. This can lead to a real comprehension of the meaning of the notes on the staff—a comprehension frequently lacking in children whose musical experience has been restricted to a singing approach. In every elementary classroom there should be a music corner that includes Song Bells and easy music to play on it. Some teachers regularly have a "song of the week" which the children learn to play in the music corner before school, after school, and during the school day. This soft-toned instrument seldom disturbs other classroom activities. (See *Keyboard Experience* further on in this chapter for more uses of Song Bells.)

The autoharp, harmolin, and other chording instruments

The Autoharp[5] is an instrument of ancient lineage which has come to be popular in both elementary and junior high schools. The model most commonly used (No. 73) has 12 push-button bars with felts that prevent the vibration of strings other than those that sound the chord tones desired. Some teachers use a five-bar model for primary grades. Although exceptional children in primary grades are able to play the Autoharp satisfactorily, it is not until the fourth grade that almost every child can do well with this instrument. In lower primary grades, teachers often press the buttons while children strum the strings. An important reason for employment of the Autoharp by teachers of primary grades is that it can help develop in the children a feeling for harmony, which is part of the preparation for part singing in intermediate grades. It is a substitute for the piano as well as being a valuable instrument for enrichment in rooms that have pianos. Hearing the chord changes and playing the correct chord at the

[5] Manufactured by Oscar Schmidt-International, Inc., 87 Ferry Street, Jersey City, New Jersey.

proper time are valuable in ear training. The act of chording is also a rhythmic response. A child who is as yet unable to sing beautifully can make as beautiful music on the Autoharp as anyone else. Success on this instrument can help individual children feel a sense of accomplishment, which is essential to good social and emotional growth.

The Autoharp is placed on a desk, a table, or in the lap with the corner between the two straight sides of the instrument pointing somewhat toward the player. Fingers of the left hand press firmly on the appropriate button while the right hand strokes the full range of the strings from left to right with a pick. Sometimes the player will stroke the strings on the left side of the bridge to produce a deeper-toned effect. Chording on the Autoharp may effectively introduce chording on the piano. The Harmolin[6] is another instrument of this general type.

These chording instruments can provide valuable listening experiences in identifying common chords. Children can learn to recognize the I-chord as the "home" chord, the V-chord as the "away-from-home" chord, and the IV-chord as the "leaning" or "longing-for-home" chord. They may identify them by appropriate motions: the "home" chord with folded arms, the "away-from-home" chord with outstretched arms, and the "leaning" chord by raising both arms to the left or to the right.

A major problem in the use of Autoharps and Harmolins is that of tuning them. There is no universally accepted method. Ordinarily, one tunes to a piano that is in proper pitch. The notes of the C Major chord may be tuned first (all C's, E's, and G's), then the notes of the G₇ chord (all B's, D's, and F's—the G's having been tuned as part of the C chord), and next the F Major chord (all A's—the F's and C's having been tuned as tones belonging to the other chords). These chords should then be played slowly to find out whether any of the strings need further adjusting. After this, the other strings may be tuned as individual tones of the chromatic[7] scale. Then every chord of the instrument is played slowly to find a possible need for further tuning. A child may play tones of the piano while the teacher adjusts the strings.

There is today a strong trend to include "Autoharp chords" in many recently published or revised music books. Besides the references to the Autoharp in the basal series books, there exists a specific litera-

---

[6] Manufactured by the Harmolin Company, P. O. Box 6157, San Diego 6, California.
[7] The chromatic scale consists of half-steps.

ture for it which is also applicable to the Harmolin. Some examples follow:

Autoharp Accompaniments to Favorite Songs, by Lillian Mohr Fox; C. C. Birchard, 285 Columbia Ave., Boston, Mass.

Autoharp Song Folio, by Evelyn Waldrop; William J. Smith Music Co., New York, N.Y.

Fun with the Classroom Harps, by Rj Staples; Follett Publishing Co., 1010 W. Washington Blvd., Chicago 7, Ill.

Golden Autoharp Melodies, by Sigmund Spaeth; National Autoharp Sales Co., 560 31st St., Des Moines 12, Iowa.

Harmony Fun with the Autoharp, by Beatrice P. Krone; Neil A. Kjos Music Co., 223 W. Lake St., Chicago 6, Ill.

Teacher's Guide for the Golden Autoharp, by Lorrain Watters; National Autoharp Sales Co., 560 31st St., Des Moines 12, Iowa.

If the desirability of chording experiences on Autoharp and Harmolin has gained deserved acceptance in elementary music education, it follows that there should be similar values in instruments like the ukulele and the steel guitar. In recent years the ukulele has found supporters from the fifth grade on, and chording on the steel guitar has been declared by one experienced music supervisor to be "more fascinating and satisfying" than chording on any of the instruments mentioned here. It is urged that teachers and children experiment to find out for themselves the comparative advantages of each instrument.

Keyboard experience and the piano

The term "keyboard experience" is defined as a use of the piano that makes a substantial contribution to the program of general music in the schools. It does not stress performing skill in the traditional sense. The piano can be used by children in primary grades in connection with songs in the same informal way the percussion instruments and the Song Bells are used. Children in intermediate grades can use it for chording in the way they use the Autoharp. Like the Song Bells, the piano keyboard provides an audio-visual tool to help the child gain keener perception of the interval relationship of tones, and of many other aspects of music, which can develop into a real understanding of notation. Through piano chording a foothold in comprehending the science of music theory is gained in a logical way. The piano can be used as an instrument of percussion, melody, harmony, and for any combination of these.

Classroom teachers do not have to be pianists to teach music through keyboard experience. They need only be introduced to it so that they can proceed in the same way as the children. At the beginning,[8] a child can play the tone that sounds "one" when the clock strikes "one" in *Hickory Dickory Dock*, just as he may have done on the Song Bells. In a song that has words of importance on one or two tones children may play these at the time they occur in the melody. The same little three-note melodies played on water glasses, bottles, and Song Bells may be played on the piano. As time goes on, four- and five-finger patterns can be used in an incidental way in both ascending and descending forms. Here are examples of such usage:

one finger: The child plays a tone on the piano, then tries to match it with his singing voice. The child also plays repeated single tones such as in the beginning of *Jingle Bells* and in chants (pp. 196-198).

two fingers: This may relate to tone-matching, where the scale tones such as 5 and 3 (sol and mi) are played as well as sung.

three fingers: The scale tones 3 2 1 may be played whenever the words "three blind mice" occur in the song of that name. The scale tones 1 2 3 1 with the words "Are you sleeping?" may be played in the song of that name.

four fingers: The scale tones 4 4 3 3 2 2 1 in *Twinkle, Twinkle, Little Star* may be played when the following words appear: "How I wonder what you are," and "Twinkle twinkle all the night." The scale tones 5 5 4 4 3 3 2 may be played along with the words "Up above the world so high" and "Like a diamond in the sky."

five fingers: The scale tones 5 43 21 are used at the end of *Row Your Boat* with the words "Life is but a dream," and the scale tones 5 4 3 2 1 or 5 443 2 1 are used with the words "Ten little Indian boys" at the end of the song of that name.

scales: Many songs in the music series books are based on scales or parts of scales and can be played on the keyboard. One example is *Round of Thanks*, Chapter Eight, p. 188. Others are *American Singer Second Edition Book Three*, 110, 111, *Book Four*, 180a, *Merry Music*, 133, *We Sing*, 42b, *Singing and Rhyming*, 125, *Singing Every Day*, 75a, *New Music Horizons Book Three*, 71, *Book Four*, 34a.

A very natural outgrowth of such piano-song relationships is the composing of little songs within the limitations of three, four, and five scale tones—songs which the children both sing and play. Eventually this activity will lead to the use of more scale tones in song composition. The resourceful teacher will gain pleasure and satisfaction in finding songs to which these simple uses of the piano are suited, knowing that by such processes children learn to listen and thus improve their singing at the same time. This type of keyboard experience merges with the listening process of tone-matching and makes it more of a game.

[8] Examples similar to those that follow are found in *Playing as We Sing* by Ahearn and Burrows (Ginn and Company, 1955).

Another simple use of the piano is the playing of the notes according to the chord names. Example: play F with the F chord, G with the G chord. (See *Chord Roots*, Chapter Eight, p. 190.) Still other of the almost limitless things to do with the piano or Song Bells include playing the rhythm patterns of children's names on the keyboard with one tone or a series of tones; playing two tones that illustrate in correct pitch high and low in connection with songs; playing short tonal patterns from songs for tone-matching; playing octave intervals of songs that emphasize this interval; playing other intervals in songs that feature them; playing running notes, walking notes, for other children to respond to; playing entire characteristic phrases (as in the beginning of *The Caisson Song*); aiding part singing by playing two-part songs from the series books with two hands, one on each line of notes; and using the piano to accompany songs by chording.

The playing of the Song Bells, a small instrument, logically comes before the playing of the piano, a very large instrument, but whatever is done on the Song Bells applies directly to the piano because the keyboard is the same—even to black and white keys on Perfection Song Bells. The playing of chords on the Autoharp logically leads to an understanding of chording on the piano. Chording is essentially an intermediate-grades activity, but some children in the second and third grades can do it in its simpler forms—particularly children who take private piano lessons.

Piano chording

Since the 1 3 5 note pattern becomes a familiar one to children, being used both in their songs and in the procedure that enables the class to have a feeling for the key before singing (Chapter Four, p. 103) this is a logical note combination to use in beginning to teach chording. This 1 3 5 chord (a major *triad* in *root position*) is also an initial concept in the formal study of music theory. From chording experiences will come understandings of elementary theory.

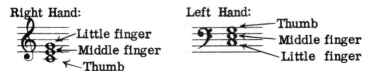

Should a child be unable to exert equal pressure through these three fingers or in any other way be unable to control them at first, he may use any combination of fingers of both hands to accomplish the playing of this chord. The teacher may help the child to play the chord in a steady walking-note rhythm, then while he continues playing in rhythm, have the class sing "Row, row, row your boat." To a child who has never played the piano, the discovery that he can accompany a well-known song in this simple manner is thrilling. There are few songs that can be accompanied by the lone 1 3 5 chord. Among them are *Row Your Boat, Are You Sleeping?* and *Little Tom Tinker.* Songs that rightfully require two chords (I and V₇) but that might be usable as one-chord songs include *Old McDonald, Farmer in the Dell, Three Blind Mice, Goodbye Old Paint, Swing Low Sweet Chariot, Taps,* and *Shortnin' Bread.* Some one-chord songs in the series books are:

New Music Horizons, Book Two, 62, 119b. Book Four, 115.
Our Singing World, Singing On Our Way, 147a, 155a. Singing Together, 18b.

ROW, ROW, ROW YOUR BOAT

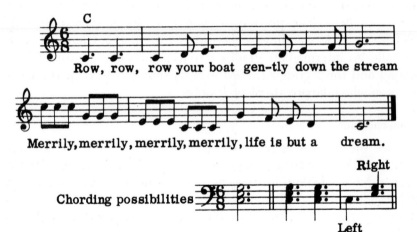

Summary of possibilities:

Play the melody with the right hand.
Play the melody with the left hand.
Play the chord with the left hand.
Play the chord with the right hand.
Play the chord with both hands.
Play the melody with the right hand and the chord with the left hand.

Play the melody with the left hand (in bass clef) and the chord with the right hand (in treble clef).

Play the chord in other forms, such as one note at a time.

How often the chord is sounded depends on how the individual feels about the song. One child may play a chord on every beat (the rhythm of the meter). Another may choose to sound the chord every other beat. Still another child may alter the steady pattern of chord-sounding by a pause at the end of a phrase. Children should be free to be as individually creative as possible in this simple way. The teacher will recognize many individual differences in the ways that children react to keyboard experience.

When a child has learned how to build 1 3 5 chords on different pitches such as C, F, G, and has learned to recognize the distinctive sound of the major chord, the 1 3 5 chord in minor may be easily taught. A child can soon learn that the minor chord has its own characteristic sound and that he can build both major and minor chords at will. Experience will expand the child's feeling for the difference in sound between major and minor. The mechanical difference between major and minor 1 3 5 chords is merely that the middle finger, which plays scale tone 3, is placed ½ step lower in minor than in major. Very few commonly known songs can be accompanied by the lone minor 1 3 5 chord, but children can compose such songs easily. An example is below:

SLAVE SONG
(Round)

D-Minor (d) chord for
autoharp and piano

Fourth Grade
Four part round

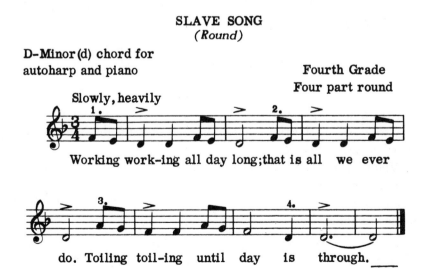

Working work-ing all day long; that is all we ever
do. Toiling toil-ing until day is through.____

Piano chording:

Suggested rhythmic responses:

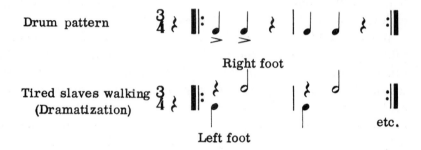

Singing and playing:
A piano part invented later which can be sung as a chant:

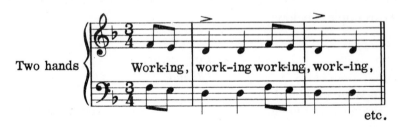

The children discovered that their song could be sung as a round.

A song of Israeli origin that can be accompanied by the G Minor chord is *Zum Gali Gali*.[8]

When numerals are used to designate scale tones, the home tone in minor is "1" just as the home tone in major is "1." However, when syllables are used for this purpose, the home tone in minor is "la" while the home tone in major is "do."

---

[8] This song is in *Open Road Song Book* (Cooperative Recreation Service, Delaware, Ohio, *Music in Our Country* (Music for Living Series) p. 169, and *Voices of the World* (Together We Sing Series) p. 132.

If children have used the Autoharp with songs requiring two or more different chords, the addition of the V_7 chord[9] to permit improvising a piano accompaniment to many familiar songs is relatively easy. A simple form of the chord change from I to V_7 and back to I is as follows:[10]

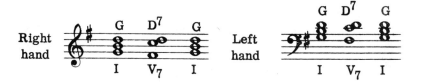

Using the hand position for the 1 3 5 chord as a starting point, the following directions apply in *all* major keys:

Right hand: The little finger remains on the same key. The fourth finger is placed ½ step higher than the third finger was. The thumb is placed ½ step lower than before.

Left hand: The thumb remains on the same key. The index finger is placed ½ step higher than the middle finger was. The little finger is placed ½ step lower than before.

Many familiar songs can be harmonized with the I and V_7 chords. Some of the most familiar are *Chop Sticks, Put Your Little Foot, Billy Boy, Listen to the Mocking Bird, Singing in the Rain, Clementine, Shoo Fly, Alouette, Deaf Woman's Courtship, Ten Little Indians, Long Long Ago, Skip to My Lou, Where Has My Little Dog Gone?, Polly-Wolly-Doodle, Hot Cross Buns, Lightly Row, Oats Peas Beans and Barley, Mary Had a Little Lamb, London Bridge, Down in the Valley, Farmer in the Dell, Three Blind Mice, Did You Ever See a Lassie?, Old Texas, Looby Lou, Buffalo Gals, Lavender Blue,* and *Bow Belinda.*

Since most songs in minor keys are based on a scale in which the seventh tone is raised ½ step, practically all minor I-V_7 chord songs will have the V_7 chord played exactly the same as it is played in the major keys of the same name, i.e., the V_7 chord in G Minor is usually the same chord as in G Major. Thus, the only difference in chording

[9] See page 75 for an explanation of the origin of the hand position for playing the V_7 chord.

[10] A more simple form omits the lowest note of each of the chords.

CLEMENTINE

Oh my dar-ling, oh my dar-ling, oh my dar-ling Clem-en-tine. You are lost and gone for ev-er, oh my dar-ling Clem-en-tine.

Piano chords:

would be in the I chord, which in minor would have its third (the middle note) ½ step lower than in the major chord. It is a simple matter, then, to play *Nobody Home* in G Minor:[11]

NOBODY HOME

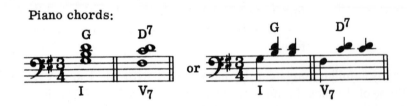

Heigh Ho, no-bo-dy at home. Food nor drink nor mo-ney have I none. Yet will I be ve-ry mer-ry.

---

11 Some musicians abbreviate G Minor by writing "g," and G Major by "G."

Piano chording:

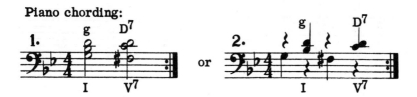

or

and yet another way:

Suggestion: Try making up an introduction with Example 3. Also, improvise an ending for this round. Add suitable percussion instruments and hand clapping.

Other interesting songs in minor that use these same chords are the French carol *Pat-a-pan* (*Merry Music*, p. 185, *Together We Sing*, Enlarged Edition, p. 234r) and the English carol *Dame, Get Up* (*Together We Sing*, Enlarged Edition, p. 54br). Percussion instruments go well with *Pat-a-pan*.

The hand position for the IV chord is easier than the hand position for the V₇ chord. The "rule" for the change from I to IV is as follows:

Left hand: The little finger remains on the same key. The index finger is placed ½ step higher than the middle finger was. The thumb moves up one whole step.

Right hand: The thumb remains on the same key. The middle finger is placed ½ step higher than before. The little finger moves up one whole step.

Left hand   Right hand

The round *Christmas Bells* provides a good introduction to this chord change. Use the above chords as marked. See page 75 for an explanation of the origin of the hand position for playing the IV chord.

CHRISTMAS BELLS

The familiar round *Lovely Evening* is an excellent example of a song such as the above that requires only the I and IV chords for accompaniment.

The IV chord in minor is played by lowering the highest of the three tones of the major IV chord ½ step. A beautiful American folk song that can be harmonized with only I and IV chords is *Wayfaring Stranger:*

WAYFARING STRANGER

D Minor (d)

I'm just a poor wayfaring stran-ger a trav'-ling

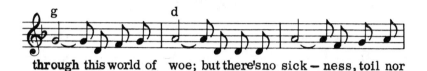

through this world of woe; but there's no sick — ness, toil nor

dan-ger in that bright world to which I go. I'm go-ing

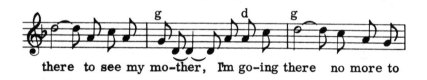

there to see my mo-ther, I'm go-ing there no more to

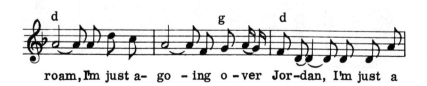

roam, I'm just a- go - ing o -ver Jor-dan, I'm just a

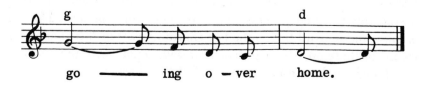

go ————— ing o - ver home.

Examples of the many songs in major keys easily chorded with I,
IV, and V₇ chords are *The Caisson Song, Oh Susanna, He's a Jolly
Good Fellow, The First Noel, Camptown Races, Home on the Range,
America, Night Herding Song, Eyes of Texas (I've Been Working on
the Railroad), All Through the Night, Sing Your Way Home, Jingle
Bells, Deck the Halls, Happy Birthday to You, Old Oaken Bucket,
Auld Lang Syne, Annie Laurie, Old Folks at Home, Old Black Joe,
Reuben and Rachel, Silent Night, Santa Lucia, The Muffin Man.*

AMERICA

This use of the piano in the classroom can result in a teacher's
learning to play comparatively well. Should any teacher desire to
hasten this learning process, there are beginning piano books that
employ and expand the method of chording used in this chapter; by
means of these an adult can teach himself to play with more skill. A
list of such books is found at the end of the chapter.

Teachers should use the loud pedal of the piano very sparingly. A common fault of piano players is overuse of this pedal, which results in a blur of tones rather than in the clarity and distinctness children need to hear.

If one can chord with I, IV, and V_7 chords in major keys, it is not difficult to chord in minor keys with I, IV, and V_7. Incidentally, minor keys are not as important as major keys as far as common usage in the United States is concerned. While peoples of Eastern Europe find in minor tonality a natural expression, the people of the United States lean rather heavily toward the major tonality. American children should be able to identify minor and major and to enjoy hearing the changes from minor to major and vice versa in songs such as *We Three Kings of Orient Are*, *When Johnny Comes Marching Home*, and *Minka*, but it is not necessary in the elementary school to do much with technical matters such as the different kinds of minor scales. However, from fourth grade on the teacher must be prepared to face certain questions. Let us try to forecast some of them.

1. From where do the V_7 and IV chords come, and why are our fingers in the positions they are on the keyboard?

A 1 3 5 chord can be built on every step of the scale. We could chord by using only 1 3 5 chords, but it would be very awkward to do, and it would not sound well. What we are trying to do with our chord positions at the piano is to move our fingers as little as possible. It is something like being "intelligently lazy"—which in this case is also being efficient. Here are the I, IV, and V chords in 1 3 5 position in the C Major scale:

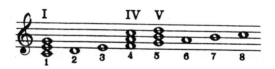

These chords can also be called C, F, and G, because they have two names, one being the Roman numeral that corresponds to the Arabic number name of the scale tone on which the chord is built, and the other being the letter name of the note that is "1" when the chord is in 1 3 5 (root) position. Here is the V_7 chord in root position.

We are still in the key of C Major. Compare the V₇ with the V above. This chord is called V₇ because a note has been added that is seven lines and spaces above G. The notes from the bottom to top in this chord are G, B, D, and F, or 1 3 5 7. It is V₇ because G is the fifth step of the scale of C, and we are using that key in this illustration.

The following illustration shows where we obtain the simple three-finger hand position for chording:

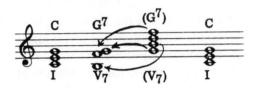

By rearranging the G 1 3 5 7 chord into another *position*, and by omitting the note D, which is the one we can most easily eliminate without injuring the sound of the chord, we can keep the hand in the same place as it was in playing the I chord and move only the fingers.

The IV chord that we use in piano chording is another position of the original 1 3 5 arrangement of the notes:

Note: Teachers may wish to have some understanding of chord positions even though this information may not be taught as such to the children. Common chord positions are:

The first inversion is called 6-3 because if one counts from the lowest note to the highest, numbering the lowest note "1," the *interval*[12] is found to be that of a *sixth*. Counting in similar manner, from the lowest note to the middle one, reveals that this

[12] For an explanation of the term "interval," see Chapter Seven, p. 173. Also see Appendix C.

interval is a *third*, hence this is a 6-3 chord. The origin of the name of the 6-4 chord can be counted out in the same way. The two intervals here are a sixth and a *fourth*, hence the name 6-4 chord.

---

2. Why do we have sharps or flats in major keys?

Every major scale has the same structure, being built of whole-steps except for the intervals between scale tones 3 and 4, and 7 and 8, which are half-steps. The teacher can explain this by holding up the Song Bells and showing the class by sight and sound why sharps or flats are in all major keys except the key of C—and why the key of C needs no sharps or flats.

3. Why is the key of G Minor in the key signature of B♭ Major?

Every minor scale begins on the sixth step of some major scale. G Minor is therefore *related* to B♭ Major—they both have the same key signature. C Minor is the *relative* minor to E♭ Major; E Minor is the relative minor to G Major. Again, the Song Bells are useful in explaining this, as is the piano keyboard.

4. Where does the sharp or natural come from when we play the V₇ chord in minor keys? What are the minor scales?

There are three kinds of minor scales: the natural, the harmonic, and the melodic. When the natural minor is used, there are no accidentals (sharps, flats, cancel signs). (See *Wayfaring Stranger*, p. 73.)

C Minor (natural)

If one listens carefully as this scale is played, he will find that there is a whole-step between scale tones 7 and 8. This is unlike the major scale, which always has a half-step between 7 and 8. Possibly in order to make this scale sound more like the major scale does, people raised that seventh step by ½ step. The new scale was called the *harmonic* minor scale. It is this raising of the seventh step that gives us our sharp or natural in the V₇ chord, and makes that chord the same as the V₇ in the major key of the same name—in this case C Major. C Minor is called the *parallel* minor to C Major since they both begin and end on the same note.

C Minor (harmonic)

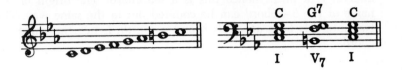

People changed the minor scale again so that its highest four notes would sound just like those notes of the major scale. To do this, they raised by ½ step the sixth step of the minor scale along with the seventh step. This resulted in making the IV chord in the melodic minor scale (ascending) just like the IV chord in the parallel major key. An interesting difference about the melodic minor scale is that when it descends, it changes back to the original natural minor.
C Minor (melodic)

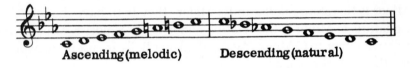

Ascending (melodic)   Descending (natural)

Recorder-type and flute-like instruments

These instruments are used most frequently in the fourth and fifth grades. However, some third grades do well with them.

The recorder is the ancestor of the present-day flute, and composers of distinction once wrote music for it. Its use in the elementary schools has been hindered by its cost, which, though not great, is more than parents are willing to spend on a non-standard instrument, and by its difficulty, which is somewhat greater than the busy classroom teacher wishes to accommodate. Hence we have the current use of low-cost imitations[13] made of plastic material. The most common are the Song Flute, the Tonette, and the Flutophone. These instruments have a range of a ninth:

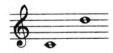

The Tonette can be tuned by lengthening the instrument by pulling out the mouthpiece. Advantages of tuning are offset by the fact that the plastic material wears when the mouthpiece is pulled in and out

---

[13] European music educators insist that a suitable recorder is preferable.

frequently, and that the teacher must be sure that all Tonettes are tuned alike when they are played by a group. After a mouthpiece has become worn, it can be kept from falling out by placing a thin strip of paper between the mouthpiece and the body of the instrument where they join. Some teachers use tape to hold the parts together. The Song Flute cannot be tuned. This disadvantage is offset by having all instruments in the same pitch, and by the assurance that no mouthpiece will fall out. Both the Song Flute and the Tonette are constructed so that children's fingers fall naturally in place on the finger-holes, which are set in a curved line, while the Flutophone has finger-holes that are set in a straight line.

The sound of these instruments is essentially soft, as is necessary for classroom use. Because all three instruments are limited to the range previously mentioned, their most common use is in connection with songs within the range of the ninth beginning on middle C. A ninth is the interval of an octave plus one whole-step. Two frequently used instruments have a larger range—each of about two octaves beginning on middle C: the Symphonette and the Melody Flute. These instruments are a little more difficult to play than those of smaller range, and, in the opinion of the authors, should seldom be used below fifth grade. Of all these simple instruments, the one with the most pleasing tone is the Melody Flute, which in some parts of the United States is used in the junior high school grades. All of these instruments except the Melody Flute finger like the saxophone, the flute, and the upper register of the clarinet. The Melody Flute's fingering is one finger removed from that of the standard instruments. This apparent defect does not seem to bother children who later change to a real flute, clarinet, or saxophone, which, for example, fingers G with three fingers while the Melody Flute fingering for the same note requires only two fingers.

There are music supervisors who object to the use of these little instruments in the classroom. Their major objections are two: (1) the children enjoy them so much that unless a teacher knows how to control the situation they may be overemphasized to the neglect of other aspects of the music program—particularly singing; (2) they are played so badly out of tune that their use constitutes a poor musical experience. It follows, then, that the teacher who uses the easy-to-play instruments must avoid these pitfalls. It is suggested that three rules be followed:

1. Use such instruments on a mass basis no more than one time per week.
2. On the day the instruments are used the children should be using their singing voices *in connection with playing the instruments* approximately one-half of the period, as will be explained below.
3. The teacher should devise ways so that the children will play the instruments in tune; otherwise they should not be used.

If a teacher can learn to teach these instruments properly, he will find that through this playing experience he can teach listening, note reading, sight singing, part singing, and music composition as well as playing.

After the teacher decides to use the little instruments, his first task is to choose the one best suited to his group. If possible, the children should participate in the choice by experimenting with several of them. Of course, when two or more children blow the same instrument the teacher should have available a sterilizing agent.[14] The teacher should learn to play the chosen instrument well before attempting to teach the class how to play it. Skill on any of them is easy to acquire, so this is not an obstacle.

The present music series books do not contain beginning lessons on these instruments, so it is best to use instruction books written for this purpose. There are many of these on the market, but few of them are suited to the general music class because the approach is not a song approach—it is the technical approach of the instrumentalist. A good beginning book of the desirable type should contain many well-known songs for children to sing and play, including some to sing and play in parts. A book that fills these requirements is *Melody Fun*, distributed by the Lyons Band Instrument Company, Chicago. Its subtitle is "For Singing and Playing with the Tonette." This implies that the playing should supplement the singing—not dominate it.

The following teaching procedure is implied by the subtitle of *Melody Fun*. On page two of this book we find the first fingering to be learned by the children, the note B on the middle line of the staff. Before attempting to play this note the children should first *hear* the pitch and *sing* the pitch. The teacher plays the note several times while the class listens to the pitch and to the tone quality. Then the teacher sings the pitch. The class sings the pitch—singing the note

---

[14] A variety of disinfectants is available at drug stores. One should be selected that will not affect plastics adversely.

name B, for the children are going to learn the note names in a highly purposeful setting. There may follow more answering back and forth from the teacher to the class (teacher plays and sings B) and from the class to the teacher (class sings B until everyone has matched the pitch vocally and has really "absorbed" it.) Thus, when the children finally play B on their instruments, they will tend to match the pitch they have heard to the extent of adjusting their lips and mouths automatically to produce it with some accuracy. Next, this book presents the note A, and we recommend that it be taught in the same manner that B was taught. Following the presentation of B and A is a little song constructed on these two pitches. Here the teacher asks the children to again sing B and A. When this is accomplished (i.e., when the children have matched tones again and remember each pitch distinctly), they are asked to sing the song *On Tip Toe* using the note names as words. This done, they next sing the song with the words. Then they play the song on the instruments. Thus the children have had, first, meaningful experiences in listening (tone matching), then in sight singing, and finally in playing the instruments. Some of them will be truly concentrating on notation for the first time in their lives.

On page three the note G should be learned in the same manner that B and A were learned. The children then sight-sing the next song, *A Safety Song*, which employs the three pitches. They sing them first with the note names, then with the words. Lastly, they play the song.

At the bottom of page three there is a song called *My First Duet*. Words can be invented by the children when they have learned to sing it with note names and to play it. It can be sung one line at a time and as a rudimentary duet introducing part singing. It is then played a line at a time and as a duet. To aid the part singing, one instrument[15] can remain on each part when the class sings.

Proceeding from this very simple introduction with the above method, F♯, B♭, and the other tones of the C scale are learned. Keen listening for proper pitch, sight singing, music notation study, and part singing are combined in this type of instrumental experience. Appropriate songs to play can be found in the series books,[16] and listening and singing based on the instrumental activity can be continued from this source of material.

---

[15] Song Bells can also aid in the teaching of part singing in this manner.

[16] A list of songs in "Tonette range" and in the keys of C, F, and G which can be accompanied by Autoharp or piano chording is found on pages 117-130 in *Basic Music for Classroom Teachers*, Nye and Bergethon (Prentice-Hall, Inc.).

The singing classroom orchestra

When children have learned to play recorder-type instruments, to chord on the piano and Autoharp, and to play Song Bells and percussion instruments, the possibility of the singing classroom orchestra presents itself. When in the series books, in *Melody Fun*, and other supplementary books, the teacher finds a melody line in the range of the recorder-type instruments with the chords named, there are opportunities for combining various instruments with voices, or alternating instruments and voices. Here is a creative activity developing musical discrimination, for the children and the teacher will have to orchestrate the song according to their own judgment. Children can also have experiences in conducting such orchestras. Songs that are not found in books at hand can be presented by means of an opaque projector or can be drawn on large (two by three feet) sheets of heavy paper or light cardboard and placed where all the children can see them. Music can be quickly drawn on such paper. A staff liner with chalk is used to mark the staff. These chalk lines are drawn over with black crayon, freehand. When two-part songs are written, the melody part may be in black crayon while the harmony part is in another color for easier reading. Examples follow:

Theme from

NINTH SYMPHONY

(Children may make up appropriate words around the concept of the brotherhood of man.)

The *Theme from the Ninth Symphony* is an example of the very simple beginning music a classroom orchestra uses. Ordinarily, themes from the great symphonies are not applicable to this type of work. This particular theme, however, has the simplicity of folk music and is understood easily by children. It can be extended to include more of the original melody than appears here. An interesting and thrilling event after words have been set to it and the song is learned is when the teacher plays a recording of a section of the last movement of the *Ninth Symphony* and watches the reaction of children who are fascinated listeners to "their song" as Beethoven used it. It is possible for "appreciation" to be at an extremely high level of effectiveness at this point. The key of C was chosen because it is easiest for the playing of the instruments. The key of F is preferable as soon as the fingering of B♭ is learned, because it places the singing voice in a better range.

Come, Ye Thankful People, Come is much more difficult and represents a later experience in the development of the classroom orchestra.

COME, YE THANKFUL PEOPLE, COME

(Children will probably know the words for this familiar song.)

In summary, the playing or instrumental activities of the general music program constitute not an end in themselves but an important aid in the teaching of better listening, singing, musical discrimination, creativity, part singing, and note reading, and serve as an introduction to simple music theory—all in a setting that children enjoy, understand, and know to be purposeful. Instrumental activities in general music are both psychologically and physiologically sound in their appeal to the natural impulses of young Americans to be active and to manipulate a variety of things. Dangers of this approach have been stated: (1) children's interest in this one segment of the general music program may cause undue emphasis on instrumental activities to the detriment of other aspects of balanced musical growth, and (2) children's playing the instruments out of tune can make such experiences worthless. In this chapter a method of teaching recorder-type instruments has been described that helps children to play in tune. It is essential that *all* instruments used in combination in the classroom be in tune with each other. It has been suggested that instruments be used en masse only one period during the week; on that day the teacher should so organize the lesson that the children are using their singing voices approximately half the time.

The place of band and orchestra instruments

Few of the standard "big" instruments blend well enough with children's voices to be usable in singing-classroom-orchestra activities. But the flute and the stringed instruments can be welcome additions. The cello provides a simple bass part. Classroom teachers should request the aid and advice of the teacher of instrumental music before adding these instruments to the classroom group.

Clarinets, trombones, cornets, saxophones, and other large instruments can be played by children in the intermediate grades. However, their tones are too powerful to blend with the light voices of children, thus they are ill-suited for inclusion in a classroom orchestra that is associated with the singing program. The authors of the basal music series books have nonetheless included some interesting uses for these instruments. These include instrumental solos, duets, descants, and true orchestrations of some of the songs. It appears that the best use for these orchestrations is in the playing of instrumental introductions and/or accompaniments for songs on special programs or for large vocal groups. They may be useful in schools experimenting with a union of vocal and instrumental music as a means of attempting to solve a scheduling problem. One publisher provides an instrumental method[17] for the large instruments that parallels the song material in one of the music series. All basal music series books should be examined in order to be aware of and to evaluate the uses suggested for the band and orchestra instruments in the general music program.

Lessons given on these instruments by the teacher of instrumental music should be scheduled in the special interest period when possible. The temporary withdrawal of some children from the classroom is a disruption unless the teacher can make plans in accordance with it. Much of the irritation that sometimes comes when children leave the classroom for these lessons can be avoided if all teachers concerned have an opportunity to plan the instrumental music schedule cooperatively.

Music Series Reference Guide for Playing Instruments

The American Singer (2nd ed.; American Book Company)

BOOK ONE

Xylophones, 170-172

BOOK TWO

Xylophone and piano keyboard, 106-109, 111, 154, 157

BOOK THREE

Violin, 122

Xylophone, piano keyboard and psaltery, 108-117, 120

BOOK FOUR

Autoharp, 45-49, 68, 72-74, 104, 106, 144, 154

Chimes, 88

Recorder-type instruments. Select songs in key of C that are in proper range. Songs in keys of F and G are: 11, 21, 22, 23, 26, 27, 28, 29, 32, 41, 45, 46, 47, 48, 49, 57b, 66, 68, 71, 72, 74b, 78, 87, 106, 109, 117, 144b, 164 (two-part), 168, 175, 184, 195 (two-part)

BOOK FIVE

Autoharp, 14, 15, 16, 17, 22, 23, 24, 28, 34, 40, 42, 46, 48, 49, 55, 59, 72, 73, 76, 77, 79, 92, 107, 112, 123, 133a, 137, 143, 158, 188

Clarinet, 142

[17] *Instrumental Music Horizons* (Silver Burdett).

Cornet, 94, 99, 142 (also clarinet)
Flute, 51, 52, 73, 75, 98, 99, 115b, 135
Orchestrations, index p. 212
Violin, 51, 52, 73, 75, 98, 99, 115b, 135

BOOK SIX

Autoharp, 12, 13, 16, 22, 24, 30, 32, 36, 37, 42, 43, 44, 46, 47, 58, 60, 63, 94, 100, 108, 116, 126, 131, 144, 146, 147, 149, 151, 153, 157, 160, 162, 193, 220, 224
Orchestrations: index p. 245
Trumpet, 9, 138, 140

Our Singing World (Ginn and Company)

SINGING ON OUR WAY

Piano, 14, 61, 117, 133
Song Bells, 14, 77, 106a, 133, 144a, 147, 155, 156a
Water glasses, 14, 61, 117, 133

SINGING AND RHYMING

Melody instruments (Song Bells, Tonettes, and so on), 98b, 115, 157, 165, 166, 167, 168
Piano chording, 47, 112
Piano playing, 47, 68, 108, 112, 144, 151, 166, 167

SINGING EVERY DAY

Clarinet, cornet, 121, 177
Melody instruments, 17, 31, 59, 123, 126, 147b, 171b, 173, 176, 178
Piano chording, 108
Piano playing, 31, 72, 84, 85, 86, 89, 90, 108, 119b, 129, 149a, 175, 178, 200
Violin, 86, 90

SINGING TOGETHER

Autoharp, 7, 24, 25, 38, 49, 56, 60, 68, 80, 180, 183, 186
Band and orchestra instruments, 59, 67, 106, 140, 151, 185, 189, 190, 192
Melody instruments, 16, 24, 28, 79, 81, 126, 153, 164, 165, 176, 181
Orchestrations, 10, 46, 86, 99, 110, 118, 127, 131, 187, 194
Piano, 74, 78, 100, 101, 105, 106, 113, 148, 170, 176, 185

SINGING IN HARMONY

Autoharp, 11, 13, 14, 23, 26, 27, 29, 30b, 37, 41, 42, 43, 58, 59, 61, 74, 75, 79, 80, 91, 93, 98, 136, 162b, 196, 200, 203
Band and orchestra instruments, 70 (flute), 86 (violin, cello), 178 (violin, cello), 204 (horns, cornet), 206 (violin), 208 (clarinets)
Melody instruments, 11, 12, 23, 29, 30, 34, 37, 40, 41, 42, 47, 50, 51, 58, 67, 74, 82, 89, 93, 98, 156, 160, 162, 165, 174, 183, 190, 199, 200
Orchestrations, 17, 62, 100, 108, 130 (strings), 140, 142 (strings), 151, 157, 212
Piano, 70, 86, 122, 123, 124, 128, 164, 166, 178, 209, 221, 225, 228, 233
Violin solo, 124

PLAYING AS WE SING (for grades one and two)

Piano

How to Teach Your Class to Play Autoharp Accompaniments
Autoharp (based on material in *Singing Every Day*)

New Music Horizons (Silver Burdett)

MUSIC FOR EARLY CHILDHOOD

Autoharp, 3, 4a, 5, 9, 16, 18a, 19b, 34b, 44a, 45a, 47, 63, 68a, 87, 102, 110, 112b, 113, 114, 115

The teacher is encouraged to play the piano score, the Autoharp, and recorder-type instruments (see p. 118), and to improvise at the piano (see p. 119)

BOOK TWO

Autoharp, 140, 142, 146, 147, 148, 149, 158
Piano, 151
Water glasses and Song Bells, 32, 33, 46, 47, 74, 119b

BOOK THREE

Autoharp, 159, 160, 165a, 169, 170, 172, 174, 175, 176, 177
Pitch-producing instruments, 184. Suggested use of instruments on tonal patterns.
Three-note songs to play on all melody instruments, 52, 71

BOOK FOUR

Autoharp, 183, 184, 185, 188, 189, 190, 191, 192, 193, 201
Piano, Song Bells, 6, 7, 22, 42, 46, 82-85, 104-105, 136-137, 156, 157, 165
Recorder-type instruments, 6, 7, 30, 31, 46, 145

BOOK FIVE

Chording (Autoharp, piano, guitar, ukulele): see *Chording*, p. 230.
Harmonica, guitar, ukulele: see *Social or Recreational Instruments*, p. 230
Orchestrations: see *Instrumental Score*, p. 230
Piano, Song Bells: see *Piano*, p. 230

BOOK SIX

Chording: see *Chording*, p. 244
Guitar, ukulele: see *Social or Recreational Instruments*, p. 244
Piano accompaniments: see *Piano Accompaniments*, p. 244
Piano, Song Bells, see *Keyboard space-frame*, p. 244
Orchestrations: see *Arrangements for instruments of the orchestra and band*, p. 245

A Singing School (C. C. Birchard)

OUR FIRST MUSIC

Publisher recommends use of "melody bells and tuned glasses." No music is designated for this activity, but songs like *The Bee*, p. 310, can be used.

OUR SONGS (New Edition)

Autoharp, 175, 176, 179, 180, 182, 183, 184, 185
Publisher recommends activities with "melody bells and tuned glasses" but no music is designated for these activities.

MERRY MUSIC (New Edition)

Publisher recommends use of melody bells and melody flutes at the discretion of the teacher.

WE SING (New Edition)

Publisher recommends use of melody bells, melody flutes, recorders, and Autoharp at the discretion of the teacher.

OUR LAND OF SONG

Publisher recommends accompanying activities with Autoharp, guitar, and ukulele.
Violin, 14, 15, 41, 52, 61, 82
New Edition only: bells, 207-215, chording, 204-215, drum, 211, 212

MUSIC EVERYWHERE

Accordion, 65, 105, 142, 144, 145, 146, 148, 149, 159
Autoharp, 65, 105, 144, 146, 148, 149
Cello, 156
Flute, 209
Guitar, 65, 105, 142, 144, 145, 146, 148, 149, 159
Piano: see Accordion above
Ukulele tablature or chords, 11, 65, 105, 118, 120, 142, 144, 145, 146, 148, 149, 159, New Edition chording, 220, 222, 225-229
Violin, 25, 209

SONGS TO PLAY

A book to help learn to play the piano.
    Supplementary material for A SINGING SCHOOL:
    Autoharp Accompaniments to Songs from Music Everywhere
    Autoharp Accompaniments to Songs from Our Land of Song
    The Play and Sing Book (with songs from *Our Land of Song*)

Together We Sing (Follett Publishing Company)

TOGETHER WE SING, Enlarged Edition

Chording: see Classified Index, p. 259, for songs marked for chording
Chording patterns (methods) for the piano, 120-121
Piano accompaniments are scattered throughout the book

MUSIC 'ROUND THE CLOCK

Autoharp and/or piano chords given for every song
Psaltery, 34, 36, 62, 63
Song Bells, 4, 13, 14, 18, 21, 22, 30, 34, 36, 39, 55, 56, 58, 59, 62, 63, 76

MUSIC ROUND THE TOWN

Autoharp and/or piano chords given for every song
Chording, 137
Song Bells employed frequently throughout
Violin, 94r, 95

MUSIC THROUGH THE YEAR

Bells and other melody instruments (notes in color), 23, 26, 27, 30, 33, 34, 36, 40, 43, 53, 65, 67, 68, 71, 79, 81, 99, 106, 108, 116, 120, 125, 126, 130, 141, 143, 147, 150
Chording for Autoharp, piano, guitar throughout the book
Piano, 33, 126, and others
Recorder, 71, 101, 123, 126
Violin, 126

MUSIC ACROSS OUR COUNTRY

Refer "Accompaniment with Chording Instruments," 178-179
Refer "With Parts for Instruments," 190 (bells, psaltery, small winds)

VOICES OF AMERICA

See Classified Index* for parts for instruments

VOICES OF THE WORLD

Parts for instruments, 223

Music For Living (Silver Burdett Company)

MUSIC THROUGH THE DAY (including children's books I LIKE THE COUNTRY
and I LIKE THE CITY)

"Instruments," 147
"Instruments" index, 151

MUSIC IN OUR TOWN

"Instruments," 153-154 (Autoharp, bell-type, piano, tone blocks)
TM distinguishing I and V$_7$ chords, 14, 43, 49
TM "Instruments," xi, "Instruments" index: Autoharp, bell-types, rhythm,
piano, countermelodies for bells or piano, and Instruments, use of, 133

MUSIC NOW AND LONG AGO

"Instruments," 169 (Autoharp, bell-type or piano, flute-type)
TM "Instruments," xi, "Instruments" (countermelodies for, Autoharp, bell-
type, flute-type), 132
TM "Instruments" (orchestral, piano, use of instruments), 132

MUSIC NEAR AND FAR

"Songs For Instruments," 184
TM "Instruments" (bell-types, piano, use of), 163, "Melody Instruments,
Scores for," 165, "Piano Music for Children to Play," 165

MUSIC IN OUR COUNTRY

(See Classified Index and Teachers Book*)

MUSIC AROUND THE WORLD

(See Classified Index and Teachers Book*)

* Not available when this textbook was written.

THINGS

TO

DO

1. Bring water glasses and bottles to class and learn how to use them in the activity discussed at the beginning of the chapter. Compose or find 3-note, 4-note, 5-note, and scale line melodies to play on glasses and bottles. Play them on Song Bells and piano.

2. Collect songs that are easy for children to play on the Song Bells on the grade level you plan to teach. Examine a series book to find appropriate songs.

3. Write in numeral notation *America* and *Twinkle, Twinkle, Little Star*.

4. Bring ukuleles and steel guitars to class and demonstrate how children can learn to play them. Teach the chords by a method that does not conflict with the chord designations in this chapter.

5. Play and compare the Autoharp and the Harmolin. Learn to accompany appropriate songs from a series book on these instruments. In what keys can they be played?

6. Analyze songs in the series books to discover in which ones the piano can be utilized as a source of interest and enrichment.

7. Collect songs that can be accompanied by one chord only and compile them in a notebook to use for your teaching purposes when you introduce chording on Autoharp and piano.

8. Compose songs for #7.

9. Identify songs that are in minor keys. One clue is the song's final note. If it is scale-tone 6, the song is in minor. Another clue, which is only partly reliable, is the appearance of accidentals. Another, and the most important of all, is the *sound* of the song when you play it or sing it.

10. Learn how to chord songs that do not have the chords marked. *Clementine*, p. 69, exemplifies how by analyzing the notes of a melody line one can decide intellectually which chord is required. In measure one, all melody notes are part of the I chord; therefore, it is the accompanying chord. In measure four, two of the three different notes are part of the V_7 chord; therefore this chord is most likely to be the

one needed. Notes on the accented beats are the ones most likely to reveal the chord. Try this procedure with songs from the series books. The better you know your piano chords, the easier this becomes. Find out if your "intelligent guesses" are correct by playing these songs on the piano with the chords. Let your ear decide.

11. Improvise piano chording to I-V$_7$ chord songs listed on p. 69.

12. A fifth grade boy asks, "Why are there two flats in the key of B♭ Major?" Explain this, using the Song Bells or the piano keyboard. (Begin the scale on B♭ and build a major scale, which has half-steps between 3 and 4, 7 and 8.)

13. Transposition (playing the same song in different keys) is not difficult when a simple method of piano chording is used. Try playing familiar songs in different keys. Begin by finding the I chord in 1 3 5 position. Learn to transpose a song one tone higher or one tone lower than written.

14. Study the methods of piano chording suggested in some of the basal music series. (See reference guide.)

15. Play the songs in this book on a recorder-type instrument.

16. Teach the class to play a recorder-type instrument according to the method suggested in this chapter.

17. Find and play on a recorder-type instrument songs of suitable range in the series books for intermediate grades. Classify them according to difficulty and by keys (mainly C, F, G).

18. Play the piano chord sequence I IV I V$_7$ I in all common keys. Play it in a hymn-like manner.

19. Improvise piano chording for songs listed on page 74 which require I, IV, and V$_7$ chords.

20. Make up a tune on a recorder-type instrument and write it in music notation. Children in intermediate grades can compose in this way.

21. Practice piano duets in which one classmate plays the melody of a song while another plays the chords.

22. Direct the singing and playing of *Nobody Home* (p. 70) as a three-part round.

23. Examine the books *Music 'round the Clock* and *Music 'round the Town* from the *Together We Sing* Series. How many types of related playing and singing activities can be found?

24. List ways in which playing activities can aid the classroom teacher who has difficulty in singing.

REFERENCES AND MATERIALS

Articles

Nye, Robert E., "The Elementary Classroom Orchestra," *Educational Music Magazine*, November-December, 1946.

Classroom Orchestra Books

Buchtel, Forrest, *Melody Fun for Singing and Playing with the Tonette*. Chicago: Neil A. Kjos Music Company.

Cheyette and Renna, *Songs to Sing with Recreational Instruments*. Bryn Mawr: Theodore Presser Company.

Slind, Lloyd H., *Melody, Rhythm, and Harmony for the Elementary Grades*. New York: Mills Music, Inc.

Snyder, Alice M., *Sing and Strum*. New York: Mills Music, Inc., 1957. Sixty-five songs.

Staples, Rj, *Classroom Teacher's Guide and Score for the Musical Fun Books*. Chicago: Follett Publishing Company, 1956.

Piano Books for Children

Eckstein, Maxwell, *The Eckstein Piano Courses*. New York: Carl Fischer, Inc.

Frisch, Fay T., *Play-Way to Music* piano series. New York: Hermitage Music Publications, Inc.

Grant, Louise and John Verrall, *Let's Make Music*. Boston: The Boston Music Company. For children in grades one and two and their teachers.

Piano Books for Chording

Dubois, Charlotte, *Songs to Play*. Boston: C. C. Birchard.

Egbert, Marion, *Seeing What We Sing*. Boston: C. C. Birchard.

Holt, Hilda, *Chord-a-tune*. Bryn Mawr: Theodore Presser Company.

McConathy, Osbourne, *Look and Play Piano Course*. New York: Carl Fischer, Inc.

Pace, Robert L., *Piano for Classroom Music*. Englewood Cliffs, N.J.: Prentice-Hall, Inc.

Rhea, Raymond, *We Play and We Sing*. New York: Bourne, Inc. Swing bass accompaniments for familiar songs with descants.

Shepard, Robert, *Harmonizing, How to Play Simple Accompaniments to Melodies at the Keyboard*. Chicago: Clayton F. Summy.

Music Fundamentals

Nye, Robert E., and Bjornar Bergethon, *Basic Music for Classroom Teachers*. Englewood Cliffs, N.J.: Prentice-Hall, Inc.

Films

   The Autoharp. Johnson Hunt Productions, 6509 De Longpre Ave., Hollywood, California.

Recorder-type Instruments

   Song Flute. C. G. Conn, Ltd., Elkhart, Indiana.

   Tonette. Lyons Band Instrument Company, 223 West Lake St., Chicago 6, Illinois.

   Flutophone. Trophy Products Company, 744 Bolivar Road, Cleveland 15, Ohio.

   Symphonette. Handy-Folio Music Company, 2821 North 9th Street, Milwaukee 6, Wisconsin.

Flute-type Instruments

   Melody Flute. Melody Flute Company, Laurel, Maryland.

Teaching
Singing

Four

In Chapter Two it was stated that a background of pleasurable rhythmic experience helps provide a basis for better singing. *When rhythm is felt in* terms of bodily movement, an individual develops sensibilities that are essential in understanding musical expression. It is believed that the ability to hear music and thus to grasp tonal relationships can improve through these experiences and the playing experiences discussed in Chapter Three. However, granted that these contribute to better singing, *good* singing is the result of special effort made by teachers to help the child to hear musical pitch and to reproduce vocally what he hears with accuracy, understanding, and good taste.

THE CHILD VOICE

The child voice is often described as light in quality as well as in volume. It is also an extremely flexible mechanism, as illustrated by the strident cries of the playground. The teacher, then, is confronted by a voice that is capable of expressing many moods in song. Since there are many moods to express, this child voice can be sweetly soft and ethereal as it sings "Lullaby and goodnight" and can be momentarily harsh as it sings "David *killed* Goliath!" A logical way of deciding upon the voice quality desired in any song is for the teacher and children to discuss what manner of voice should be used to properly express the meaning of the words. Although the child voice is light in quality, it should not sound weak or overly soft.

Many of the problems related to singing are soon solved when one adds to the above idea the following:

1. To make a generally pleasing sound (simple, natural, and clear).
2. To sing in a manner that avoids strain and tenseness.
3. To take breaths where one does when speaking the words (usually as the punctuation indicates); do not interrupt the phrase by breathing in unnatural places.
4. To enunciate clearly, but pronounce r's as Southerners do [ah(r)], and sound final consonants distinctly and in unison.

The child voice in first grade was traditionally described as being within the range from D below the staff to F on the top line. The child voice in second and third grades was considered to have a range from Middle C up to G above the staff. This remained approximately the same in the intermediate grades.

Many classroom teachers insisted over the years that songs that observed these ranges were pitched too high. It can be noted today that in the more recently published series books the range appears to be about one whole tone lower than in earlier publications. Furthermore, the more recent books on all grade levels include a large number of songs in the rather limited range of from Middle C up to fourth line D.[1] The writers of this book have the following comments to make regarding this range:

1. When used at the beginning of a school year, it is suitable for practically every voice in any classroom.
2. It should be considered a range that is to be expanded rather rapidly into the following ranges for class singing:

[1] A listing of such songs in series books graded two through six will be found in *Basic Music for Classroom Teachers*, Nye and Bergethon, Prentice-Hall, Inc., pp. 117-130.

3. Although the singing of Middle C is not injurious to the voice of the child in the primary grades, the singing of melodies that have most notes lying close to Middle C may be injurious, for such songs are believed to be pitched too low.
4. This range is apt to be comfortable for the teacher who has not used his singing voice for a time. However, the teacher's voice should increase in range with use in the same way that the children's voices will.

The range of the voice as referred to above is meant as the range of children's voices *in a group*. Individual ranges vary, particularly in the ability to sing high pitches. Many children can sing *far* above the top line of the staff, and this highest line should not be considered as the upper limit of the child voice. However, in group singing it can be considered as being *near* the upper limit.

One of the problems of some classroom teachers is that they have not learned to use their singing voices properly, and therefore hesitate to sing the notes they consider as "high." Many have used habitually a chest voice which they try to force upward in an attempt to sing higher pitches. Usually when these teachers try singing these higher notes softly in what can be termed a "half-voice" (i.e., it feels as though one is using only half of the voice he is accustomed to using; it is the head voice without the chest voice), they find that they can sing in a high voice which is very comparable to the child voice and that they can sing the high pitches with eventual ease. The classroom teacher needs a clear, natural voice, not a highly trained one. The man teacher's voice is no longer a rarity in elementary school music. Most children are well oriented to listening to and singing with the mature male voice on recordings and on the radio, as well as at home with their fathers. Once in a while a child will be momentarily confused by the octave-lower man voice. When this occurs, the male teacher should play the song on an instrument that gives proper pitch (Tonette, Song Flute, Melody Flute, Song Bells or piano) or have a child who knows the song sing it. In instances where teachers believe that they cannot sing, it should be stated that there are always ways to teach singing with the aid of recordings, musical instruments, and the children themselves.

The following are physical requirements for good singing:

1. *Posture.* Place feet on the floor; sit up straight, but not in a stiff or tense way.

2. *Breathing.* Fill the abdominal region with air first (i.e., breathe "low," not high in the chest). This is the kind of breathing we do when lying flat on the floor or flat in bed. The goal in breathing is a controlled, continuous flow of breath. A husky or breathy sound indicates wasted breath.

3. *Open Throat.* Use the open, relaxed throat one has when about to yawn. Sing with the mouth open wide, but not so wide that it causes tension. Use the neutral syllables "loo" and "ah" to relax the throat.

4. *Good Enunciation.* Open the mouth and use lips *generously* in pronouncing words. Be sure to pronounce final consonants distinctly.

Poor results often come from singing too loudly, singing too softly, not opening the mouth sufficiently, a slouching posture, a stiff and tense posture, a lack of interest, an unhealthy room temperature, and failure of the teacher to let the children comprehend the pitch and harmonic background of a song before asking them to sing it.

THE CHILD WHO DOES NOT SING IN TUNE

The fact that at a certain stage in his development a child does not sing in tune does in no way prove that he is not musical. Instances can be cited to illustrate that it is possible for an out-of-tune singer to be an excellent musician. Among the examples known to the authors are the concert master of a symphony orchestra—a superb violinist—and a boy in the second grade with a very high I.Q. who played Bach with understanding and composed music of some quality. Let us remember that inability to match tones with the voice does not necessarily mean lack of musical ability. Among the reasons for not singing in tune are:

1. *Immaturity.* These children are generally behind their classmates in all respects. They need more time in which to grow and therefore should have a variety of simple musical experiences.

2. *Lack of a background of musical experience.* If the teacher will provide this background, children in this category will eventually sing normally.

3. *Emotional and psychological blocks.* Many adults today suffer from emotional and psychological blocks to singing which were formed in the home and in the classroom. The parent who points out to a six-year-old girl that she can't sing in tune like

her older brothers and sisters may be developing in the child a sense of failure, inferiority, and frustration. The parent may not recall that the older brothers and sisters who now sing well could not do so at the little girl's age, and the girl is called upon to compete with them before she is able to do so. The teacher who tells a child that he can't sing and that he is spoiling enjoyment for others and therefore had better be only a listener from now on, can by this act turn a music lover and potential singer into a hurt person who may try to shut music out of his life from that day on.

4. *Lack of interest, failure to try.* Among these children are included those who are underfed, overindulged, and lacking in sufficient sleep. The teacher is expected to try to improve the environment of these children even though it is often difficult. Occasionally a child has so rich a musical background that it leads him to believe the activities at school are childish and unworthy of his attention. Among suggested solutions for this are (1) assign him responsibilities in helping the less mature children, and (2) provide various musical materials during the time allotted to special interests that will allow him to pursue musical interests on his own level.

5. *Physical disabilities.* This is rare, but a few children require the help of doctors of medicine.

Inability to sing in tune should disappear during the elementary years. This inability can be expected in the lower primary grades since from one-third to two-thirds of beginning first grade children cannot sing in tune. It should be corrected both there and in any of the succeeding grades. Every teacher, regardless of grade level taught, needs to be capable of helping children find their singing voices and, during the years some children continue to sing out of tune, of holding these children's interest in music through a varied program of experiences which include rhythmic response, playing simple instruments, listening, creating, and reading about music and musicians. The conscientious teacher continues trying to help the out-of-tune singer and is not discouraged. It is the duty of the teacher in the elementary grades to help each child find his singing voice and to help him to sing with accurate pitch.

To help the out-of-tune singer, there are three major points of emphasis: music activities are happy, joyous, and satisfying; the child is guided to listen, his ability to hear pitches produced both by others and by himself should be helped to develop; and the child learns to sing by trying to sing, he should be helped to continue to try.

During some stages of their development, such children can be a problem. Since some do not hear the pitch of their own voices and often sing loudly (if happily!) off pitch, there arise the following problems: (1) how to help them to listen, (2) how to keep these voices from hindering other children who are trying to keep on pitch, (3) how to help them to make as real a contribution to the group as the children who sing well, and (4) in the intermediate grades, how to tell them of their errors in such a way that they are encouraged to try harder and remain confident of eventual success.

In guiding children to listen, one of the first duties of the teacher is to establish concepts of high and low in pitch. At first, only repeated identification of these will build meaning in the minds of children. Eventually they can be low, up, and down in terms of bodily response, which builds a background for understanding the ups and downs of notes on the staff. Children are taught to play little action games in first grade such as:

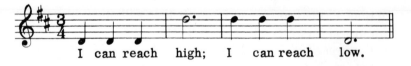

I can reach high; I can reach low.

The above example relates high and low to widely spaced pitches illustrating these words and dramatizing them in terms of physical movement. The following example is relatively more complex:

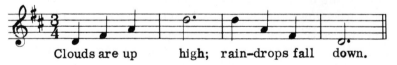

Clouds are up high; rain–drops fall down.

Many simple examples of song material useful in teaching these basic concepts are to be found in the series books and in other supplementary books, particularly those on the first grade level. However, any teacher can improvise his own songs for this purpose.

Acting out the melody line of songs in terms of pitch levels is a device that aids people of all ages to be more conscious of differences in pitch. The hand is used with a generous motion to move up, down, or to stay the same according to differences in pitch. When children are guided to respond in this manner their concepts of pitch relationships often improve to a remarkable degree. In the above example the hand would move vertically as follows:

```
                                              _____
                                               rain-
            _____
             high;
                                                            _____
       _____                                              drops
         up
   _____                                             _____
     are                                                 fall
_____                                                         _____
 Clouds                                                    down.
```

Clouds are up high;   rain-drops fall down.

Many of the children who cannot yet match tones try to sing with the same voice they use when they speak. Therefore, it is the task of the teacher to help such children find their "high" or singing voices. This is usually done in a game situation. A favorite device is to have the children pretend to be the sound of the wind, of a bird, or of a siren. Children often sense pitch differences more keenly through actions such as the teacher lifting a child's hand up high, or the children starting from a squatting position (low) and moving to a standing position (high). Another popular device is to have a child pretend he is calling someone who is far away, or pretend he is someone's mother calling him to come home from a great distance. When this is done, a sustained speech results—and when speech is thus sustained (vowels held out) singing takes place.

When a child sings but sings low and does not match the pitch expected of him, if the teacher and class will match the child's pitch and sing the song with him in the key of his own choosing, there often begins a procedure that brings success with the gradual raising of the pitch by singing this song in successively higher keys.

The use that follows of the traditional term "tone matching" is not intended to convey emphasis upon an isolated drill technique. It is the authors' intention that it be thought of as "songs and games for helping uncertain singers." Such a song or game may be sung by a class and a child may be selected to sing his part at the correct time. The part will be sung at the right time because the teacher will sing with him in case he is not yet ready to sing independently. Little or no attempt is made to correct faulty pitch or rhythm while the song is being sung. It takes patience and faith on the part of a teacher to wait weeks and months for some children to sing correctly.

A commonly used device for listening and tone matching is the calling of the roll in song and having each child sing his answer. If someone is absent, the entire class responds by singing "absent," thus adding variety to this game.

Another well known tone-matching game is one in which the teacher places various objects in the hands of the children, who may be told to put their heads down on their desks and close their eyes. The game is played by the teacher singing, "Who has the ———?" and the child who possesses the object sitting up and singing, "I have the ———."

When a child has difficulty in matching tones with the teacher in any of these tone games, matching tones to another child's singing may do the trick. It is not wise to remain working with any one child too long in any of these procedures. To do so would make the other children restless because the progress of the game would be stopped, and it would draw undue attention of the child to the fact that he is somehow not as successful as others in his class. This refers to primary grades. A further aid to listening is the suggestion that the children "tune in" their voices just as they tune in radio stations. This is a concept children can understand because they know that the dial must be in exactly the right place for the station to "come in" properly. Another suggestion is to sing a familiar grouping of tones (or even a single pitch) for the children while they listen. Then ask them to listen with their "inner ears" while this is repeated for them. Next, ask the children to sing it. Finally, ask them if they sang exactly what they heard. Some of the children who cannot yet match tones will know that they have not sung what they heard. This process when repeated over weeks and months has notably improved listening ability and tone-matching skill.

Picking out melodies by rote on the Song Bells or piano is a listening experience of value. The Song Bells can be used with songs in which it is appropriate to play the tone or group of tones the teacher is using for tone matching. Listening for the proper time to play the bells, and the playing of the correct tone or tones, constitutes a good listening experience in a situation of interest, all of which helps to build the background leading to eventual singing on pitch.

One of the most common failings of teachers of music is that of not giving the children sufficient time in which to hear the beginning pitch of songs a class is reviewing. This is because the teacher will "hear with his inner ear" the song in its proper harmonic setting, but will forget that the children, or many of them, are not hearing this. Too often these teachers sound a pitch and start the singing long before children have had time to orient themselves to this pitch, its relation to the scale in which the song is to be sung, and the harmonic setting of the first tones of the melody. This failure of teachers to help the children get a good start automatically puts some of the children at such a disadvantage that they are out-of-tune singers when they need not be. When reviewing a song with a class that includes children who need this help, the following procedure is recommended:

1. Sound the 1 3 5 chord built from the keynote[2] of the song by means of the piano, the Song Bells, or by singing it. Sound 1-3-5-3-1. This is to establish a feeling for the key, that is, a feeling for the home tone with relation to the scale. The playing of the chord sequence I V₇ I on the piano or Autoharp does this excellently.[3]
2. Sound at some length the keynote of the song. This should be sounded on an accurate instrument such as the piano, Song Bells, or pitch pipe.
3. Sing the keynote with the neutral syllable "loo."
4. Ask the children to sing this pitch, helping those who have difficulty.

[2] The keynote or home tone is found in keys having sharps in the key signature by calling the last sharp to the right "7" and counting up to the next line or space. This will be "8" (1), the keynote. The keynote or home tone is found in keys having flats in the key signature by calling the last flat to the right "4" and counting up or down to "8" or "1." Also, in keys having two or more flats in the key signature, the next to the last flat to the right *is* the keynote.

[3] See Chapter Three, p. 69 for this chord sequence.

5. Sing or otherwise sound the first note of the song if it is a note other than the keynote.
6. Ask the children to sing it and help them to match it.
7. Set the tempo by counting, directing or clapping the rhythm of the meter and saying "Sing!" or, in rhythm, "Ready, sing!", after which the singing begins on the beat following the instruction "sing."

Additional success in helping children to listen comes from working with simple repetitious songs containing note sequences that are thought to be universally easy for children to hear and sing. Among these tone groupings are:

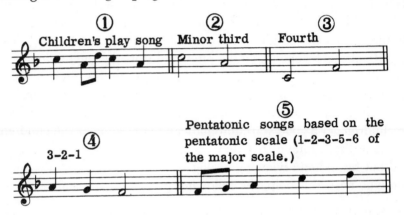

Number one of the above examples is adapted by children all over the western world to many purposes in their uninhibited play. Their own words to this chant and variations of it include thoughts such as teasing "John has a girl friend," and happy announcements, "We won the ball game," "We're going to play." Number two is believed to be the easiest of all intervals for children to reproduce vocally. Note that number one is a combination of examples two and three. Numbers four and five are self-explanatory.

Another condition for in-tune singing is that children's neck and throat muscles be relaxed.

At times it is admittedly impossible to prevent the voices of out-of-tuners from hindering to some extent the progress of those children who are further advanced in singing skills. However, one way to improve the situation momentarily is to include songs in which the out-of-tuners can make such contributions as being the "zz" of a bee, the "tick tock" of a clock either by making a clucking sound with the mouth or by using rhythm sticks or wood blocks, the "ding dong" of bells by playing appropriate tones on Song Bells or piano at the right time (which is of aid in improving listening), and by producing various sound effects or by doing various rhythmic responses instead of singing. However, since faulty singers learn to sing by singing, it is obvious that this tactic is by no means a solution to their problem. Furthermore, it would be unwise to make any seeming division of a class into singers and those who do something else, for reasons given earlier (see No. 3 on p. 98). Another allied procedure, which must also be done with care, is that of having out-of-tuners listen to the good singers. Safeguards here include the use of small groups or solo singers as the examples to be listened to so that there is no obvious division of the class into singers and out-of-tuners, and the inclusion of some good singers with the out-of-tuners when such temporary groupings are made in the classroom.

When out-of-tuners respond rhythmically to music and play the Autoharp, Song Bells, and percussion instruments, and when they offer ideas for interpretation and experimentation, they are making real contributions to group music even though they do not yet sing well. Attention should be focused on providing experiences that help them to *hear*. This brings up the question of how they should be seated during class singing. The traditional seating arrangement, much in vogue some years ago, was dictated by concern for the out-of-tuners. They were seated in a group in front of the room, with the good singing voices of other children behind them and with the good singing voice of the teacher in front of them. It was supposed that this seating arrangement, which gave them correct pitches from both behind and in front, was of great aid to them. Its disadvantage seems to have been that the obvious segregation of the out-of-tuners was a greater psychological block than the seating was an aid. It has been very largely abandoned today. If present-day children are seated in this manner, such seating is done in some way that presumably makes the children unaware of its purpose. Actually, the increasing informality of seating in today's elementary classrooms tends to make any rigid seating plans for music work unlikely.

In the intermediate grades a major problem of some teachers is how to continue to help the out-of-tuners without discouraging them. One fifth grade teacher begins each year with what she terms "making a joyful noise." Her entire emphasis at first is upon the joyous participation of every child with no regard as to whether or not he is in tune, although she is learning the capabilities of each child during this time. As soon as this first objective is achieved, she begins her work of helping every child to sing on pitch. She walks among the children as they sing, helping the ones who need her. While the singing is in progress she may tell Jimmy that he is singing lower than the song is sounding, and to listen to her as she sings. She may tell him to sit with his good friend Billy and tell Billy to help him. All of this is done in good spirit, without setting anyone apart from the group and always emphasizing to Jimmy that he is going to sing in tune soon—to listen hard and keep on trying. Usually this teacher has every child in her room singing in tune by January. The use of certain dialogue songs is of some value (Chapter Eight, p. 186).

Some boys have psychological difficulty that stems from attempting to imitate their fathers' low voices and wanting to sound like men, not like their mothers, their female teachers, or girls. This difficulty can be overcome by explaining that the boy voice changes ordinarily in grades seven through nine, adding that the beginning of the change is marked by boys having even better high voices than the girls. In fifth and sixth grades this latter point is of importance to boys and may determine whether they will use their still unchanged voices naturally or attempt to sing "down in their shoes." For psychological reasons it is best to avoid using the terms soprano and alto and use instead simply high and low. In three-part singing the three parts are called "high, middle, and low" rather than being labelled by terms descriptive of adult voices—terms not suited to describe the immature voices of children.

Two examples of tone-matching songs are given on the next page. Ways to use the second song include the children singing the echo the third time the words "hear you," "near you," and "away" appear, and the teacher asking individual children to be echoes the second and the third time these words appear.

The list below is a partial reference guide to song materials in the basic series books designed to aid the teacher in working with the out-of-tune singer. These materials should be evaluated in terms of the preceding discussion. Most songs written for tone-matching purposes are found in the books for primary grades. The teachers of intermediate grades are expected to be able to use certain parts of appropriate songs found in the books for their grade levels. Understanding of how to learn to do this will come from a thorough study of the primary grades materials and a subsequent adaptation to the intermediate grades classes.[4]

---

[4] One method is the "echoing" of identical phrases. Another is the "echoing" of the last tones of songs.

I HAVE A LITTLE BIRD

Peggy Burgess

Elementary Education Class
University of Oregon, Winter, 1955

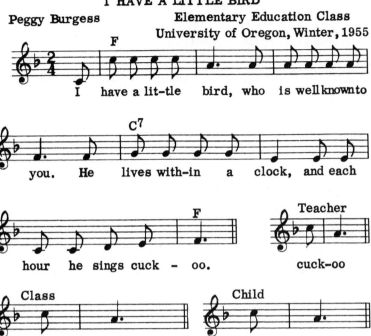

I have a lit-tle bird, who is well known to you. He lives with-in a clock, and each hour he sings cuck - oo.

Teacher: cuck-oo

Class: cuck - oo

Child: cuck - oo

THE ECHO

Kate Forman

Old Children's Air

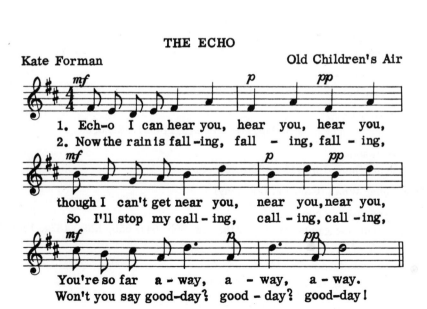

1. Ech-o I can hear you, hear you, hear you,
2. Now the rain is fall-ing, fall - ing, fall - ing,

though I can't get near you, near you, near you,
So I'll stop my call - ing, call - ing, call - ing,

You're so far a - way, a - way, a - way.
Won't you say good-day? good - day? good-day!

Music Series Reference Guide to Tone Matching

The American Singer (2nd ed.; American Book Company)

BOOK ONE

Tone matching, 6ar (see index for songs, p. 103)

BOOK TWO

Tone matching through use of tonal patterns, 117, 118, 120, 121r, 129r, 170

BOOK THREE

Tone matching, 17, 19, 30, 38r, 64, 110, 111a, 133b, 164
Tone games, 168, 191

BOOK FOUR

Tone matching, 12, 16, 21, 41, 43, 81, etc.

BOOK FIVE

Tone matching, 25a, 75, 93, 94, 105, 107, etc.

BOOK SIX

Tone matching, 44, 58, 86, 91, 96, etc.

New Music Horizons (Silver Burdett Company)

EXPERIENCES IN MUSIC FOR FIRST GRADE CHILDREN

Tone matching, tone games, and tone studies (see index, p. 142, under Singing Activities)

SECOND BOOK

Tone matching, 2a, 5, 22
Tone games, 41a, 55, 71, 101, 121

THIRD BOOK

Tonal figures, 3r, 15r, 34, 69, 90, 104a, 126r, 128, 144, 155. See TM 5

FOURTH BOOK

Tone matching, 8, 24, 38, 102, 115, 120, 162r, 177, etc.

FIFTH BOOK

Tone matching, 12, 59, 153ab, 179, 202, 212, 214, 217, 222b, etc.

SIXTH BOOK

Tone matching, 10b, 113a, 132b, 228, etc.

Our Singing World (Ginn and Company)

KINDERGARTEN BOOK

Tone-matching games, 5r, 19a, 21b, 25a, 56b, 64a, 65b, 126a, 132a, 133r, 136c, 144r

FIRST GRADE BOOK

Tone matching, 4b, 5, 6a, 6b, 53, 54a, 68a
Animal imitations, 154
Mechanical imitations, 163, 174a, 176a, 178r

SINGING ON OUR WAY

Tone matching, 30, 53, 97r, 143, 144b, 150r

SINGING AND RHYMING

Tone matching, 53a, 54a, 125, 138, 139, 160, 170r

SINGING EVERY DAY

Tone matching, 8, 9, 14, 21r, 22arbr, 33r, 70b, 153, etc.

SINGING TOGETHER

Tone matching, 23r, 25r, 26, 27r, 28ar, 29r, 31r, etc.

SINGING IN HARMONY

Tone matching, 16r, 28, 33ar, 34ar, 36, 42, 46r, etc.

A Singing School (C. C. Birchard and Company)

OUR FIRST MUSIC

(See calls and motives at the beginning of each unit.)

OUR SONGS

Teachers Manual recommends the following songs, all of which are recorded:
13, 20, 26, 35, 36, 46, 52, 57, 77, 111a, 111b, 113, 116, 127, 147

MERRY MUSIC

Tone matching, 38, 45, 53b, 54r, 56r, 58, 62a, 63, 105, 134b, etc.

WE SING

Tone matching, 9, 11r, 38a, 39r, 44b, 51b, 58br, etc.

OUR LAND OF SONG

Tone matching, 8b, 17, 27, 28, 34, 49, etc.

MUSIC EVERYWHERE

Tone matching, 12a, 13a, 34, 35, 54b, 61b, 63, 80b, etc.

Together We Sing (Follett Publishing Company)

TOGETHER WE SING, Enlarged Edition

Tone matching, 2b, 5br, 10r, 13r, 16b, 17r, 18, 22, 137b, etc.

MUSIC 'ROUND THE CLOCK

Tone matching, 11, 21, 34, 56, 73, 76

MUSIC 'ROUND THE TOWN

Tone matching, 5, 21, 30r, 34r, 71r, 73r

MUSIC THROUGH THE YEAR

Hearing tonal relations, 166-169

MUSIC ACROSS OUR COUNTRY

For echoing use such songs as 20, 24b, 31r, 32r, 33ar

VOICES OF AMERICA

Use parts of songs such as 14, 23, 41, 56, 59, 111

VOICES OF THE WORLD

Use parts of songs such as 14, 15, 57, 68, 80, 86

Music For Living (Silver Burdett Company)

MUSIC THROUGH THE DAY (including children's books I LIKE THE COUNTRY
and I LIKE THE CITY)

"Pitch" chart, 149
"Singing," 146

MUSIC IN OUR TOWN

Use songs such as 14, 25, 29r, 31, 48r, 83r, 91, 101, 104r, 109, 134r
TM "Singing," x

MUSIC NOW AND LONG AGO

Phrase and tone echoing, 2, 3, 4, 10, 26, 30, etc.
TM "Singing," xi, "Echo Effects," 132

MUSIC NEAR AND FAR

Phrase and tone echoing, 2b, 3, 12, 14r, 17, 26r, 27, 30r, etc.
TM "Singing," xii

MUSIC IN OUR COUNTRY

(See Teachers Book "Singing"*)

MUSIC AROUND THE WORLD

(See Teachers Book "Singing"*)

* Not available when this textbook was written.

ADDITIONAL REFERENCES

ROTE SINGING

A rote song is a song that is learned through the ear. The basic principle in teaching songs by rote is simply repetition. Among the earliest experiences of kindergarten and first grade children is listening to a song sung by the teacher—a song which the teacher hopes will soon be sung by the children. The teacher selects a song the content of which is interesting and meaningful to the children, and which is easy to sing. Ideally, any song is taught to children from the point of view of sharing with the children something a teacher loves and enjoys. The teacher learns the song thoroughly before attempting to teach it. Next, he sings the song to the children, not suggesting that they join with him but only that they listen. This is repeated over a number of days during which time the children gradually join in the singing. Songs are taught in a relaxed and informal manner, with the thought of enjoyment foremost in mind. It is better if the teacher sings the song from memory than if he teaches directly from a book. Recordings may be used with this process as a substitute for the teacher's voice.

When rote songs are taught to older groups, the teacher again selects songs with content that is meaningful to the children and with musical features that are suitable to the ability of the group. The exact method of presentation depends upon the song itself, and it is rare that any two are presented in exactly the same manner, since no two songs are exactly alike. Generally speaking, a short song is taught by the "whole method," i.e., singing the entire song to the children and teaching it as a unit. Longer songs are generally taught in a manner that combines the "whole method" with the "part method." The trend today is to teach as far as possible by the whole method and to introduce every song in its entirety. However, after some songs are thus presented, it is necessary to employ the part method, which means that the teacher will ask the children to repeat after him certain logical sections of the song, after which the entire song is sung again. This process goes from the whole to the parts and back to the whole again.

There are many variations in the procedures of teaching rote songs. The children's imaginations can be appealed to by an explanation or a discussion of the content of a song. (Warning: If the teacher's purpose is to provide singing experiences, talking should be reduced to a minimum.) In certain songs the words can be spoken in the rhythm of the note values of the melody. In working with these songs the teacher can make use of rhythmic speech, having the children repeat after him, or say with him, the word-rhythm that is the rhythm of the melody.

Basically, rote learning is accomplished through *guided repetition which is always kept interesting* by having children respond in a *variety* of ways—by initial listening to the story of the song as it is sung, and repeated listenings while responding with suitable bodily movement, by singing an easy characteristic part of the song while listening to the rest of it, by dramatic actions. The song on p. 113 is an example of part of this process—a process which appeals to the inventive mind of every good teacher.

Step one. The teacher sounds the pitch of the keynote F on the Song Bells or by other means, next sounds C, the starting note, and then sings the song to the children as dramatically and expressively as possible. An alternate way is to play the song on a recording as the children listen to the story it tells. Words may be on the chalkboard.

Step two. This is the part of the procedure in which the children continue to listen to the song *as it is repeated as many times as is necessary for them to learn it.* In primary grades this repetition may take place over many days while in intermediate grades some songs may be learned in a few minutes. The teacher contrives to keep interest high by leading the children to do something different almost every time the song is sung or played. The following suggestions are some of the possible ways to provide interesting variety in an essentially repetitious process. They are given here to illustrate the almost limitless variety of activities the teacher may employ in his own plan of presentation. *Only several would ordinarily be used in one lesson.* They are not listed in order of recommended use.

1. Listening and responding rhythmically
   a) Children clap hands (tips of fingers) soundlessly to the rhythm of the meter.
   b) Children clap hands soundlessly to the rhythm of the melody or words.
   c) Children stand and walk in place in time with the rhythm of the meter. (The specific type of fundamental movement done here depends upon what is possible with each song. Walking and running are possible responses to the rhythm of the above song; other movements may suit other songs.)

FIVE LITTLE PUMPKINS *

Unknown

L. B. P.

Five lit-tle pump-kins sit-ting on a gate, The first one said, "Oh my, it's get-ting late." The sec-ond one said, "There are witch-es in the air." The third one said, "But we don't care." The fourth one said, "Let's run and run and run." The fifth one said, "I'm read-y for some fun." "Oo-ool!" went the wind and out went the light, And the five lit-tle pump-kins rolled out of sight.

*From Singing and Rhyming of Our Singing World series.
Used by permission of Ginn and Company, owners of the copyright.

    d) Children act out phrases in heart-shaped movements of the hands and arms.

    e) Children conduct the meter as the song in sung or played. This is highly important in establishing correct tempo and a feeling of onward rhythmic flow.

    f) Children determine whether the music swings in two's or three's.

    g) Children act out pitch levels of the song in the rhythm of the melody. This aids in comprehending the direction of the melody (high, low, skips or a succession of scale tones).

2. Listening and responding vocally

    a) After singing the above song to the children twice, at the next repetition the teacher acts out the pitch levels every time each of the five pumpkins sings. He searches for five volunteer "pumpkins" each of whom can sing his respective part. The song is eventually sung by the teacher and the class with solo responses from the children representing the pumpkins. This aids tonal memory and develops individual singing. (In many songs there are characteristic repeated motives or phrases which can be treated in a similar but even more simple manner.)

    b) The teacher sings the "story" part of the song and all the children sing the pumpkins' parts.

    c) The children sing the "story" part of the song and the teacher sings the pumpkins' parts.

    d) The children are divided into two groups. One sings the story and the other sings the pumpkins' parts.

    e) The teacher sings the song in individual phrases (the part method) and the children echo each phrase after listening to it.

    f) Children hum the melody softly while the teacher sings or the recording is played.

3. Listening and responding in other ways

    a) Children dramatize the story as the song is sung or played.

    b) Individual children who are capable take turns playing the pumpkins' parts on a keyboard instrument when each part occurs. This can be combined with other responses.

    c) Children mouth the words (pretend to sing or whisper) while the teacher or the recording sings the song.

d) One child who sings well sings the song while the class listens. Several children may do this together rather than one doing it alone.

e) Children listen to determine the number of phrases.

f) Children listen to determine whether or not phrases are alike, unlike, or almost the same as other phrases.

Step three. Everyone sings the entire song without the aid of the teacher, unless his voice is needed to help individual children who require special attention. One of the teacher's aims should be to lead the children to achieve confidence in singing without the support of his voice or that of a recording. He uses his singing voice at first as a helpful example; later he needs to hear the singing of each child in order to better guide him, and *he cannot hear individual voices in the group distinctly when his own voice is sounding.* In the transition from children's dependence upon the sound of his voice to independence of its support, the teacher may mouth the words silently, pretending to sing, so that children will not at first realize that his vocal support is no longer there. On succeeding days the teacher will seek different ways for the children to find new interest in the song, such as:

1. Developing more dramatic actions from the children's suggestions.
2. Encouraging the children to experiment with adding their own sound effects, employing percussion instruments if they are appropriate to the song.
3. Encouraging the children to make suggestions for better musical interpretation.
4. Place on the chalkboard the tune each pumpkin sings, but not in the order in which the tunes occur in the song. Let the children try to find the tune for each pumpkin. This aids understanding of notation.
5. Suggest to the children that they bring to school their own words to this song, possibly about five little puppies or chipmunks. Call attention to the rhyming couplet. This encourages the writing of poetry.

The use of recordings in singing

A leaflet published by the American Book Company suggests the following plan for teaching a rote song from a recording:

1. Play the recording, children following the books.
2. Play the recording, children using large movements indicating phrases.
3. On third playing use one of the activities suggested above (see Step Two), depending upon the nature of the song.
4. Have children hum with record.
' 5. Have children form words with lips—no sound.
6. Have children sing with recording.
7. On another day, perhaps, when they sing with the record, let them get a good start and then pick up the needle, letting them go on without help.

It is well to emphasize teaching the words when songs are learned by rote from recordings; they are frequently written on the chalk-board. Another successful technique is having small groups of children, six or less, stand by the record player and sing with the recording while the remainder of the class listen and await their turn at doing the same thing.

The recordings that accompany the series books, as well as others not mentioned here, are of great value in teaching the songs they include. They often provide worthy examples for children to hear and to imitate. They aid the teacher who studies them even though he may prefer to present songs with his own voice. When a child tends the record machine the teacher is free to move about the room to listen to individual voices and to direct class activities. No matter how well qualified a music teacher may be, there are times when a recording will provide the most effective way to teach some songs. However, in primary grades recordings cannot completely take the place of the teacher's voice; these younger children sometimes find it difficult to understand the diction of voices strange to them.

The use of the piano

The piano or Song Bells may be substituted for the voice or recording by teachers who lack confidence in their singing voices and do not have recordings of songs they need to teach. Words for such songs may be learned by rote or written on the chalkboard. The teacher will then play the melody of the entire song. This may be repeated while the children do several of the activities listed in Step Two of the rote singing process already described in this chapter, the instrument thus taking the place of the voice or recording. For a song of some length the phrase method may be desirable. After the playing of the entire song, the melody of the first phrase will be played; the children will mouth the words silently as it is played again. Then the children may sing this phrase with the piano; and next, sing without its support. This can be continued throughout the remaining phrases, combining some of them along the way. As the song is learned, the support of the instrument is gradually withdrawn to gain independence from it. If a child in the class is a good natural musician and has a pleasing voice, he may be an excellent teacher's assistant by singing to the class phrases or entire songs that he has learned from the teacher's playing the piano or Song Bells. Recorder- and flute-type instruments are sometimes employed also in this approach to teaching singing.

Although it is highly desirable to have a piano in every classroom, the piano is not essential in teaching or in accompanying songs. In a normal situation where the teacher uses his singing voice, the piano has its greatest use at two points in the learning process—at the beginning and at the end. A song may be introduced by playing it on the piano in a simple manner. Since younger children find it difficult to hear a melody when an elaborate accompaniment is played, a simple accompaniment, permitting the melody to predominate clearly, is the most effective style of playing. During most of the learning process involved in teaching songs the piano has little use, for two reasons: (1) when the teacher is playing the piano he cannot hear the children well enough to tell if each child is singing correctly, and (2) he is in a stationary position and is unable to move through the class to hear and to help individual children with their problems. Another commonly stated reason for not using the piano at this time is that if it is used constantly the children cannot sing independently and may become semi-helpless without it. However, after a song has been learned, the addition of a piano accompaniment can be a thrilling and satisfying experience, adding greatly to the singers' enjoyment and to the musical effect of the performance.

Although the piano is not an absolute necessity, it is an important means of enrichment. It is also a very important tool for learning many things about music, as was shown in Chapter Three. Thus, the piano has its rightful place in the well-equipped classroom along with the radio, the record player, the Autoharp, the Song Bells, and the percussion instruments—but not as a dominating instrument.

MUSIC ASSEMBLIES AND CUMULATIVE SONG LISTS

Many elementary schools compile cumulative song lists[5] which suggest that certain songs be taught at various grade levels. These lists are compiled for the purpose of providing the students with a commonly known body of song material that is believed to be of value to them. Teachers plan cooperatively which songs should be on such lists, taking careful consideration of the songs most enjoyed by children. These lists should be under constant revision. The songs they include are ordinarily used in student assemblies and at other times when mass singing is of value to school morale. They are divided into classifications that assure variety, such as *patriotic and service songs* (important in the national tradition), *songs of religious and ethical value* (important in character development), *fun songs* (for group morale), *special-day songs* (Christmas, Thanksgiving), *American folk songs* (our nation at work and play), *folk songs of other lands* (the lands of our forefathers), *Stephen Foster and James Bland songs*, and *Negro spirituals*. There are many other possible classifications. Care should be taken to keep the concept of the song list sufficiently flexible so that songs of immediate and temporary value can be used.

Nothing is as effective as good group singing in building group spirit and the feeling of unity every school needs. It is, therefore, an essential element in the total school program. Singing in conjunction with assemblies should be carefully planned so that the children as a group know many songs they can sing well together. However, pleasing variety is attained when the primary grades sing a new song for the upper grades and vice versa, or when one class sings and dramatizes "something special" for the assembly in an informal way.[6]

[5] A suggested list for classroom, assembly, and community use is found in *Music in American Education*, published by the Music Educators National Conference, Chicago: 1955, p. 319.

[6] The article "Everyone Sings Together," Music Educators Journal, January, 1956, pp. 46-48, describes the organization of assembly sings in a Massachusetts elementary school.

THINGS

TO

DO

1. Have a classmate act the part of an inaccurate singer and help him to match tones by means of little song games, using parts of songs or special techniques.

2. Collect songs that can be taught in ways that give the inaccurate singer pleasurable participation.

3. Select a song and prepare to teach it to your college class by rote as suggested in this chapter. Write your plan for teaching it, remembering that the content, form, and type of melody of the song itself dictate your method.

4. Choose a recording of a song and teach this song by rote to the class through use of the recording.

5. Practice conducting songs that begin with an upbeat. Examples: *Auld Lang Syne, Star-Spangled Banner, Believe Me If All Those Endearing Young Charms.*

6. One way to add interest in classroom singing is to employ songs in which girls sing one verse or part of the song and the boys sing another. Find such dialogue songs and teach them to your class. See Music Series Reference Guide to Part Singing, Chapter Eight.

7. Plan a community sing for a Parent-Teacher Association meeting. Include a greeting song, a fun song, a sentimental ballad, a patriotic song, and a closing song. See Appendix B.

8. Practice the physical requirements of good singing as outlined in this chapter so that you can convey them to the children you will teach.

9. Bring a tape recorder to class. Tape a song that the class sings well. Play it back and ask your fellow students to suggest how their singing may be improved. When might you use the tape recorder in your music teaching?

10. Know *America* and *The Star Spangled Banner* and in what keys to play and sing them. *America* is pitched usually in G or F. *The Star Spangled Banner* is pitched in B♭ in elementary grades and in A♭ from the seventh grade on.

11. Show how tone matching is done in the intermediate grades through use of songs such as *A Merry Life* (*Singing in Harmony,* p. 28).

12. Some classroom teachers feel insecure in the use of their singing voices. What aids are available that enable these teachers to teach singing? How are they used?

13. Most lesson plans for a music period are developed from a pattern consisting of (a) a song or songs the children know (to give them confidence), (b) introducing new songs and working to improve others, (c) closing with a song or songs the children know and can sing well (to give them a feeling of success). Write a lesson plan for the grade of your choice. Include rhythmic responses and playing of instruments as aids in teaching music, in providing needed variety, in teaching notation in an incidental way, and in sustaining interest. Use the chart, p. 260.

14. Select a song and make a tape recording of it designed to help a teacher teach this song to his class by rote. Plan carefully what the children need to hear in order to learn this song. Ask an elementary school teacher to use it with his children and ask this teacher to evaluate your efforts in terms of its success in a real teaching situation.

15. Investigate the methods of the German composer Carl Orff. Refer to the book *Music for Children—Pentatonic,* by Carl Orff and Gunild Keetman, which is distributed by Associated Music Publishers, Inc., 1 West 47th Street, New York City. The Orff method stresses rhythm and the singing of melodies based on the pentatonic (five-tone) scale. Major and minor tonalities are avoided or minimized in the musical activities for the young child. Percussion instruments including xylophones and metalophones are employed. Since few songs in the series books are pentatonic in conception, creating such songs is necessary. This is easily done within the limitations described in *Music for Children—Pentatonic.*

REFERENCES

Books for Singing in Primary Grades

Coleman, Satis N. and Alice G. Thorn, *Singing Time,* 1929. *Another Singing Time,* 1937. *A New Singing Time,* 1952. New York: John Day Company.

Crowninshield, Ethel, *Mother Goose Songs,* 1948. *Sing and Play Book,* 1938. *Stories That Sing,* 1945. Boston: Boston Music Company.

Landeck, Beatrice, *Songs to Grow On,* 1952. *More Songs to Grow On,* 1954. New York: Marks and Sloane.

Songs Children Like. Washington, D.C.: Association for Childhood Education, 1954.

Seeger, Ruth Crawford, *American Folk Songs for Children,* 1948. *Animal Folk Songs for Children,* 1950. *American Folk Songs for Christmas,* 1953. New York: Doubleday and Company, Inc.

		Suggested
Recordings for Singing	*R.P.M.*	*Grade Level*
Children's Record Guild and Young People's Records, The Greystone Corporation, 100 Sixth Avenue, New York 13, New York		
Around the Campfire (community singing)	78	3-9
Hooray! Today Is Your Birthday (six songs)	78	1-4
Mother Goose (two records)	45-78	N-2
Sing Along (echoing)	45-78	K-3
Another Sing Along	45-78	1-4
Yankee Doodle (six folk songs)	78	2-6
Every Day We Grow-I-O (two records)	45-78	N-2

Albums:

Let's Sing	78	1-5
Folk Songs	78	1-5
Songs to Sing (activity songs)	78	1-4

Recordings That Teach Singing
Ginn and Company, Back Bay Post Office, Box N, Boston, Massachusetts

Albums:

Let's Sing and Play and Dance	33	1
Let's Sing of Fun and Frolic	33	2
Let's Sing and Be Merry	33	3

Filmstrips

Young America Films, Inc., 18 E. 41 Street, New York 17, New York

Songs to Sing Series: four filmstrips in color (Mother Goose songs)		K-3

Teaching
Listening

Five

Listening is, of course, part of every musical experience. The rhythmic activities given in Chapter Two were the result of first listening, then responding physically to what was heard. Creative rhythmic response and creative dramatization are also based on listening (see Chapter Six). The singing activities given in Chapter Four were made possible by listening to a teacher's singing voice, to recordings of singing, to children's voices, and to melodies played on instruments. The instrumental activities in Chapter Three began with listening to, and singing pitches of, songs before attempting to play them. Instruments were added to songs on the basis of listening with discrimination to find out whether the musical effect was what was desired. Thus, all of these activities were made possible through listening. It is from a strong background of these experiences that a more intellectual type of listening can emerge.

In this chapter a formal type of listening, that of listening to recordings, will be discussed. This type of listening experience has been one of the weaker aspects of elementary music education. One of the reasons for this is commonplace—the teacher has not been well prepared by his professional training to teach it. As in teaching in any other area the good teacher knows the material he is to present, knows why it is appropriate for his group, and knows what he expects children to learn from it.

Children in the primary grades enjoy listening to recordings that possess some of the following characteristics: (1) there can be active physical response to the music, (2) the mood is distinct, (3) the melodies heard are song-like, (4) the tone quality is beautiful, (5) the music tells a story, (6) aspects of the music relate to the experience and interest of children, and (7) the selection is short (because the attention span of these children is brief). Children in the intermediate grades can be somewhat more analytical in their response to listening; however, the above criteria are also applicable.

Formalized listening to recordings by a class is ordinarily planned for only one occasion during any school day, and it is usually not a daily occurrence. However, certain types of recordings are used daily by many teachers in connection with rest periods and in connection with art work, singing, and rhythmic responses. Types of listening differ in accordance with the function of the particular recording used. For instance, some of the records that tell stories are purely for recreation, while others offer much learning about music and musicians. The good teacher knows the function of a recording and uses it in accordance with that function.

During formal listening activities, the teacher is always an example of an interested listener, illustrating by his actions and attitude the mental concentration necessary for such listening. He listens attentively to hear the things for which he has prepared his class to listen. When such listening is properly planned, there is no talking while the recording is being played.

If there is an over-all teaching principle involved in listening, it is that the teacher so prepares for this activity that he and the children are *always* actively listening for something. If we were to ask about the basic purpose of teaching listening, we might say it is to aid children to lead happier, better lives through enjoying the best of many different types of music. This teaching is urgently needed today when the school is called upon to help children be selective and discriminating in the midst of the overwhelming amount of music of questionable taste and value being brought to them daily by recordings, radio, and television.

From enjoyment to understanding and taste to further enjoyment

As in all other aspects of music education, skill in formal listening is built upon a firm foundation of enjoyment. Earlier in this chapter were listed seven characteristics of the types of recordings children enjoy hearing. On the basis of enjoyment, the teacher undertakes to enlarge the children's musical understanding. In the primary grades, owing to the mental and physical make-up of that age group, most listening activities taking place with recordings are of three types: those that produce rhythmic and dramatic responses, those that are associated with different moods, and those that are associated with stories. It is the teacher's task to draw from the children such information as would answer the questions, "Does the music sound lively, like walking, running, marching, skipping, galloping, goblins, Indians, fairies? Does the music sound happy, sad, quiet? Could it be a lullaby?" Thus the teacher begins formal listening with information already familiar to the children. They have acquired a background of activities through which they can provide the answers to such questions. In the intermediate grades the questions can become more musically specific, as, for example: "Is this a dance (or waltz, gavotte, polka, minuet, mazurka, march)? What instrument played the melody? Do you think this was a folk song or an art song? What do you think the function of this music could be? Has this music a distinctive style? What does the music tell you about the spirit and culture of these people or of their nation? What do you know about this composer? What did you notice about the form of this music?"[1]

From these understandings come the development of discrimination and taste in listening to music. In this, the child is led to set up his own standards; they should not be adult-imposed. When children have a musical environment which provides many opportunities to choose and judge, their taste is remarkably competent. They *like* good music. The teacher guides listening with appropriate questions such as, "Do you think this music achieves what it is supposed to do? Is it sincere? Is it true to its type? Is the style one you would expect to hear? Is this music authentic—the real music of Arabia, China, the American Indian—or is it music written by composers of some other nationality or culture? Which recording of this composition do you think is the best one, and why?" Thus the teacher works toward the goal of discrimination and good taste—a goal which should further heighten enjoyment of music.

In recent years there is thought to have been an overemphasis in the use of program music (music which tells a story) and a corresponding neglect of absolute music (music which has no story). Perhaps this is because a "story" recording appears to succeed without

---

[1] With regard to musical form, see p. 51, Chapter Two, and The Music Series Reference Guide at the end of the present chapter. Only simple form is considered in the elementary school.

much effort or preparation on the part of a teacher, while absolute music requires preparation.

Children can be helped to understand almost any type of music if the teacher will "set the stage" for it. The authors once experimented in a fourth grade class by planning for the presentation of music that they considered unlikely to be accepted by the children. This music, from the layman's point of view, was disjointed rhythmically and even lacked melody in the traditional sense. Furthermore, it was a work of such length that a portion of it had to be taken out of its natural place in the work to have something short enough to use.

It all happened when the fourth grade teacher was working with a unit on the early history of the earth. The children were fascinated with their research on dinosaurs and other prehistoric life on this planet. This gave the music teacher the idea of presenting a section of Igor Stravinsky's *Le Sacre du Printemps* (The Rite of Spring) somewhat as Walt Disney had done it in the film *Fantasia*. He obtained a book of photographs of scenes from the film and showed the children the colorful illustrations of the animal and plant life and the geological conditions of prehistoric times as Disney imagined them. When the fourth grade children were told that a composer had written music about prehistoric man they wanted very much to listen to it—so one side of a 78 rpm disc was played. What went on in the children's minds is something the teachers will never know, but the rapt faces showed them that the class had been transported by means of music to a world that existed before history began. The spell was broken when the needle reached the end of the disc. One little girl said, "That music is exciting. It just wears me out!" which was a good description of the effect of Stravinsky's rhythmic complications and harsh dissonances. Later on the children asked to listen to it again, an indication that the listening experience had been successful. The teachers were satisfied with going no further than they did with that "unlikely"[2] music, being happy to have proved to themselves their contention that if a teacher plans his listening presentation well, the children will accept it. Had a fifth or sixth grade found similar attraction in this music the teachers might have brought from the children their listening observations of certain characteristics of contemporary music, more about the instruments used, and more about the com-

[2] For music by Stravinsky likely to be enjoyed in the intermediate grades, try the ballets *The Firebird,* which is a fairy tale, and *Petrouchka,* which concerns a fair and puppet show.

poser and his great influence on music composition in the first half of this century.

Fortunately, recorded material is available that can greatly help the teacher to teach formal listening. Certain albums of recordings are accompanied by many written suggestions for the use of each musical selection.[3] There are books containing information about composers and their music and there are recordings that accompany the books.[4] It is well that every elementary teacher be familiar with such material.

SUGGESTIONS TO AID LISTENING

Devote only a part of the music period to listening to recordings. Plan a variety of music activities, combining different kinds of listening experiences with singing, rhythmic responses, and playing instruments. Remember that children are normally unable to sit still and listen for very long.

Correlate listening with social studies, art, and dance.

Use *good quality recordings* on a *good quality machine*. Even the loveliest music cannot succeed if distorted by poor equipment.

Bring into the classroom *live performers* from school and community—but be sure before they are invited that they can perform suitably. Let the young children touch and feel the instruments used, for it is through physical contact that they gain in comprehension.

Use visual aids: an attractive *bulletin board* with pictures, newspaper and magazine write-ups, concert and recital programs, and clever cartoons about music and musicians. If the teacher changes the content of the bulletin board regularly, the children will read it with interest. *Films* and *filmstrips* have an important place. *Write music themes* on the chalkboard if the children do not have them to follow in their books while listening. Sing these themes before playing the recordings, if they are singable.

Bring listening to life by relating it to current events, motion pictures, radio and television programs outside the classroom, local concerts, and to newspaper and magazine feature stories.

Begin the study of musical form by leading children to discover

---

[3] The *Listening Program* record albums of the RCA Victor *Basic Record Library for Elementary Schools; Tiny Masterpieces for Very Young Listeners* (Sound Book Press).

[4] *Music for Young Listeners: The Green Book, The Crimson Book, The Blue Book,* by Lillian Baldwin (New York: Silver Burdett Co., 1951).

melodic changes and repetitions, i.e., "Is the music the same now or is it different?" See Chapter Two, p. 51.

Use appropriate *radio and television* programs in the classroom, taking care to fully prepare the children for them.

Add a Listening Post to the classroom music center. This is a control box with headphones which may be attached to any record player, thus permitting several children to listen without disturbing the class. It is manufactured by A. M. Brooks Company, 1222 West Washington Boulevard, Los Angeles, California. There are other similar teaching tools. One is The Listening Corner, devised for both music listening and speech training and accommodating eight sets of headphones and a microphone input. It is manufactured by Caliphone Corporation, 1041 North Sycamore Ave., Hollywood 28, California.

To help direct listening, place a list of key words on the chalkboard before the recording is played. Example: mood, instruments heard, meter, form, sounds of nature.

Prepare the children to understand the music of *concerts and recitals* given at the school or in the community.

Request that special *concerts and programs* for children be given at school and prepare the children to listen to them.

Employ *music notebooks* and scrap books in grades five and six— but use discretion. Children can put into them all the things listed above for the bulletin board. However, if children feel compelled to assemble bulk without true interest, such a project can defeat its purpose. Maybe all of this belongs on a lively bulletin board after all!

Children can bring favorite *recordings from home* to share with the class, explaining why they like them.

Give children the opportunity to play appropriate thematic material on piano, Song Bells, and other melody instruments.

Children can plan with the teacher a *pretend concert* of recorded music. Such programs can be organized around ideas such as music of other lands, marches of many kinds, musical instruments and soloists, music of certain composers, and American music. A variant of this was done by a student teacher in music who substituted himself and his school-of-music friends for the recordings, and substituted the school auditorium for the classroom. The children "sold" themselves tickets, provided ushers, and planned what their behavior was to be in the intermission. The university students entered wholeheartedly into the idea, dressing in formal clothes. This program was planned so that the children joined with the performers in singing at the close of the concert.

Have appropriate *books* about composers and music in the music corner and in the school library.

Give organization to listening sessions by grouping the recordings around unifying themes such as types of instruments (percussion, woodwind, brass, string), elements of music (rhythm, harmony, melody), dances, marches, different composers' concepts of sunrise, sunset, seasons, the sea, day and night, plant and animal life.

Read or tell stories about composers to make them live in children's minds. Especially appropriate are stories about these men in their childhood, and about composers' relations with children. Dioramas and puppetry may be employed.

In primary grades a lengthy recording such as *Tubby the Tuba* is too long for playing at one sitting. Make it a continued story and play one or two sides a day, reviewing them before playing another side the next day. In intermediate grades, the *Nutcracker Suite* (Tschaikowsky) is too long for one listening lesson. Therefore, play a section of it a day. Really long compositions have little or no place in elementary school music.

The piano can be used effectively for some listening experiences, particularly in the kindergarten and first grade.

By all means use the tape recorder to record children's singing and playing. Nothing stimulates interest in listening to recorded music as much as making recordings.

Children need *vocabulary* in order to discuss music they hear. This vocabulary is of two types: (1) musical terms such as *ballet* and *suite*, and (2) descriptive words. Musical terms can be written on the chalkboard and explained by the teacher before a recording is played. After the children have listened to a recording, descriptive words can be drawn from them through class discussion and written on the chalkboard as an activity in language arts.

Allow children to respond to music physically when they are listening, as long as this response is of a type that does not interfere with the listening of others. Remember that it is normal to want to move to music. Discover and notate rhythm patterns.

The RCA Victor Educational Record Catalog contains a section, "Instruments of the Orchestra," suggesting recordings of fine music that features certain instruments. The annotated listing of Red Seal Records is helpful.

Evaluation of listening programs

To aid in evaluating pupil progress in listening activities, the following evidences of success are listed:

1. The child enjoys listening to music that has meaning to him.
2. His attitude, questions, and comments reveal that he has listened actively.
3. He listens in out-of-school situations as revealed by his remarks about radio, television, and other musical programs.
4. He brings favorite recordings from home to share with the class.
5. He can hear the recurrence of melodies and rhythms in music.
6. He recognizes various moods in music.
7. He identifies musical instruments.
8. He recognizes musical compositions frequently heard.
9. He recognizes the names of composers and knows something about them.
10. He looks for pictures and stories related to music and composers.

Music Series Reference Guide to Listening

The American Singer (2d ed.; American Book Company)

BOOK ONE
(See list of recordings, 155)

BOOK TWO
Mozart, 110
(See TM 17 for list of recordings)

BOOK THREE
Famed composers, music of, 14, 60, 122, 182, 188
(See TM *The Appreciation Program* 15-17 for suggestions and list of recordings)

BOOK FOUR
Biographical sketches of composers, 52, 120, 178
Instrumental choirs of the orchestra, 43
References to works of music, 53, 54, 121, 135, 180, 182
Songs of great composers, see Classified Index, *Famous Composers*, 203
(See TM *The Appreciation Program* 9-13 for suggestions and list of recordings)
(Correlates with Hughes' *Rhythmic Games and Dances*)

BOOK FIVE
Biographical sketches of composers, see Classified Index, *Biographical Notes*, 212

References to works of music, 30, 146, 147, 154, 159

Songs by great composers, 11r, 29, 30, 34, 54, 55, 58, 75, 94, 98, 118r, 119, 121r, 132, 145r, 147, 148, 150, 152r, 154, 159, 186

(See TM *The Appreciation Program* 10-14 for suggestions and list of recordings)

(Correlates with Hughes' *Rhythmic Games and Dances*)

BOOK SIX

Biographical sketches of composers, 179

References to composers and their works, 113, 125, 133, 172, 176, 198

Songs of great composers, see Classified Index, *Famous Composers*, 244

(See TM *The Appreciation Program* 11-14 for suggestions and list of recordings and films)

New Music Horizons (Silver Burdett Company)

MUSIC FOR EARLY CHILDHOOD

Listening, 56-57, 67, 77, 78-82, 127 point 7.

Recordings listed, 78-82

EXPERIENCES IN MUSIC FOR FIRST GRADE CHILDREN

(See Reference Index, *Listening Activities*, 142)

Bodily movement, 38, 44, 86-89r

Contrasting moods, 22, 25, 109

Contrasting rhythms, 3

Descriptive music, 63b, 70, 123a

Music of great composers, 60, 85, 126

BOOK TWO

(See III *Learning to Listen*, 161)

Bodily movement, 12, 28

Contrasting moods, 12, 90

Contrasting rhythm, 60, with 77

Descriptive music, 44b, 108b

Form, creative dramatization of, 86r

BOOK THREE

(See III *Learning to Listen*, 184)

Contrasting moods, 40

Contrasting rhythms, 66

Descriptive music, 77

Listening, 156r

Music of great composers, 120

BOOK FOUR

(See V *Listening*, 207-208, see TM 48-53)

Chinese music, 31b

Contrasting moods, 68

Contrasting rhythms, 138, 179

Descriptive music, 29a

Instruments of the band and orchestra, see III D, 207

Marches, types of, 12

Mexican music, 145a

Music of great composers, 52

Our Singing World (Ginn and Company)

SINGING IN HARMONY

Beethoven, Schubert: see Contents, *Music Makers*, 4
Grieg, 219-237r
Suggested recordings: music concerned with rhythm, 16, 17, 27, 56, 194, mood, 54, 96, 138, 167, 172, stories, 39, 59, 72, 74, 75, melodic music, 27, 29, 43, 53, 84, 85, 87, 88, 175

A Singing School (C. C. Birchard)

OUR FIRST MUSIC

Cadence recognition, 158
(See *Listening Material* section in each Unit)
(See Classified Index, *Master Composers*, 364)

OUR SONGS, NEW EDITION

(See Classified Index, *Master Composers*, 187)
Form (phrase study), 171-174

MERRY MUSIC, NEW EDITION

(See Classified Index, *Master Composers*, 187)

WE SING, NEW EDITION

(See Classified Index, *Master Composers*, 188)

OUR LAND OF SONG

Figure, 152
(See Classified Index, *Master Composers*, 204)
Recordings, 8, 22, 30, 37, 45, 69

MUSIC EVERYWHERE

Form, see TM 87-90
(See Classified Index, *Master Composers*, 220, Dvořák, 100-101)
Recordings, 43, 49, 61, 63, 74, 100, 115, 193
Quiz questions, TM 96-100

Together We Sing (Follett Publishing Company)

TOGETHER WE SING, Enlarged Edition

Contrast, 147
Form, 101, 159
(See Classified Index, *Themes for Listening*, 264)

MUSIC THROUGH THE YEAR

Composers: Humperdinck, 19-21, Saint-Saëns, 41, Tschaikowsky, 60, Mozart, 74, MacDowell, 95, Haydn, 107, Brahms 136-138, Grieg, 144, Sousa, 150

MUSIC ACROSS OUR COUNTRY

Refer "Composers and Suggested Listening," 190

VOICES OF AMERICA

Examine Help for Songs section for Related Listening
(See Classified Index,* for well-known composers)

* Not available when this textbook was written.

VOICES OF THE WORLD

Examine Help for Songs, 209-221, for Related Listening

Well-known composers, 223

Music For Living (Silver Burdett Company)

MUSIC THROUGH THE DAY (including children's books I LIKE THE COUNTRY and I LIKE THE CITY)
"Listening," 146
Parallel listening references (recordings), 10, 20, 21, 30, 33, 35, 41, 57, 58, 61, 62, 63, 65, 66, 69, 70, 73, 74, 77, 81, 84, 85, 100, 104, 106, 107, 111, 112, 117, 122, 128

MUSIC IN OUR TOWN
TM "Listening," xii, distinguishing I and V_7 chords, 14, 43, 49
TM parallel listening (recordings), 2, 3, 4, 6, 9, 12, 16, 18, 21, 22, 24, 26, 28, 29, 32, 34, 66, 67, 69, 72, 73, 74, 76, 82, 83, 84, 86, 87, 94, 97, 98, 108, 113, 114, 118, 119, 121, 132

MUSIC NOW AND LONG AGO
TM "Listening," xii
TM parallel listening (recordings), 5, 7, 10, 13, 16, 21, 29, 31, 32, 37, 39, 47, 48, 53, 60, 62, 63, 66, 69, 78, 83, 85, 104, 105, 106, 107, 110, 115, 120, 122, 123, 128, 129, 130

MUSIC NEAR AND FAR
"Famous Composers," 186
"Songs From Many Lands and Many Peoples," 185-186
TM "Art Music for Listening," "Listening," xiii, "Background Material" (musical topics), vi, "Contrast Between Major and Minor," xi, "Identifying Key Center by Ear," xi, "Illustrating Phrase and Form," xi, "Index of Instrumental Material," 168, "Listening," 163, "Using Pentatonic Scale," xi, "Watch While Listening," ix

MUSIC IN OUR COUNTRY
(See Classified Index and Teachers Book*)

MUSIC AROUND THE WORLD
(See Classified Index and Teachers Book*)

* Not available when this textbook was written.

ADDITIONAL REFERENCES

134

THINGS

TO

DO

1. Examine the music series book of your choice and prepare a listening lesson for that grade level. Refer to the Music Series Reference Guide to Listening, to other suggestions in this chapter, and to the chart, p. 260.

2. Prepare a statement on why training in discriminating listening is of crucial importance in today's world of radio and TV musical offerings.

3. Plan a "concert" using recordings for an elementary classroom. Explain how children may help plan this program. Tell of the many things other than music that can be taught through this activity.

4. The term "appreciation" was not used in this chapter to describe listening to recordings because it now applies to all aspects of music learning—rhythm, singing, playing—as well as to listening. Explain why this is so.

5. A music educator said, "Good music is that music which is good for boys and girls at their current stage of development." According to this, when is the "music of the masters" good for children?

6. Listen to recordings of authentic music that employ native instruments and native voices. Could these be used in a classroom? (See the list of such recordings in the catalog of Folkways Records and Service Corporation, 117 West 46th St., New York City.)

7. Select a recording to be used in a listening lesson. Draw up a list of "key words" to be put on the chalkboard to help the children know what they might listen for.

8. Find out what impressionist music is (Debussy, Ravel, Delius) and how this music can be related to impressionism in art.

9. For your own cultural background, study various periods in music history. The following dates are approximate only: Renaissance (1450-1600), Baroque (1600-1750), Classical (1750-1820), Romantic (1820-1900), Contemporary (1900–). A convenient source of such informa-

tion is Hugh Miller's *An Outline of the History of Music* (New York: Barnes and Noble, Inc.).

10. Evidence lends support to the use of carefully selected chamber music and orchestra music of composers such as Haydn and Mozart in the primary grades. (See "An Autochthonous Approach to Music Education," *Music Educators Journal*, Feb.-March, 1949). Listen to such recordings and evaluate them in terms of possible use.

11. Select appropriate recordings for use in the rest period.

12. Examine the *Listening Program* record albums of the RCA Victor Basic Record Library for Elementary Schools and learn how to use them. Read the instructions. Note the references to these albums in the music series, particularly in the "Music for Living Series" (Silver Burdett).

13. Visit a record shop and ask what children's records the schools are buying. Listen to them and evaluate them.

14. Kindergarten and first grade teachers should study the relation between playing the piano and listening activities as demonstrated in the series books for those grades. It is clear that the ability to play simple piano pieces is one of the requirements of the professionally prepared teacher of those grades.

15. The classification and evaluation of educational records for children are greatly aided by some of the catalogs published by concerns that specialize in this area. Evaluate this aid to teachers provided by the catalogs of such companies as Children's Reading Service, 1078 St. John's Place, Brooklyn 13, New York; The Greystone Corporation, 100 Sixth Avenue, New York 13, New York; and Children's Music Center, 2858 W. Pico Blvd., Los Angeles 8, California (50¢).

16. Find out what services your state university or state system of higher education offers teachers in supplying 16 mm. films for use in this area.

17. Learn how to care for and store recordings.

18. During repeated listening to a recording that tells a story, first listen for the story. Next, listen to and analyze *how* the music portrays the story. Finally, listen to evaluate *how successfully* the composer or arranger portrayed the story by means of his music.

REFERENCES

Books for Teachers

Baldwin, Lillian, *Music for Young Listeners: The Green Book, The Blue Book, The Red Book*. New York: Silver Burdett Co., 1951. An important source of information about music and composers written for elementary school use. Recordings obtainable from Sound Book Press Society (see below under *Recordings*, 8).

Buchanan, Francis, *How Man Made Music*. Chicago: Follett Publishing Co., 1951.

Hughes, Dorothy, *Rhythmic Games and Dances*. New York: American Book Co., 1942. Used in connection with listening in the American Singer Series.

Jordalen, Marion and Alice J. Eppink, *The Who, What and Where Music Series* Book I: *Musicians*. San Francisco: Library Music Services, 1954. A listing of source materials of all types.

Mursell, James L., *Music and the Classroom Teacher*, chap. V. New York: Silver Burdett Co., 1951.

Music Educators National Conference, *Music in the Elementary School*. Chicago: the Conference, 1951. Contains list of books about music for teachers and children.

Myers, Louise, *Teaching Children Music in the Elementary School*, chap. VI. Englewood Cliffs, N.J.: Prentice-Hall, Inc., 1950.

Pitts, Lilla Belle, ed., *Handbook on 16 mm. Films in Music Education*. Chicago: Music Educators National Conference, 1952.

Books for Children

Cross, Donzella, *Music Stories for Boys and Girls*. Boston: Ginn and Co., 1926.

Goss, Madeline, *Deep Flowing Brook: the story of J. S. Bach*. New York: Henry Holt, 1938.

House, Marguerite, *O Say Can You Hear?* a workbook, 3 vols. New York: Mills Music Co., 1619 Broadway, New York City 19, 1949.

Kinscella, Hazel, *The Kinscella Readers*, 2d ed., 8 vols. Lincoln: University Publishing Co., 1949.

Wheeler, Opal and Sybil Deucher, *Bach, the Boy from Thuringia; Beethoven and His Chiming Tower of Bells; Stephen Foster and His Little Dog Tray; Grieg, Boy from the Northland; Handel at the Court of Kings; Haydn, The Merry Little Peasant; MacDowell and His Cabin in the Pines; Schubert and His Merry Friends; Curtain Calls for Haydn and Bach; Curtain Calls for Schubert; Curtain Calls for Mozart; Mozart, the Wonder Boy*. New York: E. P. Dutton Co., 1934-44.

Recordings	Suggested R.P.M. Grade Level	

1. American Book Company, 121 Second St., San Francisco 3, California — 78

    Album AS 24, *Lullabies* (lullabies from various countries) *Primary Music Series* — K-3

    Album AS 20 *Soft and Loud* (dynamics) — 1-3

    Album AS 21 *High and Low* (range) — 1-3

    Album AS 26 *Dance Suite* (dance forms and chamber music) — 4-8

2. Bowmar Records, 5415 Crenshaw Blvd., Los Angeles 43, California — 78

    Album *Listening Time*

3. Columbia Recording Corp., 1473 Branum Avenue, Bridgeport, Conn.

    Album: *Instruments of the Orchestra*, Introduction Series — 78 & 45 — 4-8

    Disc: *The Eager Piano* — 33 — 3-5

    Introducing the Masters Series — 78 45

        Great Composers Come to Life—Milton Cross, narrator — 33 1/3

        The Story and Music of Haydn

        The Story and Music of Mozart

        The Story and Music of Chopin

4. Decca Records, Inc., 50 West 57th St., New York 19, New York

    CU—106 *Tubby the Tuba* — 78 — 3-6

    4 Albums *The Symphony Orchestra* — 4-12

        90: strings, 91: woodwinds, 92: brass, 93: percussion

5. Children's Record Guild and Young People's Records, The Greystone Corp., 100 Sixth Ave., New York 13, New York

	R.P.M.	Grade
Music Listening Game (hearing pitches)	78	K-2
Golden Goose (combining melodies)	45-78	K-4
Hot Cross Buns (variation form)	45-78	1-4
Mr. Grump and Band (instruments)	78	1-3
Silly Liesl (nonsense songs for fun)	78	K-4
Clock Went Backwards (history of music)	45-78	2-5
Let's Dance (creative)	45-78	3-5
The King's Trumpet (evolution of trumpet)	78	1-5
The Wonderful Violin	78	3-6
Mozart Country Dances	78	3-7
Everybody Dances (Mozart)	78	3-7
Music of Aaron Copland	78	3-6
Said the Piano to the Harpsichord	45-78	1-5
Licorice Stick (clarinet)	78	3-6

Recordings	*R.P.M.*	*Suggested Grade Level*
Round and Round (round, canon, fugue)	78	3-7
Music of Igor Stravinsky	78	3-6
Toy Symphony (by Haydn)	78	2-4
Rondo for Bassoon and Orchestra (form)	78	3-6
Muffin in the City (learning to listen)	45-78	N-1
Muffin in the Country (learning to listen)	45-78	N-1
Little Brass Band	45-78	K-3

Albums (containing many of the above recordings):

Just Listening	78	1-4
Music Listening (2 vols.)	78	2-6
Bands, Orchestras, and Instruments	78	1-4
Musical Instruments	78	2-6

6. R.C.A. Victor Educational Services, Dept. 390, Camden, New Jersey — 78 & 45

Albums for *Listening Activities*

Albums Vol. 1 E 77, Vol. 2 E 78, Vol. 3 E 79		1-3
Albums Vol. 4 E 80, Vol. 5 E 81, Vol. 6 E 82		4-8
Indian Album E 89		4-8
Album E 104 Instruments of the Orchestra	78	4-8
Little Nipper and Bluebird Classics		

7. Sound Devices, Inc., 129 E. 124th St., New York 35, New York (Vox) — 78 & 33

Vox Music Master Series
    Examples: *Tschaikovsky, His Life and Works*
        Mozart, His Life and Works
        Schubert, His Life and Works

8. Sound Book Press Society, Inc., Scarsdale, New York (or Silver Burdett Co., 45 E. 17th St., New York 3, New York) — 78

Musical Sound Books for Young Listeners (to complement music appreciation books by Lillian Baldwin) — 78

Tiny Masterpieces for Very Young Listeners	78	N-3
Records to accompany Green Book		4-up
Records to accompany Crimson Book		5-up
Records to accompany Blue Book		6-up

9. Other Sources of Recordings

    (1) Allegro Music Inc., 5 Columbus Circle, New York 19, New York

    (2) Capitol Records, Inc., Sunset and Vine, Hollywood, Calif.

    (3) Folkways Records, 117 W. 46th St., New York 19, New York

    (4) Mercury Childcraft Records, 1733 Broadway, Room 408, New York

Suggested
R.P.M. Grade Level

Filmstrips

Jam Handy Organization, 2821 East Grand Blvd.,
Detroit 11, Michigan

Music Stories—filmstrips in color with recordings

1. *Peter and the Wolf*	33 1/3	3-5
2. *Hansel and Gretel*		3-5
3. *The Nutcracker*		3-5
4. *Peer Gynt*		6-8
5. *The Firebird*		6-8
6. *The Sorcerer's Apprentice*		3-8

Stories of Music Classics—six filmstrips in color, stories   33 1/3
of beloved classics come to life

1. *The Sleeping Beauty*	4-9
2. *William Tell*	5-9
3. *A Midsummer Night's Dream*	6-9
4. *The Swan Lake*	6-9
5. *The Bartered Bride*	6-9
6. *Scheherazade*	5-9

Films

British Information Service, 30 Rockefeller Plaza, New
York 20, New York

Instruments of the Orchestra	20 minutes	4-12

Coronet Instructional Films, 65 E. South Water St.,
Chicago, Illinois

Melody in Music	12 minutes	4-6
A young orchestra in rehearsal		

Pictures

Great Composers, The Willis Music Co., 124 E. 4th St., Cincinnati 1, Ohio

Band Instruments, Orchestra Instruments, Artist Pictures, Keyboard Junior, 1346 Chapel St., New Haven 11, Conn.

Immortal Men of Music, L. J. Morton

Portraits of Great Composers, Hall & McCreary Co., Park Avenue at Sixth Street, Minneapolis 15, Minn.

Large Size Musical Instrument Pictures (set contains 12 posters picturing 14 instruments), C. G. Conn, Ltd., Elkhart, Indiana

Magazines

Young Keyboard Junior (for grades 4-6), 1346 Chapel St., New Haven 11, Conn. It helps guide radio and television listening.

Orchestra Instruments (Books)

Huntington, Harriett E., *Tune Up—Instruments of the Orchestra and Their Players*. New York: Doubleday & Company, 1942. Includes illustrations of children playing instruments.

Lacey, Marion, *Picture Book of Musical Instruments*. New York: Lothrop, Lee & Shepherd Company, 1942. With historical sketches.

Balet, Jan, *What Makes an Orchestra*. New York: Oxford University Press, 1951.

Teaching
Music
Creatively

Six

Creativeness takes place, in an educational sense, in a learning environment where children are free to suggest and to experiment. To help children become emotionally well-adjusted, the school should provide many and varied opportunities for creative expression. What is creative at a certain time to one child may not be creative to another; it depends on the particular background of experience of the individual child. Educators consider creativeness to take place whenever the child discovers new relationships and whenever he projects himself into an activity or project and makes it something that at the time belongs uniquely to him.

One of the tests of creative teaching is whether or not the song or the activity becomes psychologically the possession of the children. They should properly think or say, "This is *our* song," (not "This is the song the teacher has told us to sing"). "*We* found a rhythm to play with our South American song which *we* decided sounded best on the tambourine." "*We* decided that the first part of the song sounded best slow so as to contrast with the last part, which *we* thought sounded best fast." "*We* made up a new dance to a favorite folk song, and changed one of our old dances to a way *we* like better." "*We* wrote a poem today to tell how we felt about the weather we're having and made a song of it." "Johnny made up an Indian tune on the Melody Flute which *we* decided to use with the Thanks-

141

giving play our class is writing." When, under the intelligent guidance of the teacher, there is freedom for children to share in the development of classroom projects, a good measure of creative activity is found. When children create constructively they learn to appreciate; therefore creative activity is one of the best avenues to appreciation. "To best appreciate the work of others one needs experience in creating."

Attempts have been made to set forth steps in the progress of a creative act. First, there is a rich, sensory, first-hand experience to which the individual makes an emotional response. This response is such that there is a desire to share emotion with others. Second, the means of expression will be selected; it may be poetry, painting, music, or some other form. Third, there follows the experimenting with the selected means. The enthusiasm and encouragement of the teacher are vital to the success of the creative act in the classroom.

Before children can be truly active in creative ways, they need to acquire a background of experience, for creative possibilities are directly related to the richness of prior experiences. Some of this necessary background comes from rhythmic activities, dramatic play, and dramatization. Some comes from class activities such as making the classroom a more beautiful place in which to live, observing beauty in nature, feeling the rhythm of poetry; and from listening to music to hear stories, to imagine pictures, and to become aware of music's tone qualities, rhythms, and harmonies.

The environment that nurtures creative activities includes the physical (space for movement, informal furniture arrangements, many materials including percussion and melody instruments, proper lighting and ventilation) and the psychological (freedom from pressure and from fear of criticism, the existence of a friendly spirit in the classroom, and the approval and acceptance of individuals by the class). The teacher is responsible for enriching the children's backgrounds and for providing the necessary physical, emotional, and social setting. He gives suggestions when they are needed, and he is careful that his suggestions stimulate the children's thinking and do not supplant it. He neither dominates nor dictates. His attitude is one of learning with the learners while guiding them in an unobtrusive way.

Through creative activities children can recognize their possibilities, limitations, and capabilities, find the joy that comes only from developing creative powers, gain confidence through the satisfaction that comes from creating, feel stronger and less inhibited, learn perseverance, grow in ability to appreciate, develop increased sensitiveness to beauty, find relaxation and release from tensions, learn to respect individual differences, share in the success of others, learn social cooperation as opposed to anti-social competition, and use leisure time wisely in the pursuit of special interests.[1] *All* music activities should be approached in a creative spirit.

Although there are creative aspects in all phases of the elementary music program, it is well to point out here what is not creative. Usually, if it is the primary goal of a teacher in a given activity to teach facts about music such as notation, key signatures, meter signatures and identification of form, the situation is seldom one in which creative elements are present. However, all of these things and many more can be taught as *by-products* of genuine creative activities. The really important purpose in these activities, aside from the act of creation itself, is bringing from the children the ideas, judgments, and consequent experiments that help them grow and effectively express their feelings. Happier living results when, in pursuit of this purpose, notation is used in composing or playing a song (and meter and key signatures are found to be useful) and when children are led to discover the form of the song they have written. Then such facts about music take on meaning because of their function in a situation real to children.

The good teacher remembers that although learning the technicalities of music is not the only goal of elementary school music today, these technicalities can be rather easily learned if they serve the children in connection with their music activities. The good teacher will make definite plans for this. He knows that school music can be sterile and uninteresting when the approach to teaching it does not include the creative aspects. Furthermore, he realizes that a primary goal of creative activities is to guide boys and girls to think for themselves.

In order for children to be creative they must be encouraged to be *different* in constructive ways. Usually, when children are found to be conforming to a set pattern it is an indication that creative activities are not present and that the teacher has imposed adult standards upon them.

[1] Elizabeth Ketchen, ed., *Living and Learning Experiences in the Elementary Schools of South Carolina* (Columbia, S.C.: State Department of Education, 1948).

Creative rhythmic activities

In Chapter Two, "doing what the music tells you to do" illustrates a creative approach to rhythm because in this activity each child is free to make his own interpretation of what he hears. When such responses take place by means of arms in the air when children are seated, the teacher should at times request that eyes be closed. With closed eyes, each child can concentrate upon his own response to the rhythm, since he is not influenced by watching the actions of others. The writing of new words to familiar melodies is considered by some to be a rhythmic activity since these words must have the same rhythm as the original ones in order to fit the melody. However, this activity should be a natural outgrowth of child interest and should not be forced. For example, a first grade class had been studying the circus when a boy began singing new words to *Hot Cross Buns*. He began, "Laugh clown laugh, laugh clown laugh." Classmates joined in the fun and added, "You are funny, I am happy, laugh clown laugh." Later, when the group was thinking of the play period to come, other words were invented: "Run boys run, run girls run; You are playing on the ball field, run boys run."

Another creative rhythm activity is inventing rhythm patterns. These can be done with percussion instruments and hand clapping or in connection with a song (Chapter Two, p. 44). Very interesting rhythmic creations may occur when a class is divided into small groups, supplied with various percussion instruments, and told to invent rhythms and act them out. Often this is done in a large play room or gymnasium, and each group presents its rhythm before the class.

When rhythm patterns are invented to accompany a song, they should be saved for future use. It is then logical for class and teacher to write such patterns in notation on the chalkboard. In the lower primary grades patterns can be notated in rhythmic notation (long and short lines as in Chapter Two, p. 25). For second grade through the intermediate grades this provides a meaningful use for music notation and is an example of incidental learning of notation as a by-product of creative rhythmic activity. When rhythm patterns are created without reference to songs, words can sometimes be supplied for them.

Still another activity is the deriving of rhythms from words. This can be done with one or two repeated words such as "Mississippi," "merrily," and "blackberry pie," and with names of boys and girls in the class. It is fun for each child to discover the rhythm pattern of his own name, and to see it in notation.

Other creative rhythm activities are the inventing of singing games, dances, and floor patterns, and the varying of known games and dances. Songs can be created from dance steps, and dances can be created from songs, particularly folk songs. Through dances there can be the discovery of aspects of form and mood in music. Interesting rhythmic expressions can be derived from dramatic play experiences. The teacher may observe certain movements which the children can be guided to develop further. Music is then added to enhance the thoughts and feelings expressed rhythmically.

Creative playing activities

The use of percussion instruments as discussed in Chapter Two emphasized the creative processes involved when children listen to music and make their own selection of the instruments and rhythmic playing responses they believe are most appropriate to the music's mood and form. Instruments can also be used to create children's concepts of different types of music. For example, the atmosphere associated with Chinese or Japanese music can be created through use of wood blocks, sticks, a gong, and drums. In addition to these, the black keys of the piano can be used with one or both hands to invent, either by chance or by melodic intent, music based on the five-tone scale,[2] and which represents to our ears some of the music of the Chinese and Japanese peoples. This same scale is characteristic of American Indian music. Children find that an open fifth in the bass of the piano represents Indian drums. To introduce this creative tool, one might play the tones G♭ and D♭ simultaneously with the left hand while the right hand creates an Indian melody on the black keys. Drums, rattles, and sticks are useful in inventing Indian music. For creating Spanish or South American music children need access to sticks, maracas, wood blocks, castanets, and tambourines. The making and testing of simple instruments is another activity that could be included here.

Adding appropriate harmony by means of Autoharp, Harmolin, ukulele, guitar, accordion, or piano chording may be taught as a crea-

[2] The black keys of the piano are mentioned because they are a ready-made example of the pentatonic scale. This five-tone scale can be played on the white keys also.

tive playing activity based on listening. Melodies can be composed on the instruments mentioned in Chapter Three.

Creative singing activities

In Chapter Four several examples of creative singing activities were discussed. The children's responses to many of the activities associated with tone matching constituted one of them. Included was the response to the teacher's sung question, "What did you see on the way to school?" and the sung responses to other questions such as, "Where do you live?" "What did you bring?" "How do church bells ring?", and pretended telephone conversations such as "Hello," "Hello," "How are you?" "I'm fine." Children can sing their own names, the names of cities, and certain word groupings that grow out of their experiences. They can also create songs—an activity to be discussed later in this chapter.

An activity of major importance is song interpretation. As stated earlier in this chapter, to have a song become the possession of children means that they have been free to contribute to its interpretation and development. The creative approach tends to have children think seriously about the meaning of the words they sing and about the connotations of this meaning in terms of musical expression. Children should be encouraged to enter into decisions as to whether the song should be sung loud or soft, fast or slow, what percussion instruments or chordal accompaniment should be used with it, and many other critical aspects—all of which should lead toward a high degree of musical sensitivity and discrimination.

Creative listening activities

Chapter Five stressed listening as an active mental and emotional activity, and stated that listening is the basic music activity from which all the others begin. When children discover or are guided to discover for themselves the many different things active listening can give them, their listening is in many instances of a highly creative type because the making of personal choices in imagination, observation, comparison, and discrimination is a creative experience. As mentioned above, adding appropriate chordal harmony to a melody by means of the piano, Autoharp, or the so-called social instruments is basically a creative listening activity.

One of the higher forms of creative listening is the dramatization of instrumental music. In connection with a unit in conservation, children[3] searched for recorded music that represented aspects of the out-of-doors, particularly trees and water, and life in the forest. *The Moldau* (Smetana) gave the mental image of the streams joining together to form a broad river which flowed through the countryside. The children wanted to show through bodily movement the flow of the water, the tall stately trees, and the animals that played in the forest. After listening many times, they dramatized these things rhythmically to the first section of *The Moldau*. Other compositions from which these children chose sections to interpret were *Contrasts* (Bartók), *Symphony No. 6 in F Major* (Beethoven), *Woodland Sketches* (MacDowell), and *Pines of Rome* (Respighi).

Another aspect of creative listening is the artwork children may do when inspired while listening to music.

Creative impersonation and dramatization

Creative dramatization of recordings of instrumental music has been mentioned immediately above. To this can be added the dramatization of piano compositions played by the teacher. Creative rhythmic dramatization was mentioned in the section on creative rhythmic activities. Impersonation as a means of introducing fundamental rhythms was discussed in Chapter Two. Chapter Four mentioned the creative dramatization of songs only incidentally. It is one of the more important creative activities, and one of the ways in which children can project themselves with great pleasure into a variety of situations.

When children "lose" themselves in such dramatizations, they forget self-consciousness and some may find their singing voices in this manner. Having children in primary grades impersonate animals and people—or having them sing for puppets—is one of the methods used by teachers to get some children started singing. Children in lower primary grades enjoy dramatizing familiar songs such as *Old Mother Hubbard*. They can create actions to songs that were not originally intended to be action songs. New singing games can be created.

Some ballads provide dramatizations growing out of interpretations of the text. Examples found in series books include *Old Woman and the Peddler; Old Woman's Courtship; Oh, No John; Wraggle Taggle Gypsies;* and *Good King Wenceslaus*. Dances are often cre-

[3] Demonstrated at the 1955 California-Western Division of the Music Educators National Conference, Berkeley, California, by Alice M. Snyder, San Francisco State College.

ated to recurring refrains. Folk dance tunes are important sources of materials for creative dramatization. Sea chanties and question-and-answer songs are also useful, as are old songs such as *Old King Cole.* The song sources for creative dramatization are unlimited and no listing can do more than direct attention to the immense possibilities at hand.

Many of the series books contain song stories that are small operettas. These should be examined and evaluated in the light of creative elements that might be present. Since the music and words are already written out and often recorded also, it is possible that few opportunities for genuine creative expression may be present. However, such song stories are valuable in that they provide necessary background for future activities which can be of more creative nature.

CREATIVE MUSIC COMPOSITION

Small children are natural composers of music. If one listens to them he will find that speech and song are interchanged quite normally in their unsupervised play.

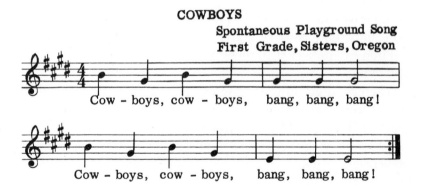

COWBOYS
Spontaneous Playground Song
First Grade, Sisters, Oregon

Cow - boys, cow - boys,   bang, bang, bang!

Cow - boys, cow - boys,   bang, bang, bang!

Teachers of lower primary grades continue this natural activity when they call the roll with their singing voices and the children reply in like manner. This was described in the section on creative singing activities in this chapter.

One sunny morning a little girl in first grade was holding her teacher's hand as she left the building to go to directed play. Deeply affected by the beauty of the day, she sang:

A BEAUTIFUL DAY

Julie McCornack
First Grade, Washington School
Eugene, Oregon

Oh what a won-der-ful day, Oh what a won-der-ful day! Oh what a beau - ti - ful day!

The teacher asked Julie to repeat her song and they sang it together so that they could remember it when they returned to the classroom and share it with others. Another teacher of a first grade group had just concluded a reading lesson in which children had learned new words. It was shortly before lunch, and the children suddenly related the new words to their interest in food:

1. One two three, come eat with me.
2. Blue and red, will we be fed?

The above examples illustrate the point that creating simple songs is an ability children possess and one that grows under the guidance of good teachers. It is only a short step from spontaneous creative activity to the point where a teacher says of a well-known poem, "Let's sing it today instead of speaking it," and the setting of poetry to music becomes a classroom activity.

Short verse that has a clearly defined rhythm may be used for a type of song improvisation that emphasizes this rhythm. As a background for this activity children should have sung many short poems and simple word rhythms. The words are spoken by the children in a regular beat pattern set by the teacher. The teacher establishes key feeling by chording the familiar I V₇ I sequence in a key of his choice, and when introducing this activity he will sing the first word of the poem, thus suggesting to the children the beginning note of the song-to-be. While he beats time (it is basic to the method that the rhythm never be interrupted) individual children are asked to sing the poem. The other children may be urged to continue to speak the words softly while they listen to the song being born. The rhythm is stressed, the assumption being that if the rhythm is maintained, a melody will appear from each child, which can be as spontaneous and uninhibited as speech. It is further assumed that it is as natural for children to have many musical ideas as it is for them to have many ideas expressed in language. This approach to song creation can be effective on any grade level and is believed by some to possess virtues that are superior, from the standpoint of creativeness, to the phrase-wise approach, which will be described later. One finds supposedly well-trained musicians who have little feeling for the onward movement of music; they often "break" the rhythm. It is believed that if children experience this type of creative expression, which keeps the rhythmic flow proceeding without interruption, there might be fewer adult musicians who lack a feeling for rhythmic consistency.

Instruments such as the Song Bells and piano are sometimes of aid in stimulating creative processes. A special music teacher brought four tone bars (from a type of bell set that can be separated) into a first grade room. The children were interested in new shoes, which

NEW SHOES
First Grade Laboratory School
Wisconsin State College
Milwaukee, Wisconsin

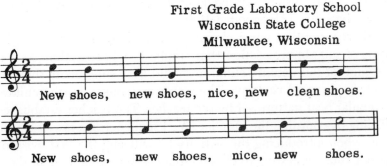

several of them wore that day, and with the aid of the four tones they created their own special song on the subject, called "New Shoes." The repetitious words are typical of first grade children. This song was sung throughout the term whenever one of the children came to school with new shoes. They learned to play it on the Song Bells also.

Melodies without words are created by children who have opportunities to experiment with tuned water bottles, xylophones, Song Bells, piano, recorder-type instruments, and the instruments of the band and orchestra. When children discover that they have the ability to compose simple instrumental melodies, they will frequently do this at home as a play activity and bring their creations to school.

Teachers save worthy compositions by writing them down in music notation. If a teacher has had special music training, he can "take dictation" when the children create a song—that is, associate at once the tones he hears with degrees of the scale. For instance, the first three song examples in this chapter are based on the same note pattern—the familiar 1-3-5 chord or the *tonic* chord. The recognition of this fact makes notating such songs a simple matter. Since few classroom teachers have had this kind of training,[4] most of them rely on other means to notate these songs. For example, the teacher who heard Julie sing *A Beautiful Day* sang it with her to remember it so that when she returned to the classroom she could find the song on the Song Bells or piano. To help remember the melody of a child's song, the inexperienced teacher can invent pictorial ways to record melodies by such means as drawing a continuous or a broken line showing the directions of the pitch and by drawing short and long dashes to represent comparative note values. Some teachers write melodies with numerals or syllables and determine the notation later. Others have the children help them remember the song until a special music teacher or another classroom teacher has time to help notate it. Some children in the intermediate grades can be of help. There is always a way to notate these songs, and any teacher who works with these activities will improve in skill as time goes on.

As soon as children understand and can use notation, the song-creating process in the classroom should include the notating of the song on the chalkboard where everyone can participate in some

---

[4] Suggestions for improving one's ability to take musical dictation are found in Appendix C.

degree in seeing that it is written in such manner that it correctly pictures what was created. Also, when good songs are notated in or transposed to keys that children find easy to use when playing recorder-type instruments, such songs may be duplicated and given to the children. When children take such songs home to play for their parents on these instruments or on the piano, they are learning about music notation as a by-product of their creative activity.

The following excerpt from the *Alabama Education Journal*[5] concerns the writing of poetry and music on the intermediate grade level. The teacher had enriched the children's background for this activity by developing vocabulary through increasing awareness to beauty in the classroom and in nature, and by reading appropriate poetry for the class.

Until the time when the writing of poetry was found to be an enjoyable activity there had been no particular relation between poetry and music. However, when the time came to try to set some of the poetry to music, the students were eager to try. At the beginning, poems with a very simple and direct rhythm were read by the class so that everyone felt the same rhythmic flow of the words. The children moved at their desks to the rhythm of the words, and they tapped the rhythm. While there was some early hesitance because of the newness of the procedure, this disappeared abruptly after the first experience with it. Children tried "walking out" the rhythm of their poems by walking while they spoke them. As a consequence, the rhythm of the words was a dominant feature of the first songs composed. Later on, the more subtle meanings of words, and the varying moods of the poems became of increasing importance and shared an equal emphasis with rhythm. All that was done with creative music was an outgrowth of the earlier and continuing efforts of the classroom teacher to guide activities in such a way that the children were free to develop their sensitivity to visual impressions, to word meanings, and to sounds.

At first, the children selected from their store of poems they had written those which they felt would be easiest to set to music. The music teacher discussed these with the class and together they examined and experimented to find those with the clearest rhythmic patterns. Then the staff was placed on the blackboard and the words were written beneath it. The music teacher chose the key in which the song would be written and played the tonic chord (1-3-5) on a bell set. This gave the children a harmonic setting in which to start to think tonally. Later on in the year this was abandoned.

5 Vernice Trousdale and Robert E. Nye, "The Fourth Grade Writes Music," *Alabama Education Journal*, December, 1950.

No one knew in what way the class would compose its song. Sometimes everyone sang phrases together and the music teacher wrote on the blackboard what he heard as majority opinion. At other times individuals volunteered phrases of the song, one after another, until it was completed. The group judged the suitability of these musical thoughts, and frequently had to discriminate between two or more versions of the same phrase. When the song was completed to the satisfaction of all, the correct meter signature was added, and bar lines and note values were determined. Here was the learning of music fundamentals in a "real" situation. Even so, the music teacher was always ready to hurry this part of the procedure whenever he felt that an over-emphasis on the mechanical details was beginning to detract from the enjoyment of the creative experience. These songs were often reproduced on a Ditto Machine so the children could take them home to show to their parents and play them on the piano and on instruments such as bell sets and Tonettes. While at the beginning the children had to be encouraged to sing their musical ideas to the class, this early stage of reluctance changed rapidly to one of nearly 100 percent participation in which the music teacher found it necessary to stress self-control in waiting one's turn. In order to express more completely the meaning of the words, the boys and girls experimented with choral reading in various combinations with singing. Almost from the first they began bringing to the class poems they had written at home, and sharing with the group their musical ideas which had been born along with the words.

Near the end of the year, a college class asked to observe the composition of songs in the fourth grade. The music teacher selected three poems of varying types. The children were not satisfied with their setting of a poem written in strict rhythm. One girl objected that it "sounded too much alike," while a boy stated flatly that "it was monotonous." This led to a revision of the last half of the song which satisfied the group's feeling of what was musically suitable. This discussion and revision revealed to the observers aesthetic discrimination at the fourth grade level. The second song was a little jingle, "The Funny Instrument." The group found this to be of such obvious tonal suggestibility that everyone began to sing together, and they sang it in unison as though they had known it always.

The third and last poem was one of mood which had no strong rhythm or rhyme to guide the composers. They solved this problem by contributing ideas phrase by phrase. This song seemed to give the children a greater feeling of accomplishment and aesthetic appreciation than any they had done before. After it was completed and on the blackboard, one of the girls suggested repeating the last four notes softly. This was tried and proved to be very effective. A boy contributed the practical thought that putting repeat marks in the right places would eliminate having to write more notes, so this was done.

MOONLIGHT

Fourth Grade
Kilby Training School
State Teachers College
Florence, Alabama

Helen Turner

Dark is the night as I lie in my bed: The stars and the moon give light. As I lie in my bed rest-ing my head, I go to sleep. I

In the course of this creative work each child developed more respect for the worth of each of the other children. The ability to contribute successfully to group action led to a feeling of security which gave, in turn, poise and self-assurance. Some who had not been able to succeed in other things found in the composition of poetry and music the satisfaction of those basic needs so frequently listed by educators: success, acceptance, belonging, and security. Some children wrote poems which showed evidence of being emotional outlets for their worries and troubles.[6]

The class had become more conscious of those intangible elements of beauty inherent in all art. They learned to enjoy many different types of poetry, not only their own, but the poems in the many books which they read voluntarily. Listening to recorded music became active and imaginative listening, perhaps due to the group's experiences in adding to the meaning of words by the use of musical composition.

The improvement in the skills of English composition was apparent. The practical use of music notation made music symbols more easily understood.[7] Due to the many socializing experiences found in this form

[6] *Little Brother*
　　My little brother, as you can see,
　　Is just as cute as cute can be.
　　My little brother makes me mad,
　　And that's why I am always sad.

[7] One of the favorite pastimes during free periods was going to the blackboard, drawing a staff, and writing tunes. Children who did this were usually those who were taking piano lessons or participating in other types of musical activities outside of school and as a consequence had richer musical backgrounds.

of creative self-expression, there was evidence of improved unity and understanding between the pupils and the teachers.

As culminating activities of some units of work, programs were presented. The original poems and songs made these programs more vital to both students and their parents.

This use of poetry and music was considered successful by those who were in contact with the fourth grade. The teachers believe that knowing the child and providing opportunity and encouragement for him to develop his powers of expression comprise the foundation on which love for poetry and music can be built.

It can be seen that when children can compose poetry and songs, the creation of simple operettas is not beyond the possibilities of intermediate grades. Since the form of most of the songs children compose is usually simple in structure, often being a question-and-answer type with repeated phrases, teachers can guide children to discover elements of form in music by having them examine their own compositions. "Is this phrase the same or different than the preceding one?" is often an interesting question when it concerns a song that a class has written. (Refer to Chapter Two, p. 51, for a discussion of music form.)

The procedure many teachers follow when they guide children in song writing in grades three and above is as follows:

1. Choose words that are simple, have rhythmic flow, and are understood by children.
2. Write the words on the chalkboard under the staff.
3. Have the class read the words together so that a definite rhythm is established. Use clapping or stepping if necessary. The most heavily accented word syllables may be underlined.
4. If this activity is comparatively new to the children, sound the tonic (1-3-5) chord by singing 1-3-5-3-1 (do-mi-sol-mi-do), or by playing it on Autoharp or piano. If these instruments are used, it is still better to play the chord sequence I-V$_7$-I to definitely establish the key feeling. If the children are experienced in song writing, this step is not necessary because they "hear with their inner ears" what they create, and the arbitrary setting of a key may interfere with the creative process.
5. Ask for suggestions to start the song. There are several approaches to this. In the earliest stages of learning to compose, a teacher may have all or part of the first phrase written and ask the class to finish that section of the song. This can be done

by the class *thinking* what the rest of the song might be (after singing the first part several times) and finally singing it, the teacher accepting the majority opinion. Soon individuals will have melodic suggestions to offer, and the process becomes one of both group and individual contribution. The group is the controlling force, however, and exercises musical and poetical discrimination in choosing between versions of parts of the song that are volunteered by individuals. The composition of these songs generally proceeds phrase by phrase with the group singing frequently from the beginning of the song. The teacher notates the song as it grows in length. Those teachers who can take musical dictation will write stemless notes on the staff. Since it is necessary to proceed with rapidity to avoid lagging interest, these are usually little lines (⁄) instead of filled out notes (●). Some teachers will prefer to use numerals or syllables and "figure" from these. Others will use the keyboard directly, and still others will employ means previously mentioned on page 151.

6. Have the class decide what the meter signature is. The teacher and class will find where the bar lines are placed by writing them before heavily accented notes. Sometimes the song will be transposed to a more suitable key. Key signatures will be determined. Note values will be determined, and stems, flags, and dots will be added.

7. Add Autoharp or piano chords for accompanying the song if desired.

8. If the song is of good quality, it should be saved by placing it in a class notebook. If it is in a key in which children can play recorder-type instruments, reproduce it on a duplicating machine so that the children may use notation at home in playing the song for their parents.

The good teacher knows that it is not the purpose of this activity to produce composers, but rather to gain the joy and confidence that come from a fascinating creative process. Below are some poems which are the result of creative efforts made by elementary school children and elementary education majors in college classes. They are included here to be used in building skill and confidence in song writing. This is a satisfying activity that is fun to do. One should forget real or imagined musical deficiencies of the moment and enjoy it!

Poems that may be set to music by primary grades

Singing and Skipping

Carol Gerlach

This is how we sing and play:
Skip two times, then gently sway.
Won't you join us in our fun?
Skip along now ev'ryone.

Choo Choo Train

Irene Amodei

Choo choo train, choo choo train,
Chugging down the track.
Choo choo train, choo choo train,
Clank, clank, clank, toot-toot!

Robins

June Bacher

Three baby robins
Have learned a new song;
It's "Tweet-a-tweet, tweet-a-tweet"
All the day long.

The Snowman

Muriel Horton

I'm a little snowman fat and white,
Here is my hat and here is my pipe.
When the sun comes out to play
Then I'll melt and go away.

Little Chick

Washington First Grade

I had a little chick
Who picked up a stick.
He went into his pen
And he sat down again.
He pecked a little worm
And oh! how it did squirm.
He ran and got his mother
To help him find another.

Poems that may be set to music by intermediate grades

The Tree

Nancy Adams

The tree outside my window
Is cold and dark and brown.
All the pretty colored leaves
Have fallen to the ground.

Pioneer Mother

Composed by a fifth grade
class for their Westward
Movement Unit

Mother was singing a lullaby
To quiet her tiny babe.
The night was cool and calm and clear;
The child was peacefully sleeping.

Autumn Leaves

Emiko Komae

Pretty leaves of red and yellow,
Colors all so warm and mellow.
Blow, wind, blow, and leaves will scatter
Before the rain comes pitter-patter.

Dreaming

Nancy Adams

As twilight draws her curtain and pins it with a star,
Two sleepy, nodding children that view it from afar,
Are whisked away to dreamland, where streets are paved with gold,
Where trees are ever silver green, and all is safe from cold.

Music Series Reference Guide to Selected Creative Activities

The American Singer (2d ed.; American Book Company)

BOOK ONE

Creative orchestration with percussion instruments: see Reference Guide in
Chapter Two of this text.
Creative rhythm described, 157-158
Dramatization suggested, 19, 20br, 30r, 70, 71, 98, 183b, 185, story, 83-92r
Verses usable as rhythmic bases for song creation, 110, 116, 118, 120, 122,
125, 127, 130, 133, 135, 136, 139, 146

BOOK TWO

Creative rhythm, 53, 68, 97-99r, 109b, 167
Dramatized stories, 35-40, 176-185
Verses usable as rhythmic bases for song creation, 19, 48, 55, 91, 161
Verse writing, 30, 65, 66, 93

BOOK THREE

Composing songs, 16, 25, 41b, 103, 129
Dance, 134
Dramatized story, 190-199
Rhythm game, 57

BOOK FOUR

Poems to set to music, 37, 55, 107, 131, 169, 185
Writing songs, method of, 156

BOOK FIVE

Composing songs, 52
Writing words for songs, 24, 49

BOOK SIX
Creative rhythm, 82, 84

New Music Horizons (Silver Burdett Company)

MUSIC FOR EARLY CHILDHOOD
Dramatic play: see Subject Index, Acting Out Life Experiences, p. 132, also 84-94

EXPERIENCES IN MUSIC FOR FIRST GRADE CHILDREN
Creative activities, 142
Dramatization, 6a, 86-89r, 100b
Impersonation, 8, 90ar, 90b

BOOK TWO
Creative listening, 12
Dramatization of form, 86r
Refer 161-162 V "Making Our Own Music," 161 II A2, A3 "Impersonation," "Dramatization," 161 IV 2 "Rhythm Band"

BOOK THREE
Dramatization, 96, 128-129, 131, 142, 162-163
Impersonation, 42, 114, 146a
Refer 184-185 V "Creative Expression," 184 IV 2 "Rhythm Band"

BOOK FOUR
Dramatization, 10, 155
Instrumentation, 79
Refer 208 VI "Creating"

BOOK FIVE
Harmonization, 70
Percussion instruments, creative use of, 20, 109, 141, 181, 186
Refer 232 VI "Creating"

BOOK SIX
Creative floor patterns, 21
Harmonization, 59, 182-183
Refer 246 V "Creating"

Our Singing World (Ginn and Company)

KINDERGARTEN BOOK
Refer xv C "Imitative Play," xvi D "Dramatic Play," xvi-xvii E "Apparatus," xvii-xix III "Creative Expression"
Song stories, 143-151r, 152-162r

FIRST GRADE BOOK
Refer xv-xvii III "Creative Expression," xiii C "Imitative Play," xiv D "Dramatic Play," xiv-xv E "Apparatus"
Song stories, 190-198r, 199-204r

SINGING ON OUR WAY
Dramatic play, 7, 8, 9, 51, 66a, 79r, 81, 86, 111, 116ar, 124r

Instrumental recordings suggested for dramatic play, 66, 73, 81, 132, 156
Song stories, 158-166r, 167-175r

SINGING AND RHYMING

Dramatic play, 8, 10, 19, 28r, 51, 60r, 67, 80r, 81r, 89, 100r, 125, 146, 160, 161r, 163r, 165
Instrumental recordings suggested for dramatic play, 79, 81, 85, 102, 145, 150, 151
Song stories, 170-181r, 182-190r
Song writing, 20, 32, 94, 115, 131, 157

SINGING EVERY DAY

Dramatic play, 7, 19, 45r, 52r, 60, 61r, 104, 105, 153, 170r
Instrumental recordings suggested for dramatic play, 19, 134
Song stories, 180-190r, 191-201r
Song writing, 18, 94, 115, 127, 133, 139, 171

SINGING TOGETHER

Dramatic play, 36, 38r, 39, 42r, 44, 45r, 49, 50, 53
Song story, 193-213r-Album 5-A
Song writing, poems for, 64, 112, 178

SINGING IN HARMONY

Dialogue songs for dramatic play, 45, 46-51r
Song story, 219-237r-Album 6-A

A Singing School (C. C. Birchard)

OUR FIRST MUSIC

Creative rhythm-band instrumentation suggested in units
Rhythmic plays and dramatization suggested in each unit
Song story, 344-362

OUR SONGS, NEW EDITION

Creative instrumentation, 110-111
Dance creation, 178
Dramatization, 9, 18, 21r, 26, 31r, 40, 56r, 100ar, 109, 116, 127, 138, 144r, 150r, 183, TM 23-24. Refer also to Teachers Manual for song analyses.
Songs for original play, 77-81
Song stories, 72-76, 155-170, TM 24-25
Song writing, words for, 42, 61, 65, 69, 71, 106, 110, 119, 178, 181
Tuneful Tim's letter, 117-118

MERRY MUSIC, NEW EDITION

Dramatization; refer Teachers Manual
Melodies for original words: see sections 117-144, 178
Song stories, 64-71, 161-170
Tuneful Tim, 114-116
Words for original melodies, 13, 38, 42, 45, 48, 72, 105, 109, 153, 179

WE SING

Dramatization: refer Teachers Manual
Song story, 170-185, TM 45-55

Song writing, 19, 33, 53, 57, 62a, 97
Verse writing, 21, 48, 85, 97, 99, 139

OUR LAND OF SONG

Creative activities, TM 34-35
Song story, 192-202, New Edition 203-215
Song writing, 31, 32, 34, 69, 90, 152
Suggestions for playlets, TM 37-41
Verse writing, 17, 30

MUSIC EVERYWHERE

Dance creation, 149
Dramatizations, suggested, TM 67-82, 95-96
Song story, New Edition, 219-230
Song writing, 70

Together We Sing (Follett Publishing Company)

MUSIC 'ROUND THE CLOCK

Words that might be set to music, 10, 17, 29, 33, 44, 61, 71, 79, 82, 84, 86

MUSIC 'ROUND THE TOWN

Dramatization, 133: 5, 13r, 14, 30r; 134: 60-67 (circus)

MUSIC THROUGH THE YEAR

Adding instrumental parts, 33 (pentatonic), 90 (drums)
Choric reading, 59, 102
Dramatization, 30, 50
Poems that might be set to music; evaluate those listed, 181

MUSIC ACROSS OUR COUNTRY

Poems that might be set to music; evaluate those listed, 191

VOICES OF AMERICA

See Classified Index* for:
    ballads and stories for possible dramatization
    poems that might be set to music

VOICES OF THE WORLD

Ballads and stories; examine for possible dramatization, 222
Poems that might be set to music, 223

Music For Living (Silver Burdett Company)

MUSIC THROUGH THE DAY (including children's books I LIKE THE COUNTRY
    and I LIKE THE CITY)
"Creative Response," 147
"Dramatizations" Index, 152

MUSIC IN OUR TOWN

TM "Creative Response," xii, "Writing Down Children's Songs," xv, "Ac-
    tivities: dances to invent, adding a coda, adding an introduction,"
    "Creating songs," "Word substitutions," 133

* Not available when this textbook was written.

° Not available when this textbook was written.

ADDITIONAL REFERENCES

THINGS

TO

DO

1. Compose three melodies: (a) one on the black keys of the piano or Song Bells, (b) one for which most of the pitches are 1-3-5, and (c) one that is based on the major scale.

2. Compose a melody on a recorder-type instrument.

3. Create Oriental and American Indian music on the piano or Song Bells according to the suggestions on page 145. Then add appropriate percussion instruments.

4. Select a folk song or a ballad that tells a story appropriate for dramatization. Present it to the class in such a way that although you guide the activity, the ideas for this dramatization and the making of choices during the process of creating the dramatization come from the students.

5. Choose recordings of instrumental music for dramatization from the RCA Victor Basic Record Library for Elementary Schools, *The Rhythm Program* and *The Listening Program,* and try them out in your college class.

6. Listen to the recordings of instrumental music suggested on page 147 or some of your own choice and create a dramatization based on them.

7. Investigate and evaluate the possibilities of choral reading as an expressive creative activity.

8. Guide the class in creating songs, using poems from this chapter, poems of your own making, or suitable poems from other sources.

9. Dramatize one of the song stories from the series books as a class committee project and evaluate it in terms of creative activities.

10. Create a song from a dance step.

11. Create a dance from a folk song.

REFERENCES

Books

Andrews, Gladys, *Creative Rhythmic Movement for Children.* Englewood Cliffs, N. J.: Prentice-Hall, Inc., 1954.

Cole, Natalie, *The Arts in the Classroom*. New York: The John Day Company, 1940.

Coleman, Satis N., *Creative Music for Children*. New York: G. P. Putnam's Sons, 1922.

———, *Creative Music in the Home*. New York: The John Day Company, 1940.

Fox, Lillian M. and L. Thomas Hopkins, *Creative School Music*. New York: Silver Burdett Company, 1936.

Murray, Ruth, *Dance in the Elementary School*. New York: Harper & Brothers, 1953.

Nye, Robert E. and Bjornar Bergethon, *Basic Music for Classroom Teachers*. Englewood Cliffs, N. J.: Prentice-Hall, Inc., 1954.

Snyder, Alice M., *Creating Music With Children*. New York: Mills Music, Inc., 1957.

Tobbit, Janet E. and Alice M. G. White, *Dramatized Ballads*. New York: E. P. Dutton Co., 1936.

Recordings	R.P.M.	*Suggested Grade Level*
Children's Record Guild and Young People's Records		
The Greystone Corporation, 100 Sixth Avenue,		
New York 13, New York.		
Dramatic Play		
Let's Help Mommy	45-78	K-2
Emperor's New Clothes (2 records)	78	2-5
Whoa, Little Horses	78	N-2
Cap, Spike, and Salty Sam	78	K-2
Puss in Boots (2 records)	78	1-5
Indoors When It Rains	45-78	K-2
Improvising Dances		
Let's Dance	45-78	3-5
Swing Your Partner	45-78	2-6
Improvising Songs		
Bring a Song, Johnny	45-78	K-3
Where Do Songs Begin?	78	1-4
Albums		
Pretending	78	K-2
Let's Act and Sing	78	2-5
More Act and Sing	78	2-5

Teaching
Music
Notation

Seven

*If music is taught fully, learning to read music notation is an integral part of it. If music reading is taught rightly, it always serves for the chil-*dren an immediately functional or interesting purpose. Since children differ in the ways they learn to understand notation and since music reading is a complex skill, a variety of approaches and emphases should be employed. Failure to gain reasonable skill in reading music bars children from important growth—social and cultural as well as musical. Although some years' time is necessary to acquire this ability, the effort toward this end should be pleasurable and purposeful.

The preceding chapters of this book contain many activities illustrating the fact that teaching understanding of notation is a part of teaching other aspects of music. The following activities associated with music reading are mentioned in the chapters indicated:

Learning notation through bodily movement (Chapter Two).

> bodily movement which eventually becomes identified with notation
>> (walking   walking notes   quarter notes)
>> (skipping   skipping notes   skipping note pattern)
> feeling physically if the music "swings" in twos or threes, leading toward understanding accent and meter
> rhythmic notation, use of

165

numeral notation, use of

translating the rhythm of children's names into notation

conducting the meter

stepping the melody-rhythm of songs (translating melody-rhythm into note values by first feeling them physically)

writing characteristic or created rhythm patterns for hand clapping or for percussion instruments in notation on the chalkboard

writing rhythm scores in notation

acting out the musical phrase in various ways

realization of similar and dissimilar parts of songs

Learning notation through playing activities (Chapter Three).

notation learned by using it to play on water glasses, bottles, Song Bells, piano, and recorder-type instruments

chord structure learned by chording on Autoharp, piano, and "social instruments"

notation used in classroom orchestra activities

notation used in writing original vocal and instrumental melodies

Learning notation through singing activities (Chapter Four).

learning concepts of high and low pitch

playing tonal figures on keyboard instruments

singing or playing the tonic chord (1-3-5-3-1) tonal pattern to orient singers to the key of songs

acting out songs in pitch levels

conducting

Learning notation through listening activities (Chapter Five).

writing on the chalkboard the themes of music to which children listen

Learning notation by creating songs (Chapter Six).

notating original music

Learning notation through part-singing activities (Chapter Eight).

notation used in part-singing activities of many types

Learning notation by use of music in related activities (Chapter Nine).

notating original music

notation used in learning related music

A GRADE LEVEL APPROACH TO NOTATION
IN MUSIC SERIES BOOKS

As in the teaching of other skills there is no definite time at which an emphasis on music reading begins, this being dependent upon the background of musical experience possessed by the individual child. *Every basal music series has its own well-organized approach to music reading; therefore it is a responsibility of every teacher to study and to understand this approach* to find whether or not it is suited to his group of children at a given time and to decide what part of the reading program as presented should be added to or eliminated from his teaching plans. A study of the series books reveals the following general outline of reading activities by grade level:

Kindergarten and Grade One. A rich, happy, and emotionally satisfying environment of many varied musical activities. From these guided activities emerge such concepts as high and low (in pitch), loud and soft, mood, the home tone (key feeling), fundamental movements, accent, rhythm patterns, fast and slow. Increasing understanding of pitch levels by acting out melody lines, and associating this in a very general way with the notation of these melodies. Playing tunes on Song Bells by ear and by numeral notation. Incidental, not direct, teaching of details of notation.

Grade Two. Increasing concern about notation develops, particularly during the last half of the school year. Clearly associating physical responses to notation (such as up and down, long and short, walking, running, skipping). After this, the naming of notes (quarter, eighth, half, whole). Use of note letter names, numbers, and/or syllables is begun. Children led to notice that melodies are constructed scalewise or skipwise, and become aware of repetitions of like phrases and note patterns. Numbers and/or syllables are associated with note patterns. Playing on Song Bells with numbers and with notation. Developing an understanding that notation is "a picture of the melody." Learning that the music "swings" in two's or three's.

Grade Three. Wider use of note names, numbers, and/or syllables. Further stressing of note patterns. Playing melodies on Song Bells and piano by notation. Noticing scale line and chord line note sequences. Introducing very simple piano chording. Seeing original songs in notation. Seeing notation as "a picture of the melody." Detecting like, different, and almost-alike phrases in notation.

Grade Four. Use of the Autoharp, the keyboard, and recorder-type instruments with notation. Use of notation in writing and playing original songs. Increasing independence in reading notation. Quick recognition of like, different, and almost-alike phrases. Mastery of familiar note and rhythm patterns. Increasing knowledge of useful technical details of notation. Chording on the piano. Making listening activities more meaningful by watching the notation of recorded melodies, in the books or on the chalkboard.

Grade Five. More playing experience with keyboard and other instruments. Chording on Autoharp, piano, and instruments such as ukulele, harmonica, guitar. Using notation in two-part singing. Making the listening program more meaningful by placing thematic material on the chalkboard or watching it in the books. Expanding knowledge of useful technical aspects of notation through their use in a variety of activities. Notating original songs.

Grade Six. "Hearing with the eyes" and "seeing with the ears." Independent sight singing a goal. Two- and three-part singing. A general knowledge of intervals. Playing and chording instruments. Using notation in writing original compositions. Making the listening program more meaningful by placing thematic material on the chalkboard or watching it in the books. Increased knowledge of useful technical aspects of notation through their use in a variety of activities.

COMMENTS AND SUGGESTIONS

Numbers, letter names, and syllables

Men have long attempted to find practical ways of learning to read music notation. Roughly one thousand years ago two monks sought to improve the skill of their respective choirs in this regard. One of them, Guido d'Arezzo, is said to have invented a system of Latin syllables used as a measuring stick to identify scale tones. This system has evolved to become the *do re me fa sol la ti do* of today. In the United States this is called the *moveable do* system because "do" represents the keynote of all major keys. In France it is called the *fixed do* system because Middle C is always "do." The other monk, Odo of Clugny, chose an instrumental approach, and is said to have had his choir learn to play the monochord, a one-stringed Greek instrument, and then apply this understanding to singing by notation. These two approaches to teaching music reading, the Latin-syllable and the instrumental, are both very much alive today.

Lowell Mason, who was appointed to teach music in the schools of Boston in 1838, was the first American school music teacher. His method of teaching music reading was a three-fold approach which began with associating the numbers 1, 2, 3, 4, 5, 6, 7, 8 with the degrees of the scale, using the Latin syllables also, and including the regular note names as a third aspect. Mason used numbers in all initial explanations of tonal relationships, and the tonic chord and all the intervals were taught by extensive numeral drills. The syllables came to be emphasized by music teachers probably because of their use in ear training and sight singing on the college level.

In 1845[1] and 1883[2] methods of teaching music reading were published that represented revolts against the use of Latin syllables, and that unsuccessfully attempted to eliminate syllables by substituting numerals. The preface of Jordan's *New Method of Sight-Singing* stated that methods of sight singing with syllables were too intricate, explaining:

> While some persons overcome the difficulties thus presented [by syllables] in reading music, the larger number are left as much in the dark as ever. . . . The distinctive features of this [numeral] method . . . are the separating of the two mental processes necessarily employed by the persons reading at sight. These processes are, 1st. Reading or comprehending the scale number of each tone. . . . 2nd. The production of the tone read. The usual custom of using the syllables Do, Re, Mi, etc., is dropped, not because it is impossible to teach a person by that method but because experience has shown that while a few learn, many fail.

The Jordan Method began with the numbered C scale, then soon transposed the numeral concept to other common keys. Finally, the neutral syllable "la" was sung while the student *thought* the numbers. Chromatics were avoided.

In the early twentieth century the names of Samuel Cole and Alfred White stand out as music educators who taught and advocated the use of numerals rather than the syllables. Still later Howard Hinga discarded both syllables and numbers in the teaching of music reading in the schools of Rochester, New York. A study made by one of the authors of the present book at Highland Park, Illinois, in 1948-49 yielded evidence that interest in devices such as syllables and numerals was highest in the third grade, indicating that if

[1] H. M. Beal, *The Boston Numeral Harmony; or Day and Beal's Phonography of Music.* Boston: 1845.

[2] Julian Jordan, *New Method of Sight-Singing.* New York: Bigelow and Main, 1883.

teachers chose to employ them, they might consider emphasizing them on that grade level. Another in-service study made at the same school yielded conclusive evidence that an approach to music reading consisting of a minimal use of numbers combined with an emphasis on easy-to-play instruments was much more effective than an approach consisting almost exclusively of the use of Latin syllables. Although the children, in this instance, preferred numbers to syllables, slightly more than half of them stated their dislike of singing with either. Their natural inclination was to sing songs with meaningful words, and they had a normal dislike of any substitute unless there was a game aspect to the teachers' presentation.

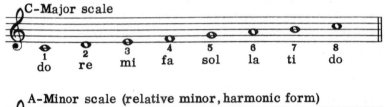

Numerals and syllables are similar devices. They represent the same idea in that both are "measuring sticks" to help one understand the relationship of the tones of the scale. "1" and "do" are two ways of naming the same thing—the key note in major keys (the home tone). Because numbers are already familiar, they are generally preferred by most elementary school teachers and children to the Latin syllables, which are unfamiliar. Either device may be introduced in connection with songs that are already well known to children. When syllables are used, some teachers believe that the first grade is the place to begin indoctrination with them, employing them as "nonsense" extra verses to songs. Other teachers believe that syllables should not be introduced earlier than in second or third grade. Gradually "do" or "1" is recognized by the children as the home tone, and other syllables or numbers acquire meaning and position in relation to "do" or "1." After children have been guided to think tonal relationships accurately in terms of numbers or syllables, the teacher usually has them sight sing with a neutral syllable such as "loo" while they *think* numbers or syllables. Theoretically, *these devices should be employed only when problems arise and when they are needed to make music activities more meaningful.* The letter names are learned also, whether the teacher is employing numerals, syllables, or both. Letter names assume real significance when easy-to-play instruments are used by the children. A comparative analysis of numerals and syllables follows:

Numerals	*Syllables*
familiar terminology; logical to children	unfamiliar terminology; meaningless when introduced
poor from standpoint of voice production	excellent from standpoint of voice production
favored by music theorists; numbers apply to harmony	not favored by music theorists; syllables do not apply to harmony
chromatics very awkward and are avoided	chromatics easily sung (but elementary school music rarely uses them)
excellent in explaining intervals	poor in explaining intervals
harmful to enjoyment if overused	harmful to enjoyment if overused

Whether or not the prospective public school teacher will employ numbers and/or syllables in his music teaching depends upon a number of circumstances. The person who can best interpret these is the teacher of the college elementary music-education class who has opportunity to study the trends and traditions of the area served by his institution. The college music-education teacher and his students are faced with a number of circumstances, trends, and facts including that (a) the syllable tradition exists most strongly in the Northeastern United States and it weakens, generally, as one proceeds westward, (b) a growing number of institutions no longer employ syllables in the training of music majors or elementary education majors, (c) among co-authors of music series books are found those who do not believe in nor practice the use of syllables in their public school teaching although their books endorse syllables quite wholeheartedly, and (d) musicians who play musical instruments have no need of syllables or numbers in order to become sight readers of music.

This state of confusion is not as serious as it first appears and may be resolved by the knowledge that all of the activities in the present book can be accomplished without the aid of syllables, and that should a teacher find himself in a teaching situation in which syllables must be employed, they can be quickly learned along with the children if this teacher has an adequate background in terms of these activities.

Note patterns and intervals

To numbers and syllables there has been added another element: the recognition of tonal patterns. With this concept music reading is taught according to the same principles as word reading. When English reading is taught, the children are guided to recognize at once certain familiar combinations of letters that are words. Likewise, the children are taught to recognize in the songs they sing certain common combinations of notes. This approach will be found used in combination with numbers and/or syllables in the basal music series books.[3]

Examples of tonal patterns:

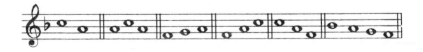

---

[3] Refer to *The American Singer*, Books Two and Three, and the *Our Singing World* Guide and Teaching Suggestions: Kindergarten and Grades One, Two, and Three (Ginn), pp. 37-42.

Since experienced sight readers of music are known to depend in large part upon their instant recognition of the interval relationship of the notes they see, it is believed that a general understanding of intervals may be introduced at about the sixth grade level. Numbers are of direct aid in comprehending intervals.

All one does to find the interval relationship of two notes is to call one of the notes "1" and count the lines and spaces to the other one. The number of this latter note is the name of the interval.

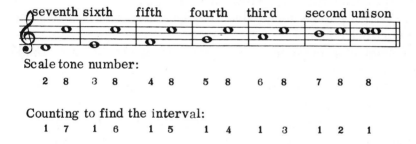

Scale tone number:

| 2 | 8 | 3 | 8 | 4 | 8 | 5 | 8 | 6 | 8 | 7 | 8 | 8 |

Counting to find the interval:

| 1 | 7 | 1 | 6 | 1 | 5 | 1 | 4 | 1 | 3 | 1 | 2 | 1 |

A common interval is the *fourth*. It is easily sung and occurs frequently in many songs. It is found in the two beginning notes of *Yankee Doodle* (5̄-1) and recurs several times in the course of the tune. The familiar *Lullaby and Goodnight* stresses the *minor third* (1½ steps) at its beginning (335·33 5-). The 1-3-5 chord pattern is made up of two thirds, a *major third* (1-3, two steps) and a minor third (3-5). The major scale is composed of *minor seconds* (½ step) and *major seconds* (one step). The *fifth* is found at the beginning of *Twinkle Twinkle Little Star* (1 1 5 5), and the *major sixth* is popularly identified with the beginning notes of *My Bonnie* (5̄-3). The *seventh* is found rarely in elementary school songs. The *octave* (1-8) is easily identifiable. It is suggested that intervals be taught only in an incidental way, and that their occurrence in song material will have more meaning to children than would their occurrence in interval drills. For example, when sixth grade children know that *My Bonnie* starts with the interval of a sixth, it may be interesting to find that interval in other songs. The keyboard is a most helpful tool in building the concept of intervals because intervals can be seen, felt, and heard by children when they play them.

Other suggestions for teaching notation

1. Music reading is not a separate and special study; it is an integral part of the other music activities. It is taught best in relation to rhythmic responses, singing, playing, listening, and creating because it takes on purpose and meaning in the minds of children.

2. Children see five lines of the staff but frequently fail to comprehend the four spaces; the concept of a space should be made clear.

3. One of the easiest ways for children to sense pitch differences and interval relationships is by their playing melody instruments.

4. Musical symbols should be learned in context, i.e., in connection with the music with which children are working.

5. "When phrases sound alike they look alike" is a valuable concept to teach children.

6. Beginning experiences in music reading should be so simple that success is virtually assured.

7. The simultaneous reading of words and notes is very difficult, and seeing the words distracts children from seeing the notes. Therefore, when emphasizing note reading, sing often without words, using a neutral syllable such as "loo," so that the children's full attention can be focused on the notes. Use songs with known words at first. When preparing to read words and music at the same time it is well first to help the children speak the words rhythmically in a manner that gives them a feeling for meter and for note values.

8. Use the approach to note reading stated in connection with the Song Bells (Chapter Three, p. 60) in which numeral notation leads to comprehending music notation.

9. Use a variety of approaches to music reading because of individual differences and the fact that there is no *one* way to teach music reading.

10. Emphasize only one aspect of music reading at a time.

11. A common formula for introducing aspects of note reading is (a) hear it (sung by the teacher or from a recording), (b) sing it (learn it by rote and act it out in pitch levels), (c) play it (on the keyboard or other instruments by ear), (d) see it (on the chalkboard or in books); remember that music notation is simply a picture or drawing of what the body has already felt and what the ear has already heard.

12. The answer to the question, "When should I teach children any specific aspect of note reading?" is "When they have need of it in their music activities." If the teacher plans a rich and varied program of activities, the children are certain to have need of notation, and will learn it because it has functions that are clearly understood by them.

13. Teach first for comprehension of phrases and groups of notes and later for the smaller details of notation.

14. The goal is to teach children "to hear with their eyes and to see with their ears."

15. Place on the chalkboard themes of the recorded music used during listening activities. The eye will help the ear, and something about notation will be learned. If the themes are singable, sing them with "loo" before recording is played.

16. The progress from rote to note should be so gradual that the child never feels that note reading is a new activity.

17. Use the skills area (Chapter One, p. 5, 7) for group instruction in reading music. Some children are ready for it and have special interest in it. Others are not ready. Many of the failures of the past stem from trying to teach music notation to every child in the classroom at the same time. This approach is no longer considered good practice in teaching children to read English, and this applies equally well in teaching children to read music.

18. Emphasize the instrumental approach to note reading through use of the Song Bells, piano, recorder-type and flute-like instruments; relate this to singing as described in Chapter Three.

Techniques and devices

1. Playing on Song Bells that have been turned on end reveals how ups and downs in pitch look. This can be related to the ups and downs of notes on the staff.

2. A flannel board can be made by stretching and taping outing flannel over heavy cardboard. Lines of the staff can be drawn with a Flo-master Pen, and notes made of black felt. Children enjoy manipulating the notes, and the appearance of the flannel board notation is superior to that of notation drawn on a chalkboard. Some teachers prefer to use no cardboard but instead fasten the top and bottom of the flannel to slender wooden rods. With this construction the device can be rolled up and stored when not in use.

3. The major scale consists of whole-steps with the exception of

half-steps between scale tones 3 and 4, and 7 and 8. The keyboard (Song Bells or piano) explains this visually. A time-honored aid to explain the structure of the major scale is the comparison of it to a ladder:

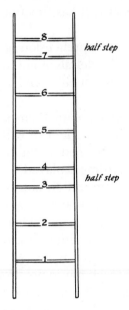

4. The scale is written on the chalkboard either in numbers, in regular notation, or in syllables. The class sings various scale tones as the teacher points to them.

5. "Singing from the hand" is useful for drill on difficult passages from song material and for intervals. The teacher uses the right hand to point to the scale tones the class sings:

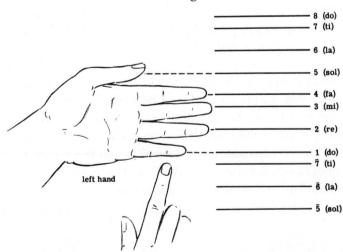

6. Place a few measures of some familiar tune on the chalkboard and hide it by pulling down a map. When students are ready, uncover the notation. The game is to guess the name of the tune without humming or playing it.

7. The *Happy Hours Staff and Note Set* and accompanying workbook is a device for individuals to play with; it is not for general class use. It is produced commercially by the Handy-Folio Music Company, 2821 North Ninth St., Milwaukee 6, Wisconsin.

8. Sing and play from music written on two-by-three-foot tag board as described in Chapter Three, p. 82.

The former strong tradition favoring the use of Latin syllables has weakened to the extent that the literature of music education now contains many statements conceding that there are other approaches. Authorities in education have for many years criticized the use of Latin syllables in the public schools, largely from three standpoints: (1) that it is an *abstract* device, (2) that it requires more time to teach than can be justified in terms of the large variety of activities that now constitute the elementary school music program, and (3) that enjoyment of music is the major goal in elementary music education.

The trend of these times favors a minimal use of numerals and a stressing of the use of easy-to-play instruments beginning with the keyboard. Two of the most important guiding principles are (1) that learning music notation should be an integral part of the various activities of the music program rather than something taught in isolation, and (2) that notation should be taught in a way that serves an immediately useful or interesting purpose to children. *Development of reasonable skill in reading music is essential to musical growth.* The classroom teacher should study the complete note-reading programs in the music series books to become familiar with the objectives planned for the various grade levels according to those books. After this study, and as a result of teaching experience, each teacher should evolve a method, which, although uniquely his own, will have to take into account the over-all approach agreed upon cooperatively by all of the teachers in the elementary school in which he teaches.

178 TEACHING MUSIC NOTATION

Music Series Reference Guide to Teaching Music Reading

The American Singer (2nd ed.; American Book Company)

BOOK ONE

Incidental learning in connection with concepts such as *high and low, walking, running.*
See TM for Second Grade *Reading Readiness,* 3

BOOK TWO

Classified Index *Notational Aspects,* 189
General approach, TM 3-4
Presenting notation, TM 9-11

BOOK THREE

Classified Index *Instrumental Relationships,* 204, *Rhythm Pattern* Index, 204, *Tonal Pattern* Index, 204-205
General approach, TM 3-4
The Note Song, TM 6-8

BOOK FOUR

Classified Index *Instrumental Relationships,* 204, *Tonal Patterns,* 205, *Rhythm Patterns,* 205
The Note Song, TM 7-8

BOOK FIVE

Classified Index *Instrumental Relationships,* 212, *Notational Aspects,* 213
The Note Song, TM 6-7

BOOK SIX

Classified Index *Instrumental Relationships,* 245, *Notational Aspects,* 245
The Note Song, TM 5

New Music Horizons (Silver Burdett Company)

EXPERIENCES IN MUSIC FOR FIRST GRADE CHILDREN

Reference Index *Music Reading Readiness,* 142
TM 56-57, 90-93

SECOND BOOK

Pitch-producing instruments, 161 IV 3
Reading readiness, 162 VI
Rhythmic symbols, 161 IV 4
TM 58-61, 94-106

THIRD BOOK

Instrumental program, 184 1., 3
Reading program, 185 VI
TM 61, 107-121

FOURTH BOOK

Music reading, 205-206 I
Playing an instrument, 207 B., C., E.
TM 2-6, 83-86, 97-112

FIFTH BOOK

Music reading, 227-229 I
Playing an instrument, 229-230 III
TM 6-10, 87-91, 113-130

SIXTH BOOK

Music reading, 246-248 VI
Playing an instrument, 244 II
TM 10-15, 91-96, 131-151

Our Singing World (Ginn and Company)

KINDERGARTEN BOOK

TM Melodic Patterns, 37-42

FIRST GRADE BOOK

Music reading, xix
TM *Melodic Patterns*, 37-42

SINGING AS WE PLAY (Primer)

TM 42-45

SINGING ON OUR WAY

TM *Music Reading*, 95-112

SINGING EVERY DAY (Primer)

TM 45

SINGING AND RHYMING

TM *Music Reading*, 163-183
We Play and Sing, 4

SINGING EVERY DAY

TM *Music Reading*, 32-75
We Sing and Play, 4

SINGING TOGETHER

TM *Music Reading*, 122-194
We Sing and Play, 4

SINGING IN HARMONY

TM *Music Reading*, 252-300
We Play and Sing, 4

A Singing School (C. C. Birchard)

OUR SONGS (NEW EDITION)

Music Road I (pamphlet)
Tonal figures, 188
TM rhythm in group bodily movements, 12-15, reading music, 17-23

MERRY MUSIC (NEW EDITION)

Music Road (pamphlet)
Tonal figures, 188
TM *Reading and Writing Music*, 21-22

WE SING (NEW EDITION)

Music Road I (pamphlet)
Time and tonal problems, 188
TM *Music Reading,* 12-41, *Rhythm Pattern Pictures,* 56-63

OUR LAND OF SONG

Music Road II (pamphlet)
Reading section, 205
TM *Music Reading,* 16-19, 21-30, *Rhythm and Tonal Pictures,* 7-8

MUSIC EVERYWHERE

Classified Index *Songs with Rhythmic Accompaniment,* 220, Tuneful Tim, 220
Music Road II (pamphlet)
Reading section, 221
TM instruments, 50-51, *Simple Bodily Movements,* 21-23, *Dalcroze Eurythmics* (stepping), 23-24, *Keyboard* (chromatics) 28, *Music Writing,* 29-34, *Minor Scales,* 47-49, *Phrase* (form), 88-90.

Together We Sing (Follett Publishing Company)

MUSIC 'ROUND THE TOWN

Reading, 130-132

MUSIC THROUGH THE YEAR

Refer "Musical Growth at This Level," 161-162, "Guides to Simplify the Learning," 162, "Being Aware of Musical Phrases," 163, "Melodic Contour," 163-164, "Hearing Endings," 164-165, "Choosing Harmonies," 165-166, "Staff Location of Key Center," 166, "Hearing Tonal Relation," 166-169, "Responding to Rhythm," 170-173, "Reading from Notation," 173

MUSIC ACROSS OUR COUNTRY

Refer "Understanding the Meaning of Notation," 179-181, "Songs with common tone groups bracketed," 191

VOICES OF AMERICA

Refer to Music Reading in "To Teachers and Parents" section*
Refer to Parts for Instruments in Classified Index*

VOICES OF THE WORLD

Music reading, 206-208
Parts for instruments, 223

Music For Living (Silver Burdett Company)

MUSIC THROUGH THE DAY (including children's books I LIKE THE COUNTRY and I LIKE THE CITY)

"Musical Snippets," 148

MUSIC IN OUR TOWN

TM "Musical Growth," vii, "Music Reading," viii-x, "Designing elements of a tune," "Instruments, use of," "Phrases," "Relating melodic direction to meaning," "Relating rhythm to meaning," 133

* Unavailable when this textbook was written.

MUSIC NOW AND LONG AGO

TM "Music Reading," viii-x
TM "Observing Elements of a Tune," 132
TM "Phrases," "Pointing Up Meter," "Pointing Up Rhythm," 133

MUSIC NEAR AND FAR

"Songs for Instruments," 184
TM "Musical growth as an organizing principle," vii, "Musical Reading: General," viii-x, "Music Reading: Specific," x-xi, "Note Lengths," 163, "Phrases," 163, "Piano Music for Children to Play," 165

MUSIC IN OUR COUNTRY

(See Classified Index and Teachers Book°)

MUSIC AROUND THE WORLD

(See Classified Index and Teachers Book°)

° Not available when this textbook was written.

ADDITIONAL REFERENCES

THINGS

TO

DO

1. Select a song from a series book and analyze it in terms of possible use for note reading in intermediate grades. Consider the key, the beginning note, note values, scale lines in the melody, chord lines in the melody, other note patterns, difficult intervals, measures and phrases that are alike, and possible rhythm problems. Present this song to your fellow students to find out whether you can guide them to help themselves to sight-sing effectively.

2. Study and compare the music-reading programs of the various basal music series.

3. Demonstrate how music reading can be taught in conjunction with rhythmic response, singing, playing, listening, and creating.

4. What is numeral notation? rhythmic notation? Give examples.

5. Compare the teaching of reading English words and the teaching of reading music by means of note patterns. Illustrate with songs.

6. Compare the Latin syllables and the numerals as means of helping teach note reading.

7. How can individual differences be provided for in the teaching of music reading in view of the fact that the grade level on which reading readiness takes place may vary greatly among children?

8. Make a flannel board and demonstrate it to the class.

9. Try out and evaluate the devices suggested in 4, 5, and 6 on pp. 176-177.

10. Evaluate from your own experience the function of the Song Bells, piano, recorder- and flute-type instruments in learning to read music.

11. Construct a visual aid to help children understand the staff. Hold the Song Bells vertically with the large bars downward. Draw a staff on either the chalkboard or light cardboard, a staff having lines that lead horizontally from the appropriate bars of the Song Bells (from bottom to top, E, G, B, D, F). This aids children in comprehending the relationship between tones sounded on the bells and notes on the staff.

12. Construct wall charts that help children understand facts of music notation.

REFERENCES

Articles and Books

Ernst, Karl, "The Place of Reading," *Music Educators Journal,* January, 1953.
Landeck, Beatrice, *Children and Music,* Appendix I, New York: William Sloane Associates, Inc. A superior reference.
Myers, Louise, *Teaching Children Music in the Elementary School,* chap. VII, Englewood Cliffs, N. J.: Prentice-Hall, Inc., 1950.
Nye, Robert E., "If You Don't Use Syllables, What Do You Use?" *Music Educators Journal,* April-May, 1953.

Song Books

Vandre, Carl, *Sight Reading Fun.* New York: Mills Music, Inc.

Filmstrips

Young America Films Inc., 18 E. 41st St.,
New York 17, New York.
  Young America Sings (Otto Meissner). Teaching filmstrips. Double-faced 12-inch LP recordings with correlated filmstrips. Bridges gap from rote-to-note singing. Units currently for grades 3, 4, 5.

Eight

Two-part singing is traditionally emphasized in fifth grade; therefore building a readiness for and introducing part singing is traditionally part of
the music program in fourth grade. Three-part singing is a goal in sixth grade. This chapter will point out the importance and relationship of certain aspects of music in the primary grades to part singing in grades four, five, and six, as well as call attention to some possible exceptions to the traditional grade placement of some types of this activity.

Before beginning part-singing activities, it is assumed that children can sing well in pitch melodies that include common tonal combinations, for if they cannot sing one part satisfactorily, they cannot do well with multiple parts. It is further assumed that the children have acquired in the primary grades both a good rhythmic sense and a good harmonic sense. Understanding music notation is also of aid in singing parts and is often considered another prerequisite, even though singing in parts can be initiated by rote.

Part singing is learned because it is pleasurable. It is a logical part of the children's musical growth and can lead to still greater appreciation of beauty and to still greater emotional and aesthetic satisfaction.

Dialogue songs, rounds, canons, and combinable songs

Among the several theories concerning introducing part singing is one exemplified by the so-called dialogue song, a song in which children are divided into two groups taking turns at singing parts of the song. Although this is not part singing in the harmonic sense, it is assumed that the singers will become oriented to the idea of being divided into groups within the class and of being responsible for singing their particular part at the right time. An example of a dialogue song for intermediate grades is *The Keeper,* on page 186.

The singing of rounds and canons[1] is believed by some to be preparation for part singing. Whether this opinion can be justified depends upon how such songs are taught. If children are taught to sing them in a manner that leads them to out-shout other parts, or to put their hands over their ears so that they cannot hear the other parts, then no real part singing is taking place. If, on the other hand, they are taught in a manner that leads the singers to hear how the other parts join with theirs, then the experience can justifiably be called a form of part singing. The teaching procedure may be outlined as follows:

1. The children learn the melody well.
2. The children learn to hear the harmony upon which the melody is based. The teacher chords this harmony on Autoharp or piano, or uses a recording that provides a clear and simple harmonization.
3. The hearing of the new part (second entrance) of the round is accomplished by the teacher singing or playing this part while the class is softly singing the first part, and is listening to how the parts join together to make interesting music.
4. Some children join with the teacher on the new part. Listening to all the parts and to how they join together in the harmonic setting is stressed. Balance of the parts so that all singers can hear all of the parts is essential.
5. If the round is of more than two parts, the new parts are added in the same general manner as above.

Rounds and canons are emphasized in fourth and fifth grades and are used less frequently in the primary grades because many of the children are not of sufficient musical maturity to be able to sing them well and to hear with understanding what they are doing. It is possible, however, for exceptional first grade children to sing simple canons like *Old Texas* because they are echo-type songs.

---

[1] Rounds and canons are similar. The difference is that a round repeats (goes back to the beginning) whereas a canon does not. A round is a "circle canon."

THE KEEPER

Unknown   Old English

The keep - er did a - shoot - ing go, And
un-der his cloak he car-ried a bow,
All for to shoot at a mer-ry lit-tle doe A-
mong the leaves so green, O!

Jack-ie boy!   Sing ye well!
Mas - ter!   Ve -ry well!

Hey down,   Der-ry der - ry down, A-
Ho down,   A-

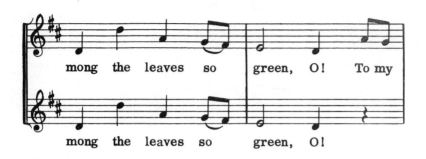

mong the leaves so   green, O!   To my

mong the leaves so   green, O!

hey,   down, down!

To my   ho,   down, down!

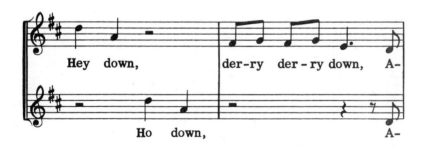

Hey down,   der-ry der-ry down,   A-

Ho   down,   A-

mong   the   leaves   so   green,   O!

mong   the   leaves   so   green,   O!

OLD TEXAS

Cowboy Song

I'm goin' to leave ol' Tex-as now They've got no use for the long-horn cow.

Other useful songs of this type are *Susan Blue* (*Singing Every Day,* p. 176), *A Thankful Song* (*New Music Horizons Book Five,* p. 125), *Taps* (*American Singer Book Six,* p. 124, *Together We Sing,* Enlarged Edition, p. 127), and *My True Love Hath My Heart* (*Music Everywhere,* p. 214).

ROUND OF THANKS

Traditional   Four-part round

For health and strength and dai - ly food we give Thee thanks, O Lord!

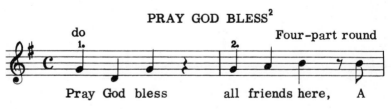

PRAY GOD BLESS[2]

Four-part round

Pray God bless all friends here, A

---

[2] From *Singing Together* of *Our Singing World* Series (Ginn and Company). Used with permission.

mer-ry mer-ry Christ-mas and a hap - py New Year.

The value of two songs sung simultaneously as an experience leading toward part singing is questionable. However, it is possible that
it might have value if taught in the manner suggested for the singing
of rounds. It is likely that the major value is recreational because the
attempt is fun. A list of songs commonly used follows:

1. *Three Blind Mice* and *Row Your Boat*
2. *Three Blind Mice* and *Are You Sleeping*
3. *Three Blind Mice* and *The Farmer in the Dell*
   (The above rounds can be sung in other combinations too.)
4. *Ten Little Indians* and *Skip To My Lou*
5. *Blue Tail Fly* and *Shoo Fly* (choruses only)
6. *Solomon Levi* and *A Spanish Cavalier*
7. *Darling Nellie Gray* and *When You and I Were Young, Maggie*
8. *Keep the Home Fires Burning* and *There's A Long Long Trail*
9. *Humoreske* and *Old Folks at Home*
10. *Ring the Banjo* and *The Girl I Left Behind Me*

Adding harmonic endings

This simple and effective way to develop a feeling for part singing
may be initiated in third grade, where two-part harmonic endings
may be used, and expanded in the fourth grade to three-part endings.
In this activity the teacher adds a part or parts to the final note or
notes of a song. For example, *Old Black Joe* ends with scale tones
3-2-1--. The children would be told to sing or hum those tones softly
while they listen to the teacher as she[3] sings the words on scale tones
3-2-3--. Next, the children who believe they can sing the new part

[3] A woman teacher is referred to here because the female voice has the same
pitch as the unchanged child voice. A man teacher would probably play the new
part on the Song Bells, piano, or a melody instrument to avoid using his octave-
lower voice.

will join with the teacher while the others continue singing the melody. It has been the experience of many teachers that some children may never before have been conscious of their ability to hear two different pitches at one time in this fashion. These children may ask to sing such a harmonic ending again and again in order that they may fully enjoy what is to them a new comprehension of beauty.

This idea can be expanded as follows:

Other examples of harmonic endings may be found in the music series books by using the Music Series Reference Guide to Selected Part Singing Activities in this chapter and the indexes of some of the books. When once understood they can be easily created by teachers and children. It is recommended that these be taught first by rote, since the aim at this juncture is to develop harmonic feeling, not note reading. Notation can then be used to show how the already-experienced harmony looks. Eventually this can lead to an understanding and purposeful use of the notation of part singing. This activity develops a helpful background for improvising parts ("barbershop harmony") and for singing in thirds and sixths.

Chord roots

The singing of chord roots as an approach to part singing is assuming new importance in light of the thinking of some music educators. In order to present this point of view, it should be stated that it is believed that the musical background of elementary school children is quite different today than it was a comparatively short time ago. Now children are brought into a world brimming with music with which they are in direct contact almost from the hour of their birth, due to the prevalence of radio, recordings, and television. Furthermore, this music with which they are daily associated does not consist of a single melody line; it is more apt to be rich and full-bodied. Dr. L. H. Slind describes this music as vertical in structure as compared to the horizontal melodic line. The music the children hear out of school is built of rhythm and harmony as well as of melody. Consequently, they may find less interest in isolated melody than did the children of 25 years ago. This leads to the theory that kindergarten and first grade children need first an emphasis on rhythm, then upon singing simple melodies to which simple harmony is later added by means of the teacher chording on Autoharp or piano and using selected recordings. It follows theoretically that if children have this rich background in rhythm and harmony they will be better able to understand, sing, and enjoy melody because of their understanding of its place in combination with the other two major components of music. There may be logic in the claim that many children are bored with music programs that are confined largely to melody because such music suffers by comparison to the more complete music heard outside the classroom. Dr. Slind advises, "Let the children have *all* of the music, not only the melody!" Another implication of this is that if children are taught rhythm, melody, and harmony, rather than mostly melody, part singing will become a much more evident and successful part of the music program than it is now.

The singing of chord roots is one of the easiest parts to add to a song because of the harmonic strength of this part, which is the foundation tone of each chord. Although this activity is primarily of intermediate grade level, it is possible for some third grade children to take part in it. The song materials employed are those that are best harmonized by only two or three chords—I, IV, and V_7. (See Chapter Three, pp. 66-74, for listings of such songs.) The following example consists of the first section of a dance, the *Varsovienne*. It can be harmonized by two chords, G (I) and D_7 (V_7). After the song is well learned, and after the harmony is taught by chording an accompaniment or by the children's hearing this song from a recording, the chord roots may be added.

The words can be sung in melody rhythm on the pitch of the chord root; or numerals, note names, or syllables can be sung on those pitches.

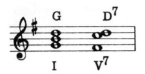

VARSOVIENNE
(Put Your Little Foot)

Traditional

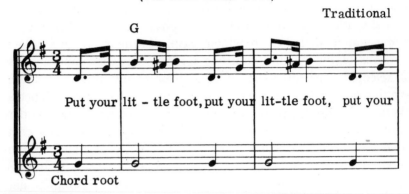

Put your | lit - tle foot, put your | lit-tle foot,　put your

Chord root

lit - tle foot right | there. Put your lit-tle foot, put your

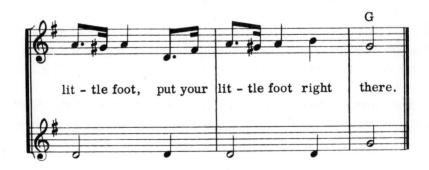

lit - tle foot,　put your | lit - tle foot　right | there.

Wait for the Wagon illustrates how one of the music series books applies this principle.

WAIT FOR THE WAGON [4]

5 (so)

Brightly   R. B. Buckley

1. Will you come with me, my Phyl-lis, To yon blue moun-tain free? Where
2. Where the riv-er runs like sil-ver, And birds they sing so sweet, I

do (1)......... do......... so (5)......... do.........

blos-soms smell the sweet-est, Come, rove a - long with   me.   It's
have a cab - in, Phyl-lis, And some-thing good to   eat.   Come,

do.............. do............. fa (4)....so....... do.........

ev-'ry Sun - day morn-ing, When   I   am   by   your   side, We'll
lis-ten   to   my   sto-ry,   It   will re-lieve my   heart, So

do.............. do............. so............... do.........

jump in - to   the   wag-on, And   all   take   a   ride.
jump in - to   the   wag-on, And   off   we   will   start!

do................. do............. fa..... so........ do....

Chorus:

Wait   for   the   wag-on,   Wait   for   the   wag- on,

do............. do......... do............... fa..............

Wait   for   the   wag - on and we'll   all   take   a   ride.

do............. do................. fa... so....... do.....

---

[4] From *Singing Together* of *Our Singing World* Series (Ginn and Company). Used by permission.

To provide for individual differences and to support the new part, children can play the chord roots on Song Bells, piano, or recorder-type instruments. In singing classroom orchestra work, the viola and the cello can make a good bass part by playing the chord roots. The type of bells that separate into individual tone bars can be employed very profitably in this activity.

The adding of this part to songs that are of simple harmonic structure can be the beginning of much meaningful activity. Let us assume that the children are going to build a score for the singing and playing of *Put Your Little Foot,* a score that will reveal their ideas about rhythm and harmony as well as about melody. The teacher has placed the melody on the chalkboard. He has also written the two chords that accompany this song. The children's first task is to find where in the song each of the chords is needed, if it is to be sounded on the piano or Autoharp to accompany the song. Since they have been taught that the note that receives the heavy accent or accents is ordinarily a tone of the required chord, they have an important clue on which to work. They know that the first beat of the measure in every meter signature is the most heavily accented beat, and that in ¾ meter there is only one primary accent (the first beat) in each measure. (In ⁴⁄₄ meter there are two—a primary accent on the first beat and a secondary accent on the third beat.) The children find that in the first three measures of *Put Your Little Foot* the note on the first beat is "B." Looking at the chords, they notice that "B" is a member of the tones of the G (I) chord, but not of the D_7 (V_7) chord. Therefore, the chord needed for those three measures (or at least at the beginning of them) is the G chord. The note at the beginning of the fourth measure is "A." The children find "A" to be a member of the D_7 chord, therefore, this is the chord needed in the fourth measure. They proceed in this manner to the end of the song, then "try out" their harmony with the melody to see if it is correct. In some songs, the note "D" may be on the first beat of a measure. In this case, the children will decide by listening which of the chords is the right one to use. They can also tell by analyzing all the notes of any measure to find to which chord most of the notes belong. This is an important clue to use any time students are determining chords for songs for which chords are not designated.

Now that the children have found the chords, they may write these on a staff below the melody. They may create a more interesting piano part later which is derived from these chords. If one knows the chord, he knows the note that is the chord root, because the note "G" is the root of the G (I) chord and the note "D" is the root of the D_7 (V_7) chord. These notes are placed on a staff below the other music already written. Next, the children may invent rhythms for the song, which they will play on suitable percussion instruments. If they know how to write chants[5] they may add one to their song. There will be continued experimenting which will involve singing and playing of parts, a use and understanding of harmony, and different ways of presenting the melody. The beginning of the score may look like this:

[5] The writing of chants is discussed on pp. 196-202.

To add to this simple melody, harmony, and rhythm, children may create more parts in the form of chants and simple counter-melodies:

The opportunities for creative experiences are very great in this approach to music. Creating and experimenting with such a score can provide truly basic experiences for understanding part singing. Singing chord roots constitutes learning a new part. Learning this part contributes markedly to the further comprehension of harmony because it forms the foundation tones of the harmonic structure that supports the melody. Since understanding chord roots comes from understanding the chords (and chording) on the piano and Autoharp, this stimulates the addition of other rhythmic and harmonic parts. All of this is assumed to result in musical growth particularly conducive to part singing.

Chants

Chants[6] have been defined as recurring rhythmic or melodic patterns or figures. As in the case of chord roots, knowledge of the harmony forms the basis for understanding chants. These added parts have value as rhythmic, creative, and part-singing activities as well as being music that some immature singers can sing in tune. Easy chants, particularly of the one-pitch (one-note) type, can be sung in the primary grades.

[6] A detailed explanation of writing chants may be found in *Basic Music for Classroom Teachers*, Nye and Bergethon, pp. 36-49.

Initial experiences in writing simple chants may be gained through the use of well-known songs that can be accompanied by only one chord such as *Row Your Boat, Are You Sleeping?* and *Little Tom Tinker*. The first tone to be used would be the chord root. Instead of using the chord root as in the preceding pages, invent a rhythm pattern that contrasts with the melody. The regular recurrence of this rhythmic pattern is sung on the pitch of the chord root (i.e., the home tone, "1," or "do"). For example, in the case of *Row Your Boat* (Chapter Three, p. 66) the patterns that can be composed to be sung in conjunction with the melody are myriad. A few of them are:

Percussion instruments are frequently used to accentuate the rhythm of a chant, and melody instruments are sometimes of aid in keeping some children on pitch. For dramatic effect those children singing the chant often begin about four measures before the melody begins, thus adding an *introduction* to the song. They also may continue for a few measures after the melody is sung, thus adding a *coda*. *Row Your Boat* may be sung as a melody with an added chant. When sung as a two-part round, addition of the chant results in a form of three-part singing, and when extended to be a four-part round, the chant adds a fifth part. With such simple song material, three- and four-part singing of this type can be done in fourth grade. Furthermore, the chant itself can be extended so that still more parts result.

For example, the above chants are pitched on "1" (C) of the 1-3-5 (tonic) chord. The chanters can be divided into two groups with one group singing on scale tone "3" at the same time the other sings on "1." When this is learned, the chanters can be divided further into three groups singing the chant on scale tones 1, 3, and 5 respectively. This is an example of vocal chording[7] done in the rhythm of a chant. The melody adds a part. If the chant now consists of three parts and the round is sung in four parts, a seven-part song results. The teacher is, of course, limited in the number of possible parts by the musical maturity of his group. However, the possibilities present in this

[7] See Vocal Chording, this chapter, p. 208.

simple music are surprising. Chording instruments can be a natural companion activity to this type of part singing. Melody instruments may be used also.

Thus far we have been concerned with the one-note chant. There are other possibilities. For example, *Are You Sleeping?* could have chants as follows:

Little Tom Tinker could have these:

Children often alter the final repetition of some chants in order that the last note sung will be the home tone. Again, creative possibilities are nearly boundless. The chant patterns upon which most of these are created for I-chord songs are shown below.

CHANT PATTERNS FOR ONE-CHORD SONGS

I

1, 3, 5 (singly and in combination)

1 8

1 $\bar{5}$ 1

1 $\bar{7}$ $\bar{6}$ $\bar{5}$

1 $\bar{5}$ $\bar{6}$ $\bar{5}$

1 $\bar{5}$ $\bar{6}$ $\bar{7}$

Multiple chants (two or more different ones) could conceivably be employed in the same song. However, if too many different words are sung at one time, the meaning of the words is lost and the effect ceases to be very musical. Experimenting by substituting neutral syllables or melody instruments may be worthwhile.

When chants are sung with two-chord songs,[8] the initial experi-

---

[8] A list of two-chord songs is found in Chapter Three, p. 69.

ences are usually with scale tone "5" because that tone is common to the two chords, I and V$_7$. This is the only tone of the scale on which it is possible to create a one-tone chant in such songs. Such rhythmic chants for *Three Blind Mice* might be:

Another commonly used chant is one based on the scale tones "5" and "6." Scale tone "6" is a member of neither I or V$_7$ chord yet it has the unusual quality of not interfering with the harmony as long as it is placed on an unaccented part of the measure. This kind of a chant for *Looby Loo* could be:

This 5-6-5 pattern works very well with songs like *Old Texas, Ten Little Indians* and *Skip To My Lou,* and children can invent many rhythmic variants of it.

Space does not permit examples of every type of chant that is possible with two-chord songs. However, the chart below reveals some of the possibilities that are interesting to explore.

CHANT PATTERNS FOR TWO-CHORD SONGS

I	V_7
5, 5 5	5, 5 5
5 6 $\bar{5}$	5 6 $\bar{5}$
1 $\bar{7}$ $\bar{6}$ $\bar{5}$	$\bar{7}$ $\bar{7}$ $\bar{6}$ $\bar{5}$, $\bar{7}$ $\bar{6}$ $\bar{5}$ $\bar{5}$
1 $\bar{5}$ $\bar{6}$ $\bar{7}$	$\bar{7}$ $\bar{5}$ $\bar{6}$ $\bar{7}$, 2 $\bar{5}$ $\bar{6}$ $\bar{7}$
1 $\bar{5}$ 1	2 $\bar{5}$ 2, $\bar{7}$ 5 $\bar{7}$
5 3 5	5 2 5, 5 4 5
1 $\bar{5}$ $\bar{6}$ $\bar{5}$	$\bar{7}$ $\bar{5}$ $\bar{6}$ $\bar{5}$, 2 $\bar{5}$ $\bar{6}$ $\bar{5}$
3 5 3	2 $\bar{5}$ 2, 4 5 4

Chants may become monotonous because of their constant repetition. Therefore it is desirable that they be omitted from sections of some songs.

Chants for three-chord songs are of necessity more complex since there are now three chords on which they must be based. An example of a chant for such a melody is the very simple one written below for *Go Down Moses*. This particular chant employs scale tone "5" for the I and V_7 chords and scale tone "6" for the IV chord in the one measure in which it appears. Other examples of chants can be found in music books included in the reference list at the end of this chapter as well as in the Music Series Reference Guide to Selected Part-Singing Activities.

The teacher can use the I, IV, and V_7 chords for piano chording. These chords are often played one octave lower. Should the constant chanting become monotonous, the children can sing in unison on the words, "Go down, Moses, way down in Egypt's land," and return to the chant after this section. A low-pitched drum is effective, and a tunable drum is ideal.

GO DOWN MOSES

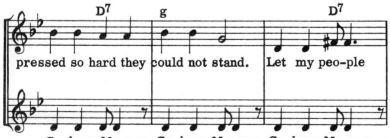

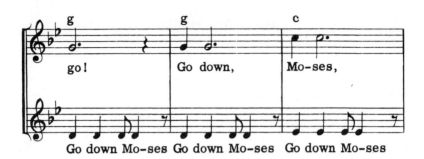

Counter melodies and descants

Singing counter melodies and descants constitutes another of the many approaches to part singing. A counter melody is an added melodic part, usually lower than the original melody, which often imitates it and often moves in contrary motion to it. Ideally, a descant is a melody in its own right although written to accompany another melody. In practice, the descant is subordinate to the melody. It is usually higher in pitch than the melody and a small group of children sing it while the majority of the children sing the melody. The reason for this is that high pitches sound relatively louder than low pitches when they are combined in part singing; therefore a small group on a high part balances with a larger group on a low part. When the teacher understands the relation between counter melodies or descants and the chords and the original melodies, he can guide children to compose them. The first example is a counter melody to *Down in the Valley*. In this case it is of such melodic nature in its own right that it is easier to sing than the real melody. This has resulted in its wide use in Oregon, where many third grade children sing this two-part song.

DOWN IN THE VALLEY

American Folk Song
Arranged by R. E. N.

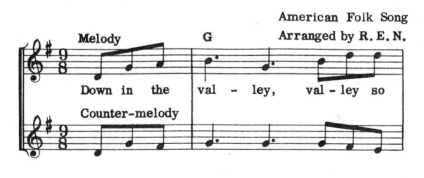

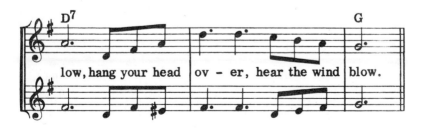

THE BREAK OF DAY[9]

Sidney Row

Czechoslovakian Folk Tune

Arranged by Gladys Pitcher

1. Bright is the day, blue is the
2. Dew on the rose spar-kles with

1. Bright, bright is the morn,
2. Dew, dew on the rose

sky, Wel-come an - oth - er fair
light Fresh is the wind from the

blue the sky, Wel-come an - oth - er fair
spar-kles, And fresh is the wind from the

day;_____ Sweet-ly the
West;_____ Morn-ing is

day, we will wel-come the day;
West, fresh the wind from the West;

lark, soar-ing on high,
come, gone is the night,

Sweet-ly the lark, soar- ing high,
Morn-ing is come, gone is night,

[9] From *Our Land of Song*, p. 74. Used by permission of C. C. Birchard & Company. Another counter melody, this appears in a fifth grade book.

Sings us   his   beau - ti - ful   lay;_____
Earth now   a - wakes from her   rest;_____

Sings us   his   beau - ti - ful   lay,   he'll
Earth now   a - wakes from her   rest,   a -

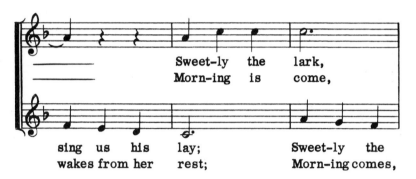

_____   Sweet-ly   the   lark,
_____   Morn-ing   is   come,

sing   us   his   lay;   Sweet-ly   the
wakes from her   rest;   Morn-ing comes,

soar-ing   on   high,   Sings   us   his
gone is   the   night,   Earth now   a-

lark   on   high,   Sings   us   his
gone   is   night,   Earth   now   a-

beau-ti - ful   lay._____
wakes from her   rest._____

beau - ti - ful,   beau-ti - ful   lay.
wakes from her   rest, from her   rest.

A beautiful traditional-type descant, higher than the melody, and therefore to be sung by a small group, is one composed by Ewald Nolte to *Silent Night*. It is designed for sixth grade and junior high.

SILENT NIGHT[10]

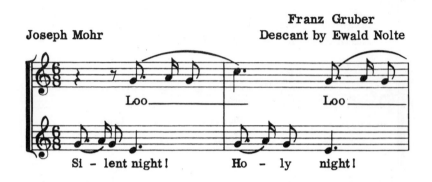

Franz Gruber
Joseph Mohr
Descant by Ewald Nolte

Loo___ Loo___
Si - lent night! Ho - ly night!

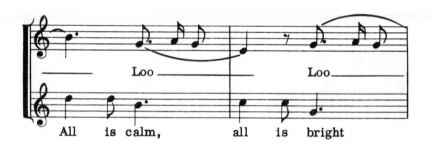

Loo___ Loo___
All is calm, all is bright

Loo___
Round yon Vir - gin Moth-er and Child,

---

[10] From Beattie, Wolverton, Wilson, and Hinga, *The American Singer, Combined Grades*. Used by permission of American Book Company, publisher.

Ideally, counter melodies and descants are learned in integral relation to the original melody, because when they are learned as separate songs and then combined, many children fail to hear the real relationship of the two parts. The melody should be well learned first of all, and a feeling for the harmony should be established.

The elementary school chorus may learn a descant or counter melody to be sung while the rest of the children sing the melody; and these elements may be combined in an assembly program. Likewise, children of superior ability may prepare descants out of school to be combined in class with the melody sung by the other children. Another use for this type of added part is by certain melody instruments —from Song Flutes, Tonettes, and Song Bells to violins and flutes. If done with discretion, employing a melody instrument is a way of strengthening either or both parts.

Vocal chording

An example of one type of vocal chording was mentioned on page 197 in connection with *Row Your Boat*. Usually, chording of the vocal type consists of the same tones that are often used for piano chording in the treble clef. The children may be divided into four groups, with one assigned the melody and the other three assigned the three chord tones. This activity would logically begin with one-chord melodies and progress to three-chord melodies or to more complicated harmonies. It may start in a simple way in fourth grade. It is sometimes emphasized in sixth grade as an approach to three-part singing. The ease with which children can learn to chord vocally will be determined by their ability to hear harmony; their ability to learn harmony will be favorably influenced by successful experiences in instrumental chording (Autoharp, piano) and by guided listening activities that aid the hearing of chord changes.

One of the music series refers to the singing of chord roots as "chording." In this text, singing chord roots and vocal chording are two clearly different activities, though harmonically related.

The chords to be sung can be arranged in several positions. The following chart not only exemplifies this but illustrates chord positions that are sometimes used as exercises to introduce children to this activity. Although numbers may be used to introduce this work, humming or the neutral syllable "loo" is used in actual performance.

The following excerpt from *Silent Night* illustrates this activity.

Si - lent night! Ho - ly night! All is calm,

Vocal chording

all is bright! 'Round yon Vir - gin

Improvising harmony parts

The improvising of harmony parts has been often overlooked as one practical approach to part singing. "Barbershopping" or "singing harmony by ear" has had a definite carry-over into the natural musical expression of boys and girls when they are on field trips or picnics, at camp and at home. The writers know of an elementary school where the improvising of parts by volunteer neighborhood quartets was an activity of importance, even affecting school and community programs. A list of songs that have had use in this activity includes *Home On the Range, Down By the Old Mill Stream, There's a Long Long Trail, Moonlight and Roses, Let the Rest of the World Go By, Eyes of Texas (I've Been Working on the Railroad), Red River Valley, Oh My Darling Clementine, A Bicycle Built for Two*. This activity is usually most effective at sixth grade level, where it develops into three-part singing, although some fifth grades can do well with it.

Using instruments

The value of types of instrumental music experience as an aid to the background and to the performance of part singing has been commented upon several times previously, both in this chapter and in Chapter Three pp. 61, 81, 84). To summarize, chording on instruments helps prepare children for part singing, and the use of melody instruments or the piano in playing one or more of the parts of a song can aid in making the activity successful. But children should not remain dependent upon hearing an instrumental part in order to "hold a singing part"; the teacher should use such aids with discretion.

Thirds and sixths

Earlier in this chapter, the singing of chord roots was pointed out as one of the easiest types of elementary part singing because of the strength of the harmonic elements involved. An approach older from the standpoint of general use is the employment of thirds and sixths. As in other ways to begin part singing, the children are first assumed to know the melody very well, and to have heard the song accompanied by the Autoharp, piano, or recording in a manner that helps them comprehend the integral relation of the melody and harmony.

The singing of thirds has been introduced in the section on harmonic endings, page 189. This use of thirds can be expanded to include parts of songs and eventually entire songs. Again using *Old Black Joe* as a familiar example, the melody accompanying the words, "I'm coming, I'm coming" can be sung softly by the children while the teacher sings (or plays) this same melodic fragment one third lower.

melody / new part
I'm com-ing, I'm com-ing

As before, children who believe they can sing the new part will join with the teacher while those who as yet feel more secure by remaining on the melody will sing that part. This section of *Old Black Joe* can be further extended in parallel thirds to include the words, "For my head is bending low." In the music series books will be found songs that rely heavily on parallel thirds to introduce part singing. A

POLLY WOLLY DOODLE

American Song

New part

Melody

Oh, I went down South for to see my Sal, Sing-ing

Pol - ly Wol - ly Doo - dle all the day; My

Sal, she is a spunk-y gal, Sing-ing

Chorus

Pol-ly Wol - ly Doo-dle all the day. Fare thee

well, fare thee well, fare thee

well my fair - y fay, For I'm

goin' to Loo-si-an-a for to see my Su-sy-an-na, Sing-ing

Pol - ly Wol - ly Doo - dle all the day.

song that can be sung in its entirety in thirds is the well-known *Polly Wolly Doodle*. As in other types of part singing, the children should know melody and harmony well before attempting the new part.

An interval[11] that sounds similar to the third is the *sixth,* which is an inversion of the third. After children have become accustomed to singing in parallel thirds, they can easily learn to sing in parallel sixths. Any song that can be sung in thirds can be sung in sixths; therefore *Polly Wolly Doodle* can illustrate this also.

Other songs such as *Lightly Row, Goodbye My Lover Goodbye, Yankee Doodle,* and *London Bridge* are often used to advantage because they are familiar and can be sung using many thirds and sixths. *London Bridge* introduces the combination of thirds and sixths:

LONDON BRIDGE

---

[11] For an explanation of intervals, see Chapter Seven, p. 173.

fall-ing down, My Fair La-dy.

There are older methods of teaching part singing, which emphasize drilling on each part, then putting them together. Today the emphasis is upon helping children to hear a new part in relation to the melody and the harmony so that they hear all of the music. This principle is applicable no matter what type of part singing is being done, whether it be round, descant, or traditional two- and three-part singing. The general outline of progress in part singing is as follows:

1. The learning of the melody.
2. The comprehension of the harmony (chord structure) that accompanies the melody by use of Autoharp chording, piano chording, or a suitable recording.
3. The introduction of the new part in a manner that permits the children to hear the integral relation of the two parts. (Children hum the melody or sing it softly while the teacher sings or plays the new part.)
4. The singing of the new part by those children who are ready for part singing, always working for a balance in volume that permits the hearing of both parts by all of the children.
5. Introducing a third part can be done by observing steps 3 and 4, adding the new part to the two parts previously learned.
6. When children have learned to feel secure in part-singing activities, then the sight reading of part songs can be an interesting and challenging activity. When this skill is developed, steps 1, 2, and 3 are eliminated. Since sight singing is a complicated skill, neutral syllables are generally used at first instead of words so that the children can concentrate on the notation. The words are added when children feel secure on the parts.

In general, the voices of fifth and sixth grade children are unchanged and have approximately the same range. Therefore each child should experience singing both high and low parts. Technically, it is incorrect to call these immature voices "soprano" or "alto." It is more accurate to abandon these adult terms and to call the children's voice parts "high," "low," and "middle," rather than "first soprano," "alto," and "second soprano." It is the aim of the teacher that every child sing each of these parts, changing from one to another according to the directions of the moment or by being assigned them in different songs.

In each of the music series fifth grade books will be found a sequence of songs that stress parallel thirds. Following songs in thirds there will be those that include both thirds and sixths, then some fourths and fifths. Every teacher in the intermediate grades should know the sequence of songs through which part singing is expected to be learned in the particular series book or books available in his school. This requires the study of the recommendations found in the teachers' manual that accompanies the books of each series.

Among the recordings that accompany each of the music series will be found those reproducing part songs. These should be examined carefully to determine their use in teaching such songs. At the time this book is being written, few of the recordings emphasize an important point stressed in this chapter—that a new part should be taught in integral relation to the melody. However, some of the recordings include this concept to a degree. In these the melody is sounded very softly at the same time the new part is sounded quite strongly.

The male teacher is at some disadvantage in teaching part singing, since his voice sounds one octave lower than the child voice. Therefore, it is necessary that he use instead of his voice some melody instrument when he wishes to illustrate part singing of unchanged voices. His voice is excellent, however, in the singing of chord roots. There is seldom a changed voice among sixth grade children, but in case there should be, the singing of special parts such as chord roots by the male teacher along with the boy will help the child adjust to his temporarily unique situation.

The elementary school chorus

Among the special interest groups in the elementary school are found the orchestra, band, and chorus. The instrumental groups are generally the responsibility of special music teachers but the chorus is frequently taught either by the music teacher or by a classroom teacher who has the interest and ability. Although some schools have a primary grades chorus which sings unison songs, the usual chorus is composed of fifth and sixth graders. Today's teachers are fortunate in having an improved selection of song materials to use, some of which are listed at the end of this chapter. Not only have the series books included chants, descants, and counter melodies in addition to the standard types of two- and three-part songs, but there are supplementary materials of value. There is no standard seating arrangement for elementary choruses. However, it is best to have the lowest and highest parts seated so that each can hear the other well. In this way the group is able to keep better on pitch. In chorus work which has a goal of public performance, the children are more or less permanently assigned to one of the parts (high, middle, or low).

Music Series Reference Guide to Selected Part-Singing Activities

The American Singer (2nd ed.; American Book Company)

BOOK FOUR

Combinable songs, 46-47, 132-133
Contrapuntal songs, 54r
Descants, 82, 88, 110, 126r, 130r, 148, 164, 192r
Part songs, 193, 195
Rounds, 17, 23, 38ar, 40r, 57b, 129, 166br, 167r, 180b

BOOK FIVE

Descants, 31r, 87
Combinable songs, 14-15, 26, 76-77
Part singing, TM 8. Suggested introductory songs, 14-15, 25ab, 26, 31, 45b
Recorded two-part songs, 73, 80, 84a, 85, 98, 123, 129, 134, 135, 144, 166, 185, 200
Rounds, 25ab, 45b, 46a, 74b, 124, 133b, 165b, 167, 183b, 184b, 192b

BOOK SIX

Combinable songs, 12-13, 124-125
Descants, 10, 116
Elementary chorus, TM 7
Part singing, TM 6-7
Recorded two-part songs, 28, 31, 45, 64, 72, 75, 91, 94, 111, 114, 128, 196, 198, 200, 202, 213, 226
Rounds and canons, 11, 29, 39b, 41, 59, 106, 107

New Music Horizons (Silver Burdett Company)

FOURTH BOOK

Descant, 168r
Dialogue songs, 115, 120, 162r, 177
Harmonic endings, 121a, 122r, 156ar
Rounds, 62, 83b, 84b, 118a

FIFTH BOOK

Refer to 2. Part singing, 228. Recorded two-part songs, 84a, 87, 90a, 119. Recorded descant, 188
See TM 22 "Beginning Two-part Singing"
Tone blending, 70, 78

Our Singing World (Ginn and Company)

A Singing School (C. C. Birchard Company)

Harmonic endings, 23, 28a, 30a, 46r, 50a, 52r, 78ar, 79a, 80r, 84, 95
Introducing singing in thirds, 28ab, 42b, 53, 65, 76a, 88, 89b, 128
Introducing singing in sixths, 45b
Recorded part songs, 8
Rounds, 28b, 36b, 37, 74a

OUR LAND OF SONG

Blending, 7, 9, 11, 17, 21
Descants, 17, 41, 61, 82, 161r
Introducing three-part songs, 178
Introducing two-part singing, 7
Partial canon, 19
Recorded part songs: two-part, 9a, 10a, 15a, 25, 32, 35, 42a, 69, 74a, 78a,
    79, 91, 150, 156, 161, 162b, 172, three-part, 61
Repartee (dialogue) songs, 13, 156r
Rounds and canons, 23, 24, 57, 75, 168

MUSIC EVERYWHERE

Blending, 26, 29, 36, 47
Descants, 25, 65r, 83r, 180
Introducing three-part singing, 26r
Introducing a three-part song, TM 100
Recorded part songs: two-part, 14b, 68, 79, 83, 86b, 88, 90b, 141, 145, 169,
    181, three-part, 26, 28b, 29, 45, 47, 48, 50, 59, 81, 98a, 147, 188a, 204,
    209
Rounds and canons, 9, 27, 38, 47, 57, 59a, 61, 96, 167, 171, 175, 182, 214,
    215
Songs for glee club, 14r, 188r, 204r, 209r, 197-218

Together We Sing (Follett Publishing Company)

TOGETHER WE SING, Enlarged Edition
Recorded part songs designated in the text
Rounds and canons, 87, 95, 104, 112, 137, 150

MUSIC THROUGH THE YEAR

Evaluate the singing of melody instrument parts (those in color), 23, 26, 27,
    30, 33, 34, 36, 40, 43, 53, 65, 67, 68, 71, 79, 81, 99, 106, 108, 116,
    120, 125, 126, 130, 141, 143, 147, 150
Rounds and canons listed, 178
Two-part songs, 9r, 14r, 16, 18, 54r, 81, 85, 89r, 105br, 123

MUSIC ACROSS OUR COUNTRY

"Rounds and Canons," 190
"Songs with Descants," 190
"Songs with Alto Part," 190

VOICES OF AMERICA

Refer to Part Singing in "To Teachers and Parents" section*
Refer to "Rounds and Canons, Songs with Descants" in Classified Index*

VOICES OF THE WORLD

Part singing, 205-206
Rounds and canons, 223
Songs with descants, 223

* Not available when this textbook was written.

Music For Living (Silver Burdett Company)

MUSIC IN OUR TOWN

TM "Dialogue Songs," "Echo Effects," 133

MUSIC NOW AND LONG AGO

TM "Dialogue Singing," "Echo Effects," 132
TM "Preparation for Two-Part Singing," 133

MUSIC NEAR AND FAR

"Song Conversation" (dialogue), 183
"Rounds," 184
TM "Harmony," xi, "Part Singing," xii, "Chord Roots," 163, "Instruments as aid to part-singing," 163, "Rounds," 166

MUSIC IN OUR COUNTRY

(See Classified Index and Teachers Book°)

MUSIC AROUND THE WORLD

(See Classified Index and Teachers Book°)

° Not available when this textbook was written.

ADDITIONAL REFERENCES

THINGS

TO

DO

1. Select a round and teach it to the college class. Become accustomed to directing the entrance of each group of singers.

2. Select a two-chord melody (I and V_7) and develop a score that provides for melody, harmony, and rhythm as suggested in this chapter on page 195.

3. Write a chant for a one-chord, a two-chord, and a three-chord song. See Chapter Three, pp. 66, 69, and 74 for suggested songs.

4. Improvise the "barbershop" harmony to some of the songs mentioned in this chapter on page 209.

5. Arrange *Lightly Row, Yankee Doodle,* or *Goodbye My Lover Goodbye* in two-part harmony, employing thirds and sixths whenever logical.

6. Find a recording of a part song and use it in teaching this song to the college class, planning each step of your presentation. Then evaluate the effectiveness of this use of the recording.

7. Evaluate the following part-singing drill. Write the scale of D Major on the chalkboard. Use either both index fingers or two short pointers. Have half the class follow your right hand and the other half follow your left hand as you point to different notes of the scale as they sing them in harmony.

8. Select from the series books a sequence of songs you would use in helping fifth grade children learn two-part singing by the use of thirds.

9. Write descants to *Hickory Dickory Dock, Oh Susanna,* and *Are You Sleeping?*

10. Select a two-part song and make a tape recording of it designed to help teach the song to fifth or sixth grade boys and girls.

REFERENCES

Books for Part Singing

Bell, Leslie, *The Festival Song Book One* (for Treble Voices). New York: Mills Music, Inc.

Cooper, Irvin, *Songs for Pre-Teentime* (Grades Six and Seven). New York: Carl Fischer, Inc.

Foltz, David, and Arthur Murphy, *Descants to Sing for Fun*. New York: Mills Music. Inc.

Gearhart, Livingston, *A Singing Bee* (Two-Part Songs for Treble Voices). Delaware Water Gap, Pa.: Shawnee Press.

Grant, Louise, *Harmony and Rhyme*. Boston: The Boston Music Co.

Krone, Beatrice, and Max Krone, *Our First Songs to Sing with Descants, Very Easy Descants, Songs to Sing with Descants, Descants for Christmas, Our Third Book of Descants, Great Songs of Faith, From Descants to Trios*. Chicago: Neil A. Kjos Music Co.

Rhea, Lois, *Singing is Fun*. New York: Bourne, Inc.

Rowen, Ruth and Bill Simon, *Jolly Come Sing and Play*. New York: Carl Fischer, Inc.

Slind, Lloyd H., *Melody, Rhythm, and Harmony for Elementary Grades*. New York: Mills Music, Inc.

———, *More Melody, Rhythm, and Harmony*. New York: Mills Music, Inc.

Wilson, Harry R., *Choral Program Series Book One*. New York: Silver Burdett Company.

Films

Coronet Instructional Films, 65 E. South Water St., Chicago, Ill.
   Harmony in Music. Introduces part singing and chording. Twelve minutes. Grades 5-8.

Johnson Hunt Productions, 6509 De Longpre Ave., Hollywood, Calif.
   Two-Part Singing. Twenty minutes. Grades 4-6.
   Music Reading. Companion to *Two-Part Singing*. Twenty minutes. Grades 4-6.

The Value
of Music in
Other Areas

Nine

A beautiful song that possesses emotional values and that describes experiences meaningful to children has universal appeal. These aesthetic, emotional, and cultural qualities point toward this song's possible use to add interest, meaning, and enjoyment to other areas of the curriculum. It is also true that the subject matter of other areas can make music activities more interesting, meaningful, and enjoyable. Thus, while the skills in any area are not to be neglected, neither the learning of music nor learning in other areas can in many instances approach completeness without each aiding the other. Music has always been man's most natural artistic medium of expression, and through its use he continually interprets his civilizations, past and present. When music assumes its rightful place throughout the curriculum, marked emphasis is given to it because of its real functions.

SUGGESTIONS FOR RELATING MUSIC AND OTHER AREAS

The following outline consists of some of the more obvious bases for relating music with other areas.

Art

Rhythm is an element common to music, art, and bodily response.

Appropriate recordings stimulate creative art.

Songs can be illustrated by children's drawings.

The making of simple musical instruments is in the area of arts and crafts.

Some ideas can be expressed in three media: art, music, and dance.

Certain artistic styles are common to both art and music. Example: impressionism.

Certain artistic concepts of form are common to both art and music. Example: classical architecture and classical form in music.

Physical education

Singing games and dances are activities considered to be in both the areas of music and physical education.

Music can be created for a known dance.

Dance can be created for known music.

Basic understanding of note values and meter signatures comes from bodily response.

Rhythm can be expressed in the dance, in music, and in art.

Certain music forms can be expressed in bodily movement.

Science

Some music concerns aspects of nature such as clouds, rain, the sea, the seasons, the steppe, stars.

There exists a science of musical sound.

Aspects of electronics include such things as recording sound, radio, television, and others.

There are many scientists who have music as an enjoyable avocation.

Making simple musical instruments involves simple acoustics.

Health and safety

There are songs that help teach health and safety.

Correct posture in singing relates to health.

Arithmetic

The study of note values and meter signatures relates to the understanding of fractions.

Language arts

Poetry and music are closely related.

Appropriate recordings can be employed to stimulate creative writing.

Poetry can be composed; music can be written to make songs based on this poetry.

Aspects of choral reading can relate to the process of learning songs.

Reading of words of songs can be an experience in the process of improving reading skills.

Music can be selected that illustrates children's literature.

Social living (*which can include problems in science, health, safety, language arts, history, geography, citizenship, art, music, and rhythms. See Chapter One, pp. 5-6.*)

Music aids in understanding ideals, religions, and traditions of contemporary and past civilizations and cultures.

Music describes geographical and climatic conditions of various countries.

Music aids in teaching history and patriotism through study of appropriate music and composers.

Music is a unifying factor and morale-builder; it aids personality development; it can relieve tensions and alleviate fatigue.

Songs can be found and also created that relate to health and safety.

Dances, instrumental compositions, songs, and music plays can be created by children in connection with units of work in social living.

Children can make musical instruments and costumes to portray the life of peoples of the past and present.

In some communities, adults from foreign countries may be invited to discuss and illustrate some aspects of their native music and customs.

Music is frequently an important aspect of culminating activities of units of work.

It can be seen that there are basic relationships between music and the other areas of the curriculum. However, the area that best lends itself to the combining of subject matter of all types is social living.

MUSIC IN SOCIAL-LIVING UNITS

The purpose of the social-living program is to help the society it represents meet the immediate and long-time needs of young people. In some schools specific units are planned in terms of a chosen theme for each grade suited to the stage of development of that age group. In developing the theme, subject matter is drawn from several areas. Social studies and language arts make up the core of the social-living program while arithmetic, science, health, physical education, music, and art are drawn upon to aid in the understanding and in the solution of the problems being studied. However, it should be kept in mind that in most schools having this type of program, additional time is allotted for the development of skills in arithmetic, science, health, physical education, music, and art.

The primary concern in the introduction of music into such units is not how much and what specific music can be used in this connection, but how music activities can contribute to further understanding and to solving of the problem under consideration. In such activities, children are free to plan for various types of musical experiences in case they relate to the solution of significant problems. The variety of musical experiences possible in a series of such units is almost limitless, and can range from song interpretation and simple dramatization to writing original song plays.

The following outline indicates how music may be used in a unit of work in the primary grades. For the purposes of this book, music in this unit is given more consideration than other activities that would normally receive equal emphasis.

A unit in social living for first grade

WHAT ANIMALS MAKE GOOD PETS?

I. Introduction

The six year old is interested primarily in problems growing out of his home and immediate community. Most children have pets in their homes or know about pets in the homes of their friends. Since children have a natural love for animals and most of them have had association with pets, this unit is based on real-life experience, which vitalizes its content.

II. Purposes

A. General

1. To provide opportunity for children to learn to plan, work, and play democratically in a group.
2. To help children assume more responsibility for the solution of their problems and the problems of others.
3. To provide for individual differences through the use of a variety of materials and activities, thus building within individuals a feeling of security, success, and happiness.
4. To make more meaningful and functional the learning of various facts and skills in language arts, science, health, arithmetic, art, music, and physical education.

B. Specific
  1. To provide the child with materials, experiences, and activities that will foster his understanding of the life of pets and its relation to his own life.
  2. To help the child to develop a sense of responsibility through caring for a pet in the classroom.
  3. To help the child understand the environment necessary for the health and safety of pets.
  4. To help the child understand how nature has equipped these pets to protect themselves.
  5. To stimulate children's creative expression through stories, poems, art, music, and rhythms.

III. Possible Means of Motivation

  A. Establishing a stimulating environment, which may include:
    1. Pictures of pets with names or sentences written beneath.
    2. Sharing experiences about pets.
    3. Pets brought to the classroom.
    4. Songs sung and recordings listened to that are concerned with pets.
    5. Films or slides about pets.
    6. The library center arranged with attractive books about pets.

  B. Excursions to:
    1. A pet shop.
    2. Homes of children having interesting pets.

IV. Content

  A. The different kinds of pets.
  B. The care and training of pets.
  C. The homes of pets.
  D. How nature protects pets.
  E. Similarities and differences between pets and children.

V. Suggested Activities

  A. Visit a pet shop and homes to study pets.
  B. Advance planning for excursions.
    1. Discuss responsibilities involved.

    2. List questions for which answers are to be found.

C. Care for pets in the classroom.

D. Show motion pictures about pets.

E. Construct a motion-picture roll using stories, songs, poems, and pictures the children have assembled or created.

F. Draw pictures and paint murals about pets.

G. Plan and present a pet show.

H. Look at pictures and read in library books to find information.

I. Discuss types of pets and their care.

J. Relate personal experiences in caring for pets.

K. Read stories and poems.

L. Write simple group stories, poems, and songs.

M. Sing songs and play singing games about pets.

N. Draw pictures to illustrate songs.

O. Do imitations and dramatizations of pets.

P. Model pets out of clay or papier-mâché.

Q. Hatch baby chicks in an incubator and care for them.

R. Discuss making charts of experience in activities with pets, and then make these experience charts.

S. Invite a member of the Humane Society to speak on the care and safe handling of pets.

VI. Suggested Activities in Subject-Matter Areas

    A. Language Arts

        1. Read experience charts.

        2. Read labels on pets' cages and on pictures.

        3. Read suggested work lists in caring for pets.

        4. Match names of animals with pictures.

        5. Read pre-primers in basic reading series containing stories on kinds of pets and their care.

        6. Make individual and group booklets.

        7. Compose original stories, poems, and songs.

        8. Provide experiences in choral reading of poems.

        9. Write letters such as requests to visit pet shop, invitations to speakers and visitors, and thank-you notes.

      10. Dramatize stories, poems, and songs.

      11. Discuss experiences in relation to pets.

      12. Read stories, legends, and poems to the children.

B. Number Activities
1. Count the number of legs various pets have.
2. Keep a record of how much pets are fed.
3. Weigh the pets to see how much they gain or lose.
4. List the kinds of pets owned by the children and count them.
5. Count the number of children who work in a group.
6. Draw a picture of a pet on each of ten pages; make them into a booklet and number the pages.
7. Use words of comparison in discussions of animals such as big, bigger, biggest, small, smaller, smallest.

C. Health and Science
1. Observe and study body structure of animals and how they are protected by nature.
2. Observe and study animals' eating habits and methods of obtaining food.
3. Compare the basic needs of animals with those of man.
4. Observe and study ways animals keep clean.
5. Learn how climate and seasons affect the lives of animals.

D. Art
1. Illustrate individual and group stories, poems, and songs.
2. Model animals from clay or papier-mâché.
3. Make murals depicting pets.
4. Use charcoal, crayon, and paint to illustrate various activities of the unit.
5. Make posters showing the care of certain pets.
6. Make a moving-picture roll and the pictures for it.
7. Study famous pictures of pets.

E. Citizenship
Participating in the planning, executing, and evaluation of various activities:
   a) Excursions.
   b) Care of pets.
   c) Making murals.
   d) Pet show.
   e) Seeing films.
   f) Discussions.
   g) Group writing of stories, poems, and songs.
   h) Dramatization and creative play.

i) Experience charts.
j) Hatching chicks.
k) Writing letters of invitation and thanks.

F. Music and Physical Education

In order for children to act in creative ways in this work unit, they require a relaxed and happy environment. The teacher should understand each child and provide a flexible program with a variety of materials for experimentation. He is fully aware that young children are naturally and normally creative; thus he is alert to the spontaneous creative activity that is usually in evidence. These children enjoy playing with words and creating chants and jingles for all occasions. For example, upon returning from the pet shop there may have been a singing conversation based on the familiar 5 365 3 chant, the teacher singing, "What did you see?" and individual children singing an answer, "I saw a puppy," (or some other animal) in a variety of ways. The teacher may have continued the singing conversation with other questions such as, "What did it say?" and the child answering, "It said 'bow wow.' " Each child could be asked to describe the pet he liked best, telling in his own words the movements and sounds it made. One such description could be, "Soft, soft kitty-cat walked, walked, walked." The children could say these words together to learn them and to feel their rhythm, and eventually the teacher might ask if they thought they could sing it instead of speaking it. From attempts at this, the following melody could result.

KITTY CAT

Soft, soft   kit-ty cat,   walked, walked, walked.

As such a melody is learned, there can be experiences for uncertain singers and in playing on the bells and piano the tones 1 2 345, which accompany the words "Soft, soft kitty-cat," and on the tones 3 2 1, which accompany the words "walked, walked, walked." Eventually children can sing such a song as they walk, and pretend they are kittens. Sometimes part of a class may sing while other children imitate kittens. Other words developed in the same way could be the following:

LITTLE DUCK

(Tone matching and bells on "quack, quack, quack" tone matching
on "Little duck")

Lit-tle duck, lit - tle duck, quack, quack, quack.

Lit-tle duck, lit - tle duck, quack, quack, quack.

LITTLE DUCKY WADDLES

(Imitate "waddle" and play on bells and piano.)

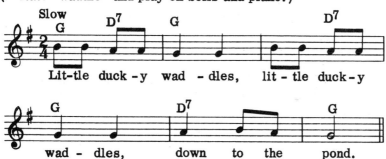

Lit-tle duck -y wad - dles, lit - tle duck-y

wad - dles, down to the pond.

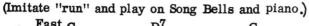

(Imitate "run" and play on Song Bells and piano.)

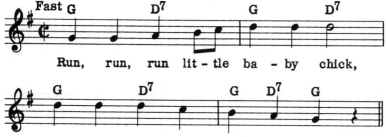

Run, run, run lit - tle ba - by chick,

run, run, run, run, quick, quick, quick.

ANIMAL TALK

(Tone matching, bells and piano)

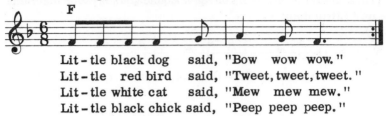

Lit - tle black dog   said, "Bow   wow   wow."
Lit - tle   red bird   said, "Tweet, tweet, tweet."
Lit - tle white cat   said, "Mew   mew mew."
Lit - tle black chick said, "Peep peep peep."
Lit - tle white duck   said, "Quack, quack, quack."

LITTLE FROG

(Jumping)

Jump, jump, lit-tle frog,   jump, jump,   on the log.

After further discussing the eating habits and the homes of the animals they have seen, the children may be interested in developing similar word-phrases and songs about these things.

RABBITS EAT LETTUCE

(Song Bells, Piano on scale)

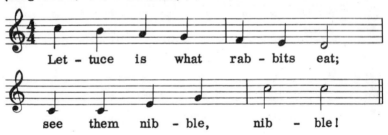

Let - tuce   is   what   rab - bits   eat;

see   them   nib - ble,   nib - ble!

BIRD IN A CAGE

(Tone matching on "singing")

Lit-tle   bird   in   a   cage   is   singing, singing,

sing-ing high! Please come out and play with   me._____

The following song was created by children to inform the children in another first grade room of an event that took place in the life of one of their pets, a white rat. Notice the change of meter, which adds to the drama of the situation.

A SURPRISE

First Grade
Frances Willard School
Eugene, Oregon

A sur - prise,___ a sur - prise,___ Oh, we have a sur - prise! Mo-ther Rat had ba-bies last night; There were nine with their eyes shut tight. Oh, my, what a sight for you. Take a look, please do!___

A list can be made of the pets the children saw, and songs about these pets can be found in the music series books. Appropriate ones can be selected and learned. Examples of such songs follow:

AMERICAN SINGER BOOK ONE

Fluffy, 77a, *Skipper,* 77b, *Kittens,* 78b (dramatization), *My Wish,* 79 (running), *Cat and Bird,* 81, *The Toad,* 82 (hopping), *The Duck,* 181c (waddle), *My Old Dog,* 182a, *Animal Talk,* 182b (add sounds of other animals and clap hands as indicated)

MUSIC FOR EARLY CHILDHOOD

(See classified lists, 131)

EXPERIENCES IN MUSIC FOR FIRST GRADE CHILDREN

Kittens, 9a, *What Does Puppy Say?*, 9b (dialogue), *My Airedale Dog*, 14b, *Cloppity, Cloppity*, 15a (step, run, jump, dramatize), *Gallop*, 15b, *My Little Pony*, 84 (hop, trot, jump), *Mary Had a Little Lamb*, 102b (Song Bells, piano), *Three Little Kittens*, 100a (dramatize), *Familiar Friends*, 80a (dramatization, percussion instruments)

MUSIC 'ROUND THE CLOCK

My Little Ducklings, 21 (Song Bells, piano), *Frisky Wisk*, 22 (Song Bells), *I Love Little Pussy*, 23 (see suggestions 62), *See My Pony*, 24 (coconut shells), *Surprise!*, 33, *My Little Kitten*, 34 (Song Bells or psaltery)

THE KINDERGARTEN BOOK

Doggy and Kitty, 110a (dialogue), *My Pony Bill*, 111b (galloping), *Puppy's Tail*, 112b, *Two Little Kitty-Cats*, 112c (dramatization), *Little Dog, What Do You Say?*, 113b (dialogue), *A Getting Up Song*, 114 (dialogue), *Mary Had a Little Lamb*, 116a (Song Bells, piano), *My Black Hen*, 177a, *Six Little Mice*, 117b, *The Hen*, 118a, *Little Ducky Duddle*, 118b, *The Little Red Hen*, 143-151 (song story)

THE FIRST GRADE BOOK

Galloping, 22, *Trot*, 23a, *Galloping Horse*, 24a, *Little Dog, What Do You Say?*, 143a (dialogue), *Margaret's Kitten*, 145, *Bunny in the Garden*, 146a, *Bunny Eats*, 146b, *My Pony*, 148b, *Trot, Trot, Trot*, 149a, *The Ducks*, 152a, *Over in the Meadow*, 156, *Little Frog*, 158a (hop, jump), *Baa Baa Black Sheep*, 155, *The Chickens*, 150a, *Tone Matching Songs* (animal sounds)

OUR FIRST MUSIC

My Bunny, 23, *My Dog Teddy*, 17b, *The Stray Cat*, 214, *Dinner Time*, 142a, *Quack! Quack! Quack!*, 142b, *The Barnyard*, 149, *The Turkey*, 164, *Come Kitty*, 206b, *My Pets*, 207b (dramatization), *Good Morning, Little Pussy!*, 209a (dialogue), *The Pony Cart*, 207 (action song), *Tame Animals*, 251b (dialogue), *Mister Turtle*, 278c (plodding)

The children may write additional verses for some of these songs and add impersonations, dramatizations, rhythmic movements, percussion instruments, and keyboard instruments when suitable.

After a visit to a farm home, children may be interested in larger pets such as ponies, goats, lambs, pigs, and calves. Experiences involving fundamental movements such as running, trotting, and galloping can result from children's observations. Concepts of high and low in pitch can be made meaningful in terms of imitating the sounds of animals. Concepts of heavy and light can be clarified in terms of dramatizing the movements of animals and be sounded with appropriate-sounding percussion instruments. Simple rhythms of animal names can be spoken, played on percussion instruments, and responded to with bodily movements. Examples: horse, horse (walk, walk), chick-en, chick-en (run run run run).

Free rhythmic expression can come from children's responses to selected recordings and piano compositions played by the teacher. A few examples of recordings are: The Decca Album *Animal Pictures in Music,* some of the Phoebe James *Animal Rhythms, Hens and Roosters* from "Carnival of the Animals" (Saint-Saëns), *Ballet of the Unhatched Chickens* from "Pictures at an Exhibition" (Moussorgsky), and selections from Victor Rhythm Album I. Examples of piano compositions are *The American Singer Book One:* for walking: *Sonata,* 111, *March of the Tin Soldiers,* 113, *Soldier's March,* 115; for running: *Badinage,* 116, *The Fair,* 117, *Gypsy Song,* 118; for tiptoeing: *Hall of the Mountain King,* 121; for jumping: *Bagatelle,* 123a, *The Strange Man,* 123b, *Leap for Life,* 124; for hopping: *Ecossaises,* 126; for galloping: *Hunting Song,* 127, *The Wild Horseman,* 128. *Experiences in Music for First Grade Children: Catch My Doggie,* 14a, *Waddling Ducks,* 70a, *The Crested Hen,* 80b, *Pony Ride* 91. *The First Grade Book: Trotting Horse,* 23b, *High Stepping Horses,* 148b, *Waddling Ducks,* 152b, *Our First Music:* for galloping: *Little Hunting Song,* 43, *The Wild Horseman,* 232b; for walking: *Soldier's March,* 97b, *March,* 234, *March,* 328a, *Pantomime,* 330a; for running: *Running Horses,* 329a.

Needless to say, there are infinite possibilities resulting from the use of recordings and from piano compositions. The titles of many of these bear no relation whatever to pets or animals, yet their musical and rhythmic content may be fitting to stimulate creative rhythmic expression about the pets being studied. Through bodily responses the children can increase their comprehension of such elements as loud, soft, high, low, restful, exciting, light and heavy. They can discover music to which they can walk, run, gallop, and they can learn to identify certain types of music such as the march and the lullaby. They can find by listening that certain parts of the music repeat while other parts are different, that some music tells a story while other music may tell only of a mood, a rhythm, or a melody, and that some musical instruments can be identified. Some children may bring in recordings having to do with pets. However, since six-year-olds are by nature active listeners in a physical sense rather than analytical listeners in an intellectual sense, the creative experience of these children is more valuable to them than their growth in abstract musical knowledge.

A source of other activities is the physical education manual published by most state departments of education, from which appropriate exercises and games can be selected. Examples of exercises may include prancing horses, the cat walk, and the rabbit hop, and examples of games may include those such as bird catcher, ducks fly, and lame fox and chickens.

Singing games may be found in music series books. For example, in *The Kindergarten Book* are *Cat and Mouse*, 40b, *Squirrels and Trees*, 41a, and *Frog in the Middle*, 41b. In *Music for Early Childhood* one finds *The Little Cat*, 59, *Song and Dance of the Pigs*, 60, and *John the Rabbit*, 63.

VII. Anticipated Outcomes

    A. Culminating Activities

        A culminating activity does not necessarily have to come at the end of a unit; it may take place at the close of any phase of a unit. These activities are usually presented in the classroom for the children themselves, for another class, or for parents. Sometimes they are given in the school auditorium for a larger group of children and parents. Possible types of culminating activities for a unit on pets may include:

        1. A pet show.

            a) A display of experience stories, poems, and songs, with illustrations.

            b) Announcers.

            c) A pet parade with rhythm band playing a march for children and their pets. (Some children might be dressed as pets.)

            d) Sing songs about pets, employing dramatization and percussion-instrument and Song-Bells accompaniments when suitable.

            e) Display pets and tell about their eating habits, how their health and safety may be protected, and the types of homes in which they live.

            f) Singing games, action songs, and a demonstration of rhythms created to describe various pets.

            g) Class sings an appropriate concluding song.

            h) Announcers thank audience for their attendance and attention.

2. An original play that includes songs, percussion-instrument and Song-Bells accompaniments to appropriate songs, rhythms, and singing games both from books and from among those created by the children.
3. An "open house" to show various activities done in connection with pets, displaying experience stories, poems, and songs, motion-picture rolls made by the children, pictures, booklets, pets modeled from clay and papier-mâché, and live pets.

VIII. Anticipated Learnings

A. An increased understanding of the child's relation to pets in the basic needs of air, water, food, shelter, and gentle care.
B. An attitude of kindness toward animals.
C. A better understanding of the characteristics of some animals and their habits.
D. A comprehension of how animals are protected by nature.
E. A broader understanding of the importance of cooperation in planning, initiating, and evaluating group activities.
F. Growth in personality adjustment evidenced by:

1. A greater willingness in the individual child to assume his share of responsibilities.
2. An appreciation of the work of others.
3. An improvement in attitudes necessary for efficient working with others.
   a) A desire to observe work standards agreed upon by the group.
   b) Consideration of the rights of others.
   c) Taking turns in group work.
   d) Caring for materials and sharing them.
   e) Taking and giving criticism in good spirit.

G. A greater feeling of security in self-expression through art, music, rhythms, and language activities.
H. More curiosity about the surrounding environment and the life in it.
I. Evidence of increasing skill in:
1. Helping to make plans, carrying problems and projects to completion.

2. Using time and materials wisely.
3. Listening attentively.
4. Thinking critically about the solution of problems and experimenting toward that end.
5. Reading a variety of materials with enjoyment and understanding.
6. Using a variety of sources of information to find answers to problems: excursions, letter-writing, speakers, films, books, pictures, and observation.
7. More effective oral and written communication.
8. Using number concepts to solve problems in meaningful situations.
9. Singing, playing instruments, rhythmic responses to music, listening to music, and creating music.

The next unit is designed for use in grade five or six. As in the preceding unit, the sections other than the one concerning music are not expanded.

A unit in social living for fifth or sixth grade

HOW CAN WE BETTER UNDERSTAND OUR MEXICAN NEIGHBORS?

I. Introduction

As indicated on page 244, the major emphases in the social living area for grades five and six are on problems of the community, state, and nation, and their relationship to equivalent problems in other countries. Therefore the geographical and economic relationships of the United States and Mexico as neighbors aid in the motivation of learning in this unit. The increasing incidence of American travel in Mexico gives added color, interest, and meaning to this popular topic.

II. Purposes

A. To find out how Mexico of today compares with early Mexico.
B. To find out the relationships existing between the United States and Mexico.
C. To develop a growing understanding of the problems of the Mexicans.

D. To develop an appreciation of Mexican art, music, and dance.

E. To develop in the child increased ability in:

1. Working together by sharing, planning, initiating, and evaluating activities.
2. Preparing and giving oral reports.
3. Using effectively a variety of materials and sources of information.
4. Thinking critically and using facts to solve problems.
5. Expressing oneself through the media of creative arts— art, writing, music, dance, and dramatics.

F. To develop skills in:
1. Reading for enjoyment and information: maps, fiction, references.
2. Participating effectively in discussions.
   a) Making thoughtful comments.
   b) Listening courteously.
3. Expressing ideas effectively through writing.
4. Music, by means of related activities.
5. Art, by means of related activities.
6. Dance, by means of related activities.

III. Suggested Approaches
A. Arrange an attractive display or exhibit on bulletin board, wall, or table:

1. Pictures of Mexico.
2. Books and articles about Mexico.
3. Mexican dolls, serapes, rebozos, sombreros, leather, pottery, weaving, and silver handicrafts.

B. Show films.
C. Invite a speaker to discuss life in Mexico, including music and art.

IV. Suggested Content
A. History and culture—Indian, Spanish, Mestizo.
B. Geographical and climatic conditions.
C. Products, resources, and industry.
D. Mechanization and transportation.
E. Living conditions in Mexico.
F. Education, religion, and customs.

G. The future of Mexico.

H. Art and handicrafts.

I. Music and dance. Songs from the series books and other sources should be used when they serve to enrich other activities of the unit. For example, in the study of the fiesta, appropriate music and dance activities are essential and integral parts of the study. When the Mexican Christmas is taken up, a piñata can be constructed in arts and crafts, and a song and dance can be written about it. Authentic Mexican folk songs depict the Mexican way of life in the same way in which authentic Negro folk songs depict a particular way of life, and they have emotional qualities as the Negro songs have. Songs can be found (or created) that tell of the Mexican's food, clothing, transportation, holidays, customs, occupations, religion, superstitions, poverty and subsequent suppressed desires. The Mexican dance, music, and art are related in their color, rhythm, and spirited character. The songs and suggestions in the list that follows have significant meaning when they are a part of the problem-solving activities of the unit.

	Suggested Activities
AMERICAN SINGER BOOK FIVE	
Claves, castanets, rattles, 108-109	Making instruments, playing rhythms
The Cowboy, 112	Chording (Autoharp, ukulele, guitar)
The Jarabe, 172	Directions given for the dance
Come and Drink, 174	Two-part singing; dance
The Doves, 175	Directions given for the dance
Play the Bugle, 176	Directions given for the dance
NEW MUSIC HORIZONS BOOK FIVE	
Down in Mexico, 43	Chording; dance directions given
Old Mexican Woman, 71	Two-part song; chording
NEW MUSIC HORIZONS BOOK SIX	
Fiesta, 173	Chording
SINGING TOGETHER	
In the Plaza, 48	Two-part song; percussion instrument accompaniment suggested
SINGING IN HARMONY	
Carmen Carmela, 62	Two-part song; percussion instrument and piano accompaniment, 65
Cielito Lindo, 68	Two-part song; create dance and a percussion-instrument score

OUR LAND OF SONG

Simple Latin-American rhythm pattern,[1] 150	Compose a song based on a Mexican rhythm pattern; write a percussion-instrument score

MUSIC EVERYWHERE

La Raspe, 159	Directions given for dance
La Cucaracha, 149	Chording; write a percussion score; descant; create a dance for the song
Fiesta, 146	Chording; descant; percussion instruments
Waltz of the Broom, 142	Compose words; chording; melody for violin; directions given for dance
Meander in Mexico, 68	Two-part song; concerns trip to Mexico, thus may be used to introduce a unit or to begin a culminating activity presentation

MUSIC THROUGH THE YEAR

Break the Piñata, 57	Refer to page 175 for further sources of information: chording, creating a harmony part, Christmas
Sweet Oranges, 56	Christmas, chording

Other suggested activities:

1. Listen to recordings of authentic Mexican music and play appropriate percussion instruments with them. Write the rhythm patterns in notation.
2. Evaluate radio and television programs concerning Mexico, particularly those including music.
3. Compose original poems, dances, and songs (both unison songs and part songs) about life in Mexico.
4. Collect and demonstrate Mexican musical instruments: guitar, castanets, claves, tambourine, maracas, guiro, drums (conga and bongo). (The ukulele and Autoharp may substitute for the guitar in classroom activities.)
5. Make instruments:
   a) Guiro, a long gourd or a grooved cowhorn scratched with a stick.
   b) Maracas, a pair of gourds[2] in which pebbles or large seeds have been placed. They are usually gaily colored, as is the guiro.

[1] More advanced rhythms may be found in the song book *Inter-Americana*, by the Krones. (Chicago: Neil A. Kjos Music Company.) These may be used in accompanying Mexican songs and in creating songs. The book also contains Spanish pronunciations and *Las Posadas*, Mexican Christmas festival in song. Another book by the Krones, *More Descants and Easy Bases*, contains the popular song *Chiapanecas* with drum and maracas accompaniment.

[2] One source of gourds is Pearson's Gourd Farm, 1409 North Merced Avenue, El Monte, California.

c) Claves, two thick hardwood sticks. Some old broomhandles will do, cut in six-inch lengths.

d) Drums. Bongo drums are open at one end, having only one drum head. They are played with the hand, and each has a different pitch. The conga is a large drum, with a low resonant tone. Some of the large compressed cardboard drums made by the Continental Can Company for shipments of valuable seed, ice cream mix, and expensive chinaware can be used for the conga. Paint them with authentic Mexican designs.

6. Paint colorful pictures to illustrate Mexican music as it is heard from a recording.
7. Dramatize a Mexican legend and include original or native rhythm patterns, flute music, and dances.
8. Plan and present a round-table discussion or panel on native Mexican music.
9. Listen to recordings of the music of Carlos Chavez. Investigate Chavez and other Mexican composers of today.
10. Write and dramatize a play about Mexicans, using original poems, rhythm patterns on percussion instruments, songs, dances, accompaniments, and Mexican musical instruments.
11. Dramatize a Mexican Christmas.
12. Dramatize suitable Mexican songs.
13. Study, demonstrate, and evaluate the guitar, both as an important musical instrument in Mexico and as an important Spanish musical instrument in history. Listen to recordings of Segovia and other famed guitarists who are serious musicians.
14. Study characteristic Mexican rhythm patterns and compose a song based on one or more of them.
15. Create a dance to an appropriate Mexican folk song.

V. Suggested Activities in Other Areas

A. Language Arts
1. Report on visits to Mexico, films seen, and materials read.
2. Discuss pictures.
3. Plan a round-table discussion on life in Mexico.
4. Discuss outstanding Mexicans of the past and present.
5. Learn new words and how to use them.
6. Write invitations and thank-you notes to speakers.
7. Write requests for travel information.
8. Write and present original plays dealing with aspects of Mexican life.
9. Write stories and poems.
10. Give oral and written reports.

11. Explain the processes used in weaving, pottery making, leather work, and metal work.
12. Explain how to prepare tamales, frijoles, and tortillas.
13. Give book reports.
14. Present oral and written summaries of films seen.
15. Write letters to pen pals in Mexico.
16. Organize a story hour, sharing stories about Mexico.

B. Research and Use of the Community to Solve Problems
1. Use books, magazines, maps, and bulletins to find answers to questions.
2. Bring books, maps, and magazines from home to share.
3. Read graphs and charts.
4. Invite people from the community to speak to the group about Mexico.
5. Show films, film strips, and slides.
6. Visit a museum.
7. Plan and participate in an interview with people who know about Mexico.

C. Art and Handicrafts
1. Paint pictures of Mexican activities, landscapes, and architecture.
2. Make a mural representing Mexico.
3. Make a class book containing art each child produces.
4. Make dresses and dress dolls in Mexican style.
5. See films on arts and crafts in Mexico.
6. Construct a model of a Mexican village.
7. Weave rugs, serapes, belts.
8. Mold Mexican pottery and paint designs.
9. Construct dioramas and motion-picture and television boxes for rolls containing drawings of Mexico.
10. Draw and make maps of Mexico from papier-mâché, sawdust or salt.

   a) Political   d) Products
   b) Physical   e) Minerals and industry
   c) Climatic

11. Draw pictorial maps showing distribution of population.
12. Make articles from leather, silver, and other metals, and weave baskets.

VI. Culminating Activities

    A. Invite another room or parents to a program, which may include:

       1. Mexican music and dances learned from the music series books or created by the children, using percussion instruments and costumes both collected by the children and made by the class.

       2. An original play (which may include music and dances).

       3. Children dressed in Mexican costumes who serve tea to parents, with Mexican music as background atmosphere along with Mexican art.

       4. Exhibit articles from Mexico and tell about them.

    B. Invite another group to hear a planned class discussion about life in Mexico.

VII. Suggested Outcomes

    A. Increased knowledge and understanding of Mexico's problems and Mexico's contributions to the world.

    B. Development of an understanding and appreciation of Mexico's place as our neighbor.

    C. A greater knowledge and understanding of Mexican music and art.

    D. Increased efficiency in the ability to:

       1. Work democratically by sharing, planning, initiating, and evaluating activities.

       2. Prepare and present written and oral reports.

       3. Use effectively a variety of materials and sources of information.

       4. Think critically and use facts skillfully in the solution of problems.

       5. Express ideas through creative media such as art, music, dance, dramatics, and writing.

    E. Development of increased skill in:

       1. Reading and organizing research materials.

       2. Participating in discussions.

          a) Sharing ideas.

          b) Listening attentively to others.

          c) Critically evaluating information presented.

          d) Writing effectively.

Some suggested topics for units in grades one through six

How the social living program should be organized and developed at the various grade levels will depend upon many factors, including the age and maturity of the children, and the problems and conditions of the school and community. This program should be organized in a way that helps children to meet and to solve their own problems of home, school, and community living, in relation to such areas as health, recreation, safety, beautification, conservation, government and citizenship, transportation and communication, and economic life. Through their attempts to meet and to solve these problems they should develop ability to live and to work democratically with others in individual and group relationships. They should also develop an understanding of being a part of an ever-expanding community. Furthermore, they should be guided in their understanding of the processes of physical and social change, and of man's responsibility for the kinds of change that take place.

Classroom teachers have the task of planning many units. Music consultants have the responsibility of aiding teachers in selecting and planning appropriate music and music activities for the amplification and enrichment of the subject matter involved in these units. In schools that have a music specialist he will find it to his advantage to make music activities more meaningful to boys and girls by relating part of the work in the music period to units of work undertaken by the classroom teacher. In terms of current educational thought, it is also necessary for special music teachers to encourage the concept that music is the property of everyone to be used by all; it is no longer the exclusive province of the music teacher. Some suggested problems to be developed as units are as follows:

Grades One and Two. (The immediate community—home, neighborhood, school.) How can we make our school a safe place in which to live? How can we make our homes safe? How can we make our classroom and school a good place in which to live, work, and play? How can we make a school garden? How can we take care of our toys? Where should we store our food? What animals make good pets and how can we care for pets? How do farmers, firemen, policemen, bakers, and others in the community help us?

Grades Three and Four. (The community and its relationships to other communities.) How can we help make our home, school, and community safe? What are the harmful insects found in our home, school, and community and how can we help destroy them? What types of recreation are found in our community, and how can we select wisely from among these types? How can we make our community a more attractive place in which to live? How can we choose suitable clothing? How do we get our food? How did our community develop? How do the people in our community make a living? In what ways are animals of today like and different from animals of long ago? What effect does climate have on the types of homes built in this and in other communities?

Grades Five and Six. (The community, state, and nation and their relationship to other countries.) How can we improve the appearance of the school, home, community, and ourselves? What are the state and nation doing to beautify our country? What are the leading natural resources of our community, state, and nation, and how can we conserve them? What are the sources of electric power in our state and nation? What are some of the improved farming methods used in our state and nation? How do many parts of the nation and of the world help us obtain food? How does the way we keep time today compare with keeping time long ago? How has mail been carried in the United States from colonial days to the present? How have writing and printing been developed? How have roads and railway systems developed in our state and in the nation? How do other countries influence the price of commodities? How was our country discovered and explored? How did the people live in the early days of our country? How has our country grown to its present size? How can we better understand our neighbors of North and South America?

MUSIC AND SCHOOL PROGRAMS

Most programs presented in the elementary school are comprised of related or integrated activities, including or stressing music as an important aspect. The term "program" is used to denote many types of presentations, from a unit-culminating activity done by boys and girls for themselves in their own classroom to a festival-type affair encompassing the entire school or groups of schools and presented before large public audiences. Programs should possess high educational values. They should correctly be logical culminations of interesting daily activities, not something unrelated to normal school experience. Children should enter into the planning along with teachers and administrators. Good programs inform parents of the types of activities with which their children are occupied in their daily school living.

It is entirely possible that pressures from school and community can result in programs that are contrary to good educational practice. Should this occur, the teacher should strive to orient parents and others as to the types of program that are, and are not, justifiable from the standpoint of education. Neither children nor teachers should be exploited. Children's interests and development should come first; they should not be sacrificed for dubious entertainment or public relations values.

Since the reason for the existence of programs is the value they have in building feelings of confidence, security, and belonging, all children should appear in them whenever possible. When it is impossible for every child to take part, perhaps scheduling two performances with alternate casts might remedy the difficulty. When there is no solution to this problem, the class should choose those of their number whom they wish to represent them.

Costumes should be kept simple and inexpensive. Whenever possible, they should be made by the children in school. When parents are assigned this responsibility, unhappiness can result from some children being underdressed or overdressed by comparison with others. When the children are dressed simply and identically (as much as the performance permits), this problem is minimized.

Large-scale programs are apt to interrupt the normal school day. When such programs are contemplated, teachers and administrators should decide whether their educational values are great enough to offset the losses due to interruption of normal class activities.

Although good performance is a worthy goal, too much emphasis on drill and "perfection" can destroy spontaneity and joy. Such programs are not worth the placing of children and teachers in an atmosphere of tension and emotional disturbance. A happier situation comes from an atmosphere of calm encouragement and relaxed enjoyment, stemming from well-laid plans organized by the children and teachers. After all, the major consideration should be what is happening to the boys and girls. This is often overlooked when adult standards of performance are mistakenly sought.

Programs presented for and by children in primary grades should be brief, with 30 minutes as a maximum length. Those presented for and by children in intermediate grades are ordinarily limited to not more than one hour. A trend has been in evidence toward shorter programs than were once presented in elementary schools, and it can be added that many parents are averse to lengthy presentations. Perhaps the competition of television has spurred the trend toward brief and fast-moving programs for adults as well as for children. The most common faults of school presentations are (1) they are too lengthy, (2) the action is too slow-moving, (3) the children's speaking voices cannot be heard by the audience.

Although the emphasis today is to place educational values uppermost in school programs, entertainment values need not be shunned, for the one does not eliminate the other. The best programs are probably those in which educational and entertainment values are so well combined that they are inseparable.

Programs that include a number of classrooms require joint faculty planning and cooperation. One teacher explains,

In our school the fifth grade teacher, the art teacher and the music teacher plan a tentative program which is submitted at the next teachers' meeting for discussion. After changes have been made and it is acceptable to all concerned, each teacher selects a project or part of the program to work out with her class. The music teacher is the coordinator, the fifth grade teacher handles the speaking parts, and the art teacher takes care of props and stage. Classroom teachers are responsible for their own class's part in the whole program. We try to let every child "in on the act" whether it be in the chorus, participating in pantomimes, stagework, props, lighting, costumes, speaking parts, ushers, and publicity so that everyone feels that he has had a part. Parent help also aids in developing a closer tie with the home, and it can improve public relations.

Programs resulting from culmination activities

This type of program has been discussed earlier in this chapter. It represents a contemporary trend toward programs that grow directly out of normal classroom activities and that convey to parents the learnings that have taken place, revealing growth not only in subject-matter skills but in all areas—especially in democratic processes and emotional security. The following song was written by children for such a program, which concerned the culmination of a unit on clothing.

MY RAYON COAT

Annette Koonce

Fourth Grade
Kilby Training School
State Teachers College
Florence, Alabama

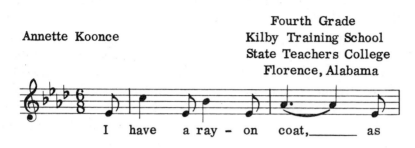

I have a ray - on coat,_____ as

cute   as cute   can   be,   but   to

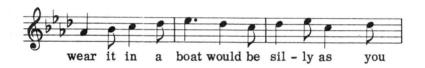

wear it in   a   boat would be sil - ly as   you

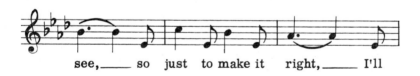

see,____ so just to make it   right,_____ I'll

leave it home to - night and____ wear in-stead my

bright lace and ny - lon be - ret._____

Programs for special days

Special-day programs include Thanksgiving, Christmas, Lincoln's Birthday, Valentine's Day, Washington's Birthday, Easter, and others. Contributing to such programs are appropriate songs and dances from the music series books and from supplementary sources including those chosen from among the songs and dances created by children. Original scripts and plays can be much more meaningful than set plans found in books and magazines, yet much good can come from the creative adapting of such material by children and teachers to better fill their own needs. The song on p. 249 was written by a fifth grade class for its Hallowe'en program.

The most important special-day programs are ordinarily those at Christmas time. They have two general aspects, the sacred and the secular, the latter having to do with the fun and gaiety of holiday good fellowship, Santa Claus, and the exchange or the giving of presents. The most common type of program is probably the one that relates the singing of Christmas songs to a script read by one or more readers. This has the advantage of being one of the easier types to prepare, but has the disadvantage of being without action. It usually offers fewer opportunities for creative effort than some of the other types of programs. Upon examining the titles of Christmas programs presented over a period of years in a large city system, the following kinds of programs and titles of plays were in evidence:

Those presented and attended by entire schools, by intermediate grades, by primary grades, or by individual rooms
Customs and carols of many lands
Original play with carols and dances
Tableau with choral reading, carols, and choral music (possible themes: the Nativity, Christmas around the world, Christmas cards)
Dramatized carols
Contrasting holy day and holiday
Carols and dances
Carols and shadow plays
Hanukkah and Christmas
Combined singing, instrumental, and drama
The Nutcracker Suite with dances, singing, and orchestra
Christmas cantata
Operetta, "Santa Claus Is Coming to Town"
Band and choral music with tableau
A carol sing
Creative rhythms, songs, and dances

HALLOWE'EN FUN

Ellen Wagner

Mysteriously

Ravinia Fifth Grade

Highland Park, Illinois

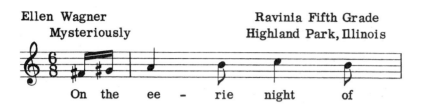

On the ee - rie night of

Hal - lo - we'en, we are sure to meet a

scar - y scene, the trees are sway - ing

to and fro, the witch - es lan - terns

are a - glow, it's beg - gar's night, you're

(Shout)

sure to know!   BOO!

Plays:

Why the Chimes Rang
Dickens' Christmas Carol
Birds' Christmas Carol
Night before Christmas
Spirit of Christmas
No Room at the Inn
Christmas Blessing
Magi's Gift
Littlest Angel
Melody of Christmas
Man Who Found the King

Festivals

Elementary school music festivals are held most frequently in the spring, and thus are often considered a culminating project that is a logical outgrowth of the school year's work. A festival implies a large number of participants. Advantages of the festival include the thrill of participating in large groups, the uniting of many teachers and students in one project, and the opportunity to display progress in music to the school and community. Disadvantages include children tiring of the music in repeated rehearsals, the near absence (in many situations) of creative elements, and the lack of democratic elements due to dictatorial direction impossible to avoid in most large festivals. The selecting of songs is ordinarily done by the classroom teachers. For example, the third grade teachers and their pupils agree upon the songs they desire to sing, thus making a higher standard of cooperation likely than when a music director dictates the list of songs. However, no list of songs can suit every third grade group and, while the majority of the children may be well served by the selection, there will always be those who find the songs too difficult or too easy. As in the case of other large-scale programs which sometimes disrupt the normal school day, teachers, children, and administrators should evaluate each festival carefully to determine whether the results are worth the effort involved. It is likely that the music festival's educational value for children is greater in small school systems than in large systems. For example, a four-room rural school or one city elementary school can conceivably produce a festival with many original and creative aspects, while a large city or county festival may become a routinized end within itself rather than an avenue that opens the door to further musical growth.

Many festivals bear no title except general ones such as "All City

Music Festival" and "Spring Music Festival." Others have titles or even slogans or themes such as "This is Music!" "Make Your Life More Musical," "Music Enriches Life," "A Montana Ranch Corral," "Pioneer Times," "Music, a Universal Language," "Music for Every Child, Every Child for Music," "The Old South," "Music Through History," and "Music of the Americas." In some localities, games are included with music to make the spring festival a "play day" for children.

Operettas. The elementary school operetta has the advantages of any activity that requires the working together of many teachers and children, such as developing a spirit of unity in the school, furthering the ability of children to work together in groups, and developing individual personalities—but the disadvantages have outweighed these if the frequency of programs of this type is a reliable criterion. Teachers have found a shortage of suitable material, that few children's voices are capable of singing leading roles, that there is often little opportunity found for creative aspects, that the rehearsing of the leading parts can result in the neglect of the other children, and that too much time may be required to properly prepare the operetta for public performance. Tiny original "operettas" are found today in some unit-culmination programs, thus illustrating the fact that it is possible for children to write their own small-form operettas.

THINGS

TO

DO

1. Examine the catalogs of educational recordings published by such firms as the Children's Music Center, 2858 W. Pico Blvd., Los Angeles 8, California (50¢); Children's Reading Service, 1078 St. John's Place, Brooklyn 13, New York; The Greystone Corporation, 100 Sixth Ave., New York; Radio Corporation of America, Camden, New Jersey; Currlin Music Center, 84 East San Fernando St., San Jose, California, for classified listings and other descriptions of recordings for use in social studies, nature, science, and all areas that concern the relation of music to the rest of the curriculum. Evaluate the assistance offered you by such catalogs.

2. Examine the indexes of the different music series books and report on their helpfulness to the teacher who is using music in other curricular areas. Do you find good classified indexes, or could these be improved?

3. For the elementary education major: Select a unit suitable for the grade level of your choice. Develop it according to the general pattern found in this chapter, selecting suitable music and music activities.

4. For the music education major: Put yourself in the place of a special music teacher who teaches music in each grade three periods each week. There has been, up to this time, no attempt to relate music to other areas of the curriculum. How may a knowledge of the characteristics of children (Chapter One) and of the content of the curriculum (this chapter) help you plan for a good music class? Why is it necessary for you to confer frequently with each classroom teacher about your plans for your music classes? On what basis should you encourage each classroom teacher to utilize music at other times during the school day?

5. Select a type of program, choose what specific kind it is to be, and develop it. What various learnings do you expect to result from this program?

REFERENCES

Books

Kinscella, Hazel, *The Kinscella Readers*. 2d ed.; Lincoln, Nebraska: University Publishing Company, 1949. *Storyland* (Second Grade), *Man in the Drum* (Third Grade), *Folk Tales from Many Lands* (Fourth Grade), *Conrad's Magic Flight* (Fifth Grade), *Tales of Olden Days* (Sixth Grade), *Around the World in Story, History Sings.*

Murray, Josephine, and Effie Bathurst, *Creative Ways for Children's Programs.* New York: Silver Burdett Company, 1938.

Myers, Louise, *Teaching Children Music in the Elementary School,* Chap. 12. Englewood Cliffs, N.J.: Prentice-Hall, Inc., 1950.

Pitts, Lilla Belle, ed., *Handbook on 16 mm. Films for Music Education.* Chicago: Music Educators National Conference, 1952. Contains annotated listing of films for correlated units of study and for music and the sciences.

Tooze, Ruth and Beatrice Krone, *Literature and Music as Resources for Social Studies.* Englewood Cliffs, N.J.: Prentice-Hall, Inc., 1955.

Music and Dance

Christmas Song Books

Christmas in Song, Preuss. Rubank, Inc., 1947.

Christmas, Its Carols, Customs and Legends, Heller. Hall and McCreary, 1948.

Songs for Christmas, Bryant-Luvas. American Book Company, 1940.

Christmas Carols from Many Countries, Coleman and Jorgensen. G. Schirmer, 1934.

Descants for Christmas, the Krones. Neil A. Kjos Music Company, 1949.

A Little Carol Book. Cooperative Recreation Service, Delaware, Ohio.

Christmas Caroler's Book in Song and Story, Kvamme. Hall and McCreary, 1935.

Descants on Christmas Carols, Vernon and others. Hall and McCreary, 1952.

Duggan, Anne, Jeanette Schlottmann, and Abbie Rutledge, *Folk Dances of the British Isles, Folk Dances of European Countries, Folk Dances of Scandinavia, Folk Dances of the United States and Mexico, The Teaching of Folk Dances.* New York: A. S. Barnes and Company, 1948.

Grime, William, *New Songs and Carols for Children,* Carl Fischer, Inc., 1955.

Krone, Beatrice Perham, *Janet and Jerry on the Farm; Come, Let Us Make a Garden; Songs of Travel and Transport.* Chicago: Neil A. Kjos Music Company, 1937.

Krone, Max and Beatrice Krone, *Songs of Norway and Denmark, Songs of Sweden and Finland, Spanish and Latin-American Songs, Inter-Americana, Songs of Many Lands, Folksongs of Brazil, Mexican Folk Songs, Songs and Stories of Our American Indians.* Chicago: Neil A. Kjos Music Company, 1941.

Krugman, Lillian and Alice Ludwig, *Little Calypsos.* Songs and stories about the West Indies arranged for rhythm instruments. Tells how to write calypsos. Brooklyn: Peripole Products Co., distributors, 1955.

Rhorbough, Lynn, *Songs of Many Nations, Treasures from Abroad* (Play Party Kit O folk dances), *The Folk Dance Set.* Delaware, Ohio: Cooperative Recreation Service.

Recordings	R.P.M.	*Suggested Grade Level*
Bowmar Records, 4921 Santa Monica Blvd., Los Angeles 29, California	78	1-3
Album: *Songs of Home, Neighborhood & Community*		
Albums of Folk Songs (social studies area)	78	4-8
Folk Songs of the U.S.A., Folk Songs of Many People, Latin American Folk Songs, Folk Songs of Canada, Folk Songs of Our Pacific Neighbors, Folk Songs of California and the Old West		
Children's Record Guild and Young People's Records, The Greystone Corporation, 100 Sixth Ave., New York 13, New York		
Individual discs		
Fog Boat Story (transport)	45-78	1-3
Jump Back, Little Toad (safety)	78	K-3
Ship Ahoy (transport) (dramatization)	45-78	2-5
Build Me a House (social studies)	78	1-3
Creepy Crawly Caterpillar (nature)	45-78	K-3
Little Pedro in Brazil (social studies)	78	4-6
Pedro in Argentina (social studies)	78	4-6
Going West (westward movement)	78	3-6
Folk Songs for Orchestra (social studies) (Russia)	78	3-6

Recordings	R.P.M.	Suggested Grade Level
Chisholm Trail (westward movement)	45-78	2-6
Daniel Boone (westward movement)	45-78	2-6
Working on the Railroad (transport)	45-78	2-5
By Rocket to the Moon (astronomy)	45-78	2-6
Timber-r-r (occupations)	45-78	3-6
Pony Express (westward movement)	78	3-6
Christopher Columbus (exploration)	78	1-6
Around the World (modes of travel)	78	N-1
Yankee Doodle (westward movement)	78	2-6
Let's Be Policemen (occupations)	78	K-2
Peter the Pusher (manners)	78	N-1
The Singing Water (nature and science)	45-78	1-4
Let's Play Together (cooperation)	45-78	N-2
Albums		
Children's Almanac (12 discs on seasons)	78	1-8
America the Beautiful (history)	78	2-6
Places and Things (two albums, social studies)	78	K-4

Decca Records, Inc., 50 West 57th St.,
New York 19, New York

Albums
Songs of Safety (safety)

Columbia Recording Corporation,
1473 Branum Ave., Bridgeport, Connecticut

*Columbia World Library of Folk and
Primitive Music*

	R.P.M.	Suggested Grade Level
Individual 12" discs	33	5-12

Irish Folk Songs, African Music from the French Colonies, English Folk Songs, French Folk Songs, Australian Aboriginal Songs and Songs from the Eastern New Guinea, Folk Songs from Scotland, Indonesian Music, Canadian Folk Music, Venezuelan Folk and Aboriginal Music, Bantu Music from British East Africa, Folk Music from Japan, Indian Folk Music, Spanish Folk Music, Yugoslav Folk Music

Follett Publishing Company, 1010 West Washington
Blvd., Chicago 7, Illinois

Albums

	R.P.M.	Suggested Grade Level
Christmas Carols (Album 20)	78	4-8
Patriotic Songs (Album 21)	78	4-8
American Folk Songs (Album 22)	78	1-8
In Joyous Song (Album RA 1, religious)	78	1-8

Suggested
Grade Level

Films

Music and Art

International Film Bureau, Suite 1500,
6 North Michigan Ave., Chicago 2, Illinois

    Design to Music, relates melodic-rhythmic   3-9
        patterns and linear design

National Film Board of Canada, 510 West
Sixth St., Los Angeles 14, California

    Hen Hop, pictorial fantasy suggested by folk music   1-12

    Fiddle de Dee, color patterns synchronized with violin   1-12

    Stars and Stripes, visual rhythmic acrobatics   1-12

Music and Social Living

Brandon Films, Inc., 200 West
57th St., New York, New York

    The River, the Mississippi River basin   5-12

National Film Board of Canada, 510 West
Sixth St., Los Angeles 14, California

    Story of a Violin, construction of a violin   5-9

What Have You Learned About Music Education?

**What is your philosophy of
music education?**

Ten

In order for a music program to function satisfactorily in any school there must be a philosophy of music education that is commonly understood by the teachers and the administration. Faculty committees or entire faculties sometimes study and discuss what the philosophy of their particular school shall be with regard to the teaching of music. It is urged that the cornerstone of such a philosophy be that music activities are *enjoyable* to both children and teachers. It is on the basis of pleasurable experiences that learnings emerge most readily and most successfully.

Every child, according to Lilla Belle Pitts, is "a special kind of musician," and has the capacity to respond to music in ways that are satisfying to him as a unique individual. As a consequence, music activities should be sufficiently varied so that they provide many different types of experiences through which each child discovers his particular musical interests, talents, and potentialities, and there should be group work within a class to provide for the various degrees of ability levels and interests.

Music experiences for children should be planned so that immediate success is possible, yet graduated in difficulty so that progress is always being made in some of the many aspects of music. These experiences should be *meaningful to children* so that boys and girls always understand clearly the purpose of whatever is being undertaken. Music notation, with its symbols and terminology, is of real value when its use is apparent to children in their music activities; it has little or no value as isolated subject matter. Therefore, an important aspect of the art of music teaching is that the teacher guide the children to types of activities interesting to them that include the introduction and *use* of music notation on the level of difficulty appropriate to the particular situation.

When grades must be given, children's work should be evaluated according to personal improvement, not on a basis of comparison and competition, and made primarily on the aesthetic growth of the individual, not on his ability to reproduce technical subject matter. The main objective in music education is to help each child develop an appreciation and a love of music and some degree of skill in understanding and interpreting the written symbols of music—not to develop professional musicians.

Special opportunities (private or group lessons, access to books for reference and research, membership in special vocal and instrumental groups) should be available to children who have the interest and ability.

The classroom teacher is in a superior position to use music when it can be most meaningful in daily classroom living. Music should be combined with other subjects whenever this is appropriate and meaningful. The teaching of music, like the teaching of reading, should be planned in terms of each individual child and his current level of attainment. At every grade level music should offer for children and teachers relaxation, enrichment, variety in the daily routine, group spirit and morale, leisure time interests, and personal and emotional adjustment and growth. The classroom teacher and the music specialist should work together in friendly, cooperative spirit to improve the music program for the children.

What are the major areas of activity in music teaching?

The music program provides experiences in three areas of activity, *listening to music, moving to music,* and *making music* by means of singing and playing instruments.

Listening is basic to all music activities. Through listening, skill is gained in hearing the different aspects of music and responding to them. Increased personal enjoyment of listening to music should result from the teaching of this activity. Children are not "born listeners" and they must be helped and guided to hear dynamics (loud, soft), pitch (high, low), tempo (fast, slow), and mood (sad, happy), and the various gradations of these elements. They should be helped to recognize simple form, the differences in sound and appearance of the various band and orchestra instruments, and the four principal classifications of adult voices—soprano, alto, tenor, and bass. Factors conducive to effective listening include physical comfort, the presenting of material in such a way that the children always have something for which to listen, and a teacher who sets an example of attentive, interested listening. The attention span of children should be taken into consideration, since children in primary grades have a much shorter attention span than those in the intermediate grades, and require a type of listening that includes more physical action. However, the attention span even in intermediate grades is comparatively short. A varied collection of appropriate recorded material should be present, and a good record player should be readily available. The many other listening activities include tone matching, voice blending in part singing, listening critically to other children, and listening to self-made music by means of a tape recorder.

Boys and girls should learn to move to the rhythm of various kinds of music through the use of their bodies. Some type of rhythmic response is nearly always a part of every music activity. Children should be at times guided to make associations between their patterns of movement and the musical notation for those movements (e.g., walking: quarter notes; running: eighth notes). New singing games should be learned each month, and children should commonly participate in folk dances and games that employ music. Individual help should be given to those children who are awkward, and creative individual differences should be encouraged. Boys and girls should take part in activities through which they build concepts of fast and slow, long and short, heavy and light, in terms of physical action.

Children should be taught to make music with their singing voices with confidence and pleasure. They should acquire a repertory of songs suitable for use in classroom, school assembly, home, and community. Steps should be taken to assist children to "find their singing voices" and to sing in tune with tone quality appropriate to the songs. Correct pitch should be designated (by Song Bells, pitch pipe, simple melody instrument, or piano) and well comprehended before children are asked to sing. Songs should be sung so that the words are clearly heard. Some children should have opportunities to direct classroom singing and thus develop conducting ability and leadership. In the intermediate grades children should be taught to sing part songs. Chorus, small ensemble, and solo experiences should be available.

The playing of percussion and simple melody and harmony instruments adds interest and meaning to rhythmic, listening, singing, and creative activities. Through playing percussion instruments children should be made aware of differences in quality of sounds and possibilities for "sound effects" in connection with music. They should have opportunities to play many different instruments. Through use of simple melody instruments, music notation can be learned in a functional setting, and by use of chording instruments (Autoharp, piano, ukulele) an elementary understanding of music theory may be achieved. A music corner should be one of the centers of interest in the classroom. Opportunities on band and orchestra instruments should be provided by the school. Such instruments are commonly taught by music specialists, thus are not normally the responsibility of the classroom teacher. However, children studying such instruments (and piano) should be encouraged to play before the class at appropriate times.

The creative aspect of the learning process should be a part of all music activities. When a child projects himself into an activity to the extent of freely offering suggestions for interpretation, dramatization, rhythmic possibilities, harmonization, and "orchestration" of song material, learning is usually taking place at a rapid rate because interest is at a high level. Rhythmic dramatization of recorded music, the composition of songs and instrumental music, and the adding of harmony parts should be natural outgrowths of a creative classroom environment. The study of music notation is another aspect of music that is an integral part of each of the major areas.

It should be understood that music possesses sufficient subject matter in its own right so that its use with other areas is not essential from a narrow point of view. However, when such use is appropriate it strengthens both music and the other areas under consideration by adding to the meaning of both. The social-studies area is particularly rich in its capacity to draw into it music, art, and other fields. Poetry, art, and music have especially meaningful relationships when children are led to find out how an idea can be expressed in each of these media. Teachers should plan for the inclusion of music in units of work from the very beginning, provided that music is a logical and meaningful part of such units. When a classroom teacher uses and teaches music and other subjects fully, music may appear quite naturally at many times during the day outside scheduled music periods.

The three major areas of music activity, and the goals that experiences in those areas should accomplish, were concisely charted in February, 1956, by a sub-committee[1] meeting at the State Department of Education, Salem, Oregon.

EACH OF THESE MUSIC EXPERIENCES	SHOULD
Listening to music	give pleasure
Moving to music	develop skill
Making music:	develop creative capacities
singing	develop knowledge of music literature
playing	develop understanding of music symbols and vocabulary
	develop understanding of the structure of music
	develop understanding of human feelings and their expression

How can pupil achievement be measured?

When the major goal of music teaching became to instill in children a life-long love and appreciation of music rather than to implant an exact knowledge of symbols and terms of music notation, objective grading of pupil achievement became practically impossible. Subjectively, by observation, teachers can state whether or not a particular child has such characteristics as a growing confidence in use of the singing voice and musical instruments, a consistent desire to take part in various musical activities, a growing skill in using and interpreting notation, an enthusiasm for music, the ability to take part in activities appropriate for his individual maturity, and an ex-

[1] The members were Mrs. Florence Hutchinson of Oregon College of Education and Dr. D. Evan Davis of Oregon State College.

panding knowledge about music and musicians. Sometimes grades are estimated by considering these factors. Some music educators suggest that keeping an anecdotal record of each child's reactions is as good a method as any on which to base grades subjectively. Dykema and Cundiff[2] write of a method of grading whereby each child is rated according to his musical potentialities and his musical attainment in seven categories (five areas of music activities, also music notation, and "home and social arts") on a scale of 1 to 5, with 5 excellent, 4 above average, 3 average, 2 below average, and 1 poor. This results in two columns of seven numbers. The total of the potentialities column is divided by the total of the attainments column to find the grade.

Since the majority of teachers realize that grades can be a serious psychological barrier between the child and his love of music, they usually try to avoid giving them. When they are compelled to do so by traditional grading systems, they tend to give high grades. When grades must be given, it is recommended that teachers do their best to collect evidence of pupil progress (such as the anecdotal record suggested above) or devise some system such as Dykema and Cundiff suggest in order to attempt to explain to children and parents as exactly as possible how grades are determined.

Since there has existed for some time a trend toward abolishing traditional grading, it is hoped that it will not be long before all teachers will be relieved of grading children by letters or numerals. Music is a particularly revealing area in which to illustrate the futility of trying to make accurate evaluations of children's achievement because the aim of music education is something that cannot be measured in any precise way. It is to instill in children a love of music with the long-term result that the developing individual becomes more sensitive and mature emotionally, more refined morally, uplifted spiritually; his life is otherwise enriched by having music as a life-long interest and source of relaxation and inspiration. How progress in this kind of development can be represented by numbers or letters on report cards is likely to remain an unanswered question.

There is another kind of evaluation, not for individuals, but indicative of the progress of a class as a group. In some intermediate grades a committee of children may keep notes on all music activities during each day. These notes are compiled weekly and kept in a

[2] Peter W. Dykema and Hannah M. Cundiff, *School Music Handbook*, new ed. (Boston: C. C. Birchard, 1955), p. 298.

notebook or wall chart. This is so organized that it can be useful for review purposes, useful also as a summary of the types and amount of music activities during the year, and constitutes something that can be given to next year's teacher along with other cumulative records for the purpose of providing continuity in the music program.

What music equipment and materials are needed in the classroom?

No area of instruction can be taught effectively without adequate equipment and materials. This is particularly true of music today. Classroom teachers are not music majors, and cannot be expected, as a group, to possess all of the skills of the specially trained musician. Therefore, it is just to state that *if classroom teachers are assigned responsibility for the teaching of music, it is to be expected that they be generously provided with the tools by use of which they can do more effective teaching.*

A piano should be easily available. (A small upright piano with full-length strings is recommended.) It should be closed when not in use, tuned at least every six months, protected from extremes of hot and cold, and equipped with workable rollers for ease in moving. At least one Autoharp is needed. Teachers use the Autoharp for harmonic accompaniments in the primary grades, and both children and teachers play it in the intermediate grades. The 12-bar model is preferable for most situations. Some types of simple percussion instruments should be in each room, the variety being influenced somewhat by the grade level concerned. An instrument of the Song Bells type (metal xylophone) should be in every classroom. Simple melody instruments such as the Flutophone, Song Flute, Tonette, and Melody Flute are often used in the intermediate grades. These are generally purchased by the children at local music dealers. A record player of good quality that can play 33, 45, and 78 rpm's is essential. Recordings that accompany the basal music series books should be available, as well as other recordings of a varied nature, both vocal and instrumental. The RCA Victor Record Library for Elementary Schools is considered basic equipment in many schools. If other means of establishing pitch are not available, a pitch pipe is necessary. A chalk liner to draw the staff quickly and easily should be in every classroom. Electrical outlets for record machines and other equipment should be placed for convenience. Projectors, both 16 mm., film-strip, and opaque, should be available. Each child should have a music text book and have access to supplementary music books and other books for recreational, reference, and research reading. The teacher should see that appropriate pictures concerning music appear on the bulletin board from time to time.

Are you adequately prepared to teach music?

No beginning teacher is *fully* prepared to teach any subject. Most experienced teachers say that they feel as though they learned more in their first year's teaching experience than they did in their four years of college preparation. Therefore, let it be granted that the art of teaching is continually a learning situation for the teacher, and that the good teacher is continually striving to be a better teacher each successive year that he teaches. It is fair to state that the musical preparation of the classroom teacher in teacher-training institutions is generally rather limited, and that most classroom teachers require the friendly aid and encouragement of music consultants or supervisors if they are to become successful teachers of music. Consequently, there is a marked emphasis today on the need for in-service training in music for elementary classroom teachers.

There is little doubt that many school systems have provided insufficient numbers of music specialists who are trained to work with classroom teachers to help them improve their teaching. Inadequacy of college preparation combined with inadequate in-service aid has resulted in a number of failures. This has caused some persons to doubt the wisdom of permitting classroom teachers to teach music, and voices have been raised that call for a return to music as a special subject taught only by music specialists. It is the opinion of the writers of this text that the college courses in music have improved in content and manner of approach and are becoming increasingly effective, that more school administrators are seeing the necessity for additional music specialists to assist classroom teachers, and that more classroom teachers are becoming successful in music teaching. They also realize that the present quality of elementary school music teaching needs great improvement. However, they believe that the philosophy of education that recognizes the elementary classroom teacher as the central figure in all subject-matter areas, including music, will eventually be successful in practice. It is hoped that every classroom teacher who reads these words is professionally minded and thus is anxious to do his part to justify the confidence that current educational philosophy has placed in his ability, for he is the person best able to teach music effectively when he is prepared to do it.

What are the duties of the music specialist who supervises on a consultant basis?

The music consultant in city and county school systems works with teachers and pupils in planning music activities both for the classroom and for school programs. He helps teachers select suitable music and dances for units of work in which music has a part. He may teach new songs in the classroom (do demonstration teaching); introduce new music activities, new materials, and equipment; and aid any phase of the music program that needs his assistance or in which he is requested to assist.

He is a resource person who locates special materials needed by teachers. He may prepare lists of source materials to help teachers find appropriate music and recordings quickly and easily. He frequently acts as an agent for the teacher in contacting people who will come to the classroom for special musical demonstrations or performances. He helps the teacher and children evaluate their progress in music. He offers expert aid to the uncertain singer and helps provide special opportunities for the gifted child. He suggests and demonstrates activities that the retarded child can do with satisfaction and pleasure. He sometimes takes the role of a special music teacher while helping prepare a classroom teacher to take eventual responsibility for music teaching.

The music consultant plans with the teacher before working with the children and gives individual instruction to teachers who desire this aid. He is generally available for help by way of the telephone at almost any hour of the day. When he is asked to observe a classroom teacher teach music, he does not take notes, because this is poor psychology from the standpoint of both children and teacher. Instead, he has an early conference with this teacher before important items are forgotten. He usually watches the children, not the teacher, to find out how effective the teaching is.

When he works with teachers who have not taught music before, he finds one thing they can do well, and advances from there. He is apt to find subtle ways to feature the excellent classroom teacher of music (to show others that "it can be done") and he encourages intervisitation as an important type of in-service training. He keeps continually in mind that genuine personal interest and friendship, not coercion, form the foundations for modern supervision. He knows that each classroom teacher is *an individual* with talents, interests, and problems that make him, to some extent, different from any other teacher. Therefore, his aid is planned on an individual basis much of the time. To do this effectively he should know each teacher well, and he should not be assigned too large a number of teachers to assist. Although there has been established no exact number of teachers for which a music consultant should be responsible, it has been stated that he should be expected to aid no more than 75 as a full-time position. He should frequent the classroom and know the children.

The consultant plans teachers' meetings with great care. Immediately after school in the afternoon is the most common time for such gatherings, and the drinking of coffee may help to restore some energy to tired teachers who are psychologically at the close of their work day. The content of the meeting should be cooperatively planned and the consultant should strive to cover only a comparatively small amount of material—but to cover it thoroughly. A common fault of music specialists is that of attempting to treat too many things in a given time. There are many possible purposes for such teachers' meetings. Some of them are the planning of public programs and school-wide programs, helping the teachers of a specific grade level with common problems, helping a group of teachers who express special interest in learning a specific activity or skill, solving scheduling problems, demonstrating new materials and equipment, selecting new materials such as basal series books and supplementary books, and orienting teachers new to the school.

Another duty of the music consultant is aiding teachers in the use of audio-visual materials. This may include guidance in locating illustrative materials for bulletin boards, use of Song Bells as an audio-visual aid, use of the record machine and recordings, use of the tape recorder in music teaching, use of various film and slide projectors, and use of radio programs and the planning of live ones. It follows that the consultant evaluates commercial radio, television, and films for school use, and evaluates the new educational and children's recordings which are constantly being placed on the market. He may prepare special bulletins on audio-visual aids. These may contain help in the teachers' preparation for class listening to radio programs and viewing of television programs and films.

An additional responsibility is to recommend materials for the school library as well as for the teachers' resource library.

The consultant realizes that when the music program is an educational program in the best sense, it contains elements that can cement school and community relations. He is expected to be a member of community music groups and other groups. He supplies information about music activities of the school to the local press. He cooperates with local radio stations on programs that concern the school. He speaks at various meetings of civic groups to inform the public of the school music program, and frequently he presents students in musical performance and performs himself as well. He works actively with the Parent-Teacher Association. He aids schools, teachers, and children in preparing for all-school and all-city programs and festivals, and stimulates public interest in such performances. He frequently becomes the best-known teacher in the community because of his many duties which help unite school and community. In the performance of these duties he must strive to make the children's experiences educational, and to take care that children are not exploited for adult amusement.

In addition to the above, the consultant works closely with administrators, for he knows that if school principals do not understand and support the music program and help him and the teachers plan it, there will seldom be united faculty opinion or action for music. Consequently there must be preplanning with administrators, and conferences with them throughout the school year so that they are fully informed and have a positive, favorable attitude. Working with the administration in preparation of the music budget, inventory, and scheduling is another important phase of the consultant's duties unless a head supervisor or a director of music has these responsibilities.

Finally, the music consultant seeks ways to guide teachers into college extension courses and workshops that will aid their musical growth. He often plans with college staffs to help make possible such courses and summer session classes for his teachers. He may provide workshops in which he directs activities for his teachers at the beginning of the school year. He may also arrange for helpful visitations by the music education consultants employed by publishers of basal music series. He provides leadership for music education.

What is the position of the special music teacher?

When a music teacher is assigned to teach music as a special subject and thus perhaps has no official responsibility to help classroom teachers, he finds that he is unable to do his best for music without taking upon himself many of the duties of the music consultant. Although his time is limited, he will offer friendly aid to classroom teachers and he will be actively interested in expanding the use of music by all of the teachers because this assists his own program of teaching. It will be to his advantage to be able to relate some of the music he uses to the units of work being carried on in the various classrooms. The closer the relationship he establishes between himself and the classroom teachers, the more help he will be able to receive from them with regard to knowledge about the children under his instruction. He needs such help because he may teach several hundred children and thus knows them only superficially while each classroom teacher may have no more than 30 and thus knows them well. Since each needs the assistance of the other, there should always be close cooperation between the classroom teacher and this type of music teacher.

The professionally-minded classroom teacher is not content to teach without music. Therefore, even though a school district may consider music as a special subject to be taught by a special music teacher, the classroom teacher continues to accept certain responsibilities. He participates with his children when the specialist comes, aids him and learns from him. Since this classroom teacher draws upon music at any time it is needed during the school day, he is in effect a music teacher even though official responsibility in this instance happens to rest with the music specialist.

THINGS **TO** **DO**	1. Answer the questions stated in this chapter.
	2. If you are a teacher in service, use this chapter as a means of evaluating the music program in the school in which you now teach.
	3. If you are a student who is preparing to teach, use this chapter to evaluate the music program in the elementary school of your own childhood experience.

REFERENCES

Dykema, Peter W. and Hannah M. Cundiff, *School Music Handbook*, new ed. Boston: C. C. Birchard & Company, 1955.

Hartsell, O. M., *How Good Is Your Elementary Music Program?* Helena, Montana: Department of Public Instruction, 1953.

Morgan, Hazel N., ed., *Music in American Education,* Music Education Source
Book Number Two. Chicago: Music Educators National Conference, 1955.

Morgan, Russell V., *Music, a Living Power in Education.* New York: Silver Burdett Company, 1953.

Mursell, James L., *Music Education: Principles and Programs.* New York: Silver
Burdett Company, 1956.

Appendix

CODE OF ETHICS FOR THE TEACHING PROFESSION[1]

WE, THE MEMBERS of the National Education Association of the United States, hold these truths to be self-evident—
—that the primary purpose of education in the United States is to develop citizens who will safeguard, strengthen, and improve the democracy obtained thru a representative government;
—that the achievement of effective democracy in all aspects of American life and the maintenance of our national ideals depend upon making acceptable educational opportunities available to all;
—that the quality of education reflects the ideals, motives, preparation, and conduct of the members of the teaching profession;
—that whoever chooses teaching as a career assumes the obligation to conduct himself in accordance with the ideals of the profession.
As a guide for the teaching profession, the members of the National Education Association have adopted this code of professional ethics. Since all teachers should be members of a united profession, the basic principles herein enumerated apply to all persons engaged in the professional aspects of education—elementary, secondary, and collegiate.
First Principle: The primary obligation of the teaching profession is to guide children, youth, and adults in the pursuit of knowledge and skills, to prepare them in the ways of democracy, and to help them to become happy, useful, self-supporting citizens. The ultimate strength of the nation lies in the social responsibility, economic competence, and moral strength of the individual American.

In fulfilling the obligations of this first principle the teacher will—

(1) Deal justly and impartially with students regardless of their physical, mental, emotional, political, economic, social, racial, or religious characteristics.

[1] *NEA Handbook for Local, State, and National Associations* (Washington: National Education Association of the United States, 1954), pp. 361-363.

(2) Recognize the differences among students and seek to meet their individual needs.

(3) Encourage students to formulate and work for high individual goals in the development of their physical, intellectual, creative, and spiritual endowments.

(4) Aid students to develop an understanding and appreciation not only of the opportunities and benefits of American democracy but also of their obligations to it.

(5) Respect the right of every student to have confidential information about himself withheld except when its release is to authorized agencies or is required by law.

(6) Accept no remuneration for tutoring except in accordance with approved policies of the governing board.

Second Principle: The members of the teaching profession share with parents the task of shaping each student's purposes and acts toward socially acceptable ends. The effectiveness of many methods of teaching is dependent upon cooperative relationships with the home.

In fulfilling the obligations of this second principle the teacher will—

(1) Respect the basic responsibility of parents for their children.

(2) Seek to establish friendly and cooperative relationships with the home.

(3) Help to increase the student's confidence in his own home and avoid disparaging remarks which might undermine that confidence.

(4) Provide parents with information that will serve the best interests of their children, and be discreet with information received from parents.

(5) Keep parents informed about the progress of their children as interpreted in terms of the purposes of the school.

Third Principle: The teaching profession occupies a position of public trust involving not only the individual teacher's personal conduct, but also the interaction of the school and the community. Education is most effective when these many relationships operate in a friendly, cooperative, and constructive manner.

In fulfilling the obligations of this third principle the teacher will—

(1) Adhere to any reasonable pattern of behavior accepted by the community for professional persons.

(2) Perform the duties of citizenship, and participate in community activities with due consideration for his obligations to his students, his family, and himself.

(3) Discuss controversial issues from an objective point of view, thereby keeping his class free from partisan opinions.

(4) Recognize that the public schools belong to the people of the community, encourage lay participation in shaping the purposes of the school,

and strive to keep the public informed of the educational program which is being provided.

(5) Respect the community in which he is employed and be loyal to the school system, community, state, and nation.

(6) Work to improve education in the community and to strengthen the community's moral, spiritual, and intellectual life.

Fourth Principle: The members of the teaching profession have inescapable obligations with respect to employment. These obligations are nearly always shared employer-employee responsibilities based upon mutual respect and good faith.

In fulfilling the obligations of this fourth principle the teacher will—

(1) Conduct professional business thru the proper channels.

(2) Refrain from discussing confidential and official information with unauthorized persons.

(3) Apply for employment on the basis of competence only, and avoid asking for a specific position known to be filled by another teacher.

(4) Seek employment in a professional manner, avoiding such practices as the indiscriminate distribution of applications.

(5) Refuse to accept a position when the vacancy has been created thru unprofessional activity or pending controversy over professional policy or the application of unjust personal practices and procedures.

(6) Adhere to the conditions of a contract until service thereunder has been performed, the contract has been terminated by mutual consent, or the contract has otherwise been legally terminated.

(7) Give and expect due notice before a change of position is to be made.

(8) Be fair in all recommendations that are given concerning the work of other teachers.

(9) Accept no compensation from producers of instructional supplies when one's recommendations affect the local purchase or use of such teaching aids.

(10) Engage in no gainful employment, outside of his contract, where the employment affects adversely his professional status or impairs his standing with students, associates, and the community.

(11) Cooperate in the development of school policies and assume one's professional obligations thereby incurred.

(12) Accept one's obligation to the employing board for maintaining a professional level of service.

Fifth Principle: The teaching profession is distinguished from many other occupations by the uniqueness and quality of the professional relationships among all teachers. Community support and respect are influenced by the standards of teachers and their attitudes toward teaching and other teachers.

In fulfilling the obligations of this fifth principle the teacher will—

(1) Deal with other members of the profession in the same manner as he himself wishes to be treated.

(2) Stand by other teachers who have acted on his behalf and at his request.

(3) Speak constructively of other teachers, but report honestly to responsible persons in matters involving the welfare of students, the school system, and the profession.

(4) Maintain active membership in professional organizations and, thru participation, strive to attain the objectives that justify such organized groups.

(5) Seek to make professional growth continuous by such procedures as study, research, travel, conferences, and attendance at professional meetings.

(6) Make the teaching profession so attractive in ideals and practices that sincere and able young people will want to enter it.

CLASSIFIED LIST OF SONGS FOR COMMUNITY SINGING

Opening Songs

Hail, Hail, the Gang's All Here (using appropriate words)
S-M-I-L-E
He's a Jolly Good Fellow
Pack Up Your Troubles
Vive l'Amour
Hello Song (*Singing in Harmony*, p. 22)

Sentimental Songs

Let Me Call You Sweetheart
When Your Hair Has Turned to Silver
Moonlight and Roses
When Irish Eyes Are Smiling
When I Grow Too Old to Dream
My Wild Irish Rose
There's a Long, Long Trail
Keep the Home Fires Burning
Till We Meet Again
Let the Rest of the World Go By
The Bells of St. Mary's
I Want a Girl Just Like the Girl that Married Dear Old Dad
Shine On, Harvest Moon

Gay Nineties Songs

A Bicycle Built for Two
Sidewalks of New York (Eastside, Westside)
When You and I Were Young, Maggie
In the Shade of the Old Apple Tree
That Old Gang of Mine
After the Ball Is Over
School Days
In the Good Old Summertime
The Band Played On

Fun Songs

Polly Wolly Doodle
Old MacDonald
The Camptown Races
The Horses Run Around (Go Get the Axe)
I've Been Workin' on the Railroad
She'll Be Comin' Round the Mountain
Little Tom Tinker (action song: stand and sit when singing "Ma-a")
John Brown's Baby (action song. Tune: Battle Hymn of the Republic)
Oh! Susanna
Cindy

Folk Songs of Other Lands

Marianina (Italian)
Weggis Walking Song (Swiss)
Came a'Riding (Czech)
The Little Ole (Norwegian)
Over the Meadows (Czech)
Marching to Pretoria (Dutch South African)
All Through the Night (English)
Vrenily (Swiss)
Stellenbosche Boys (Dutch South African)
Alpine Morning (Swiss)
Cielito Lindo (Mexican)
Waltzing Matilda (Australian)
Santa Lucia (Italian)
Drink to Me Only with Thine Eyes (English)
John Peel (English)

Rounds

White Coral Bells
Kookaburra
Are You Sleeping?
Row, Row, Row Your Boat
Lovely Evening
Three Blind Mice
Puffer Billies (Down By the Station)

Old Favorites

Aunt Dinah's Quilting Party (Seeing Nellie Home)
Juanita

Long, Long Ago
Old Black Joe
My Old Kentucky Home
Carry Me Back to Old Virginny
Love's Old Sweet Song
Listen to the Mocking Bird
Silver Threads Among the Gold
Coming through the Rye
Tenting Tonight
Stars of the Summer Night
Darling Nellie Gray
Keep the Home Fires Burning
Home, Sweet Home
Old Folks at Home

American Folk Songs

Billy Boy
Red River Valley
Nellie Bly
Cape Cod Chantey
Short'nin' Bread
Down in the Valley
Clementine
Yellow Rose of Texas
Erie Canal
Home on the Range
Dear Evelina
The Old Gray Goose

Service Songs

The Marine's Hymn
The Caisson Song
I've Got Sixpence
Anchors Aweigh
The Army Air Corps

Spirituals

I Ain't Gonna Grieve No More
Dry Bones
Oh, Won't You Sit Down?
Were You There When They Crucified My Lord?
Standin' in the Need of Prayer
I Want to be Ready
Every Time I Feel the Spirit
I've Got Shoes
O, Dem Golden Slippers
The Old Ark's a'Moverin'
Swing Low, Sweet Chariot
Little David
Joshua Fit de Battle of Jericho

National and State Songs

America
The Star-Spangled Banner
America the Beautiful
Battle Hymn of the Republic
Columbia, the Gem of the Ocean
Dixie
Yankee Doodle
(appropriate state songs)

Songs for Grace

For Health and Strength (p. 188)
The Doxology
O, Give Thanks (round)

Sacred Songs

Onward Christian Soldiers
Song of Peace (Tune: Finlandia)
God of Our Fathers
Faith of Our Fathers
The Netherlands Hymn
A Mighty Fortress Is Our God

Closing Songs

Han Skal Leve (Danish)
God Be With You
Auld Lang Syne
A Perfect Day
Aloha Oe
Goodnight Ladies
Lullaby (Brahms)
Now the Day Is Over
Taps
In the Evening by the Moonlight (ending with Hear Them Bells)

SUGGESTIONS FOR SELF HELP IN EAR TRAINING

Most classroom teachers would like to write easily in music notation the songs the children create. This skill usually is attained only
after long study and drill. However, if the teacher will learn to be
more and more conscious of the relationships of scale tones, intervals, and chord tones, he will grow in his ability to *see* in notation
what he hears sung in the classroom.

The scale

When the steps of the scale are superimposed on the 1-3-5 chord (I chord), scale tones 1, 3, 5, and 8 are stable and the listener does not feel compelled to move from them to another tone. Because they are the home tones, 1 and 8 are highly stable; 3 will sometimes desire to move down to 1, and 5 will sometimes desire to move to 8 or 1. Scale tones 2, 4, 6, and 7 are definitely restless and wish to move to tones of the 1-3-5 chord. Tone 7 leads strongly to 8, and 4 leads strongly to 3. Tone 6 finds satisfaction in leading to 5, and 2 leads to 1 (and, less strongly, to 3). The illustration represents the usual movement of tones in melody lines or parts of melodies that are accompanied by the I chord. Although one will find many exceptions to this, a valuable exercise for the learner of ear training is to write on staff paper his own melody lines in which the pitches are kept moving in accordance with those of the drawing. Then he should sing what he has written, using the piano or bells as a temporary guide if necessary.

Intervals

Another suggestion is to sing interval drills, learning to identify intervals first based on the scale, then later independent of the scale, and in connection with songs. Relating the different intervals to the scale and to particular songs aids in learning to identify them, i.e., "see" them in notation. (Refer to Chapter Seven, p. 173.) Playing intervals on piano or bells will aid at first. Learn to sing them independently of such help.

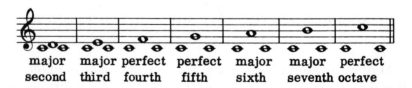

major	major	perfect	perfect	major	major	perfect
second	third	fourth	fifth	sixth	seventh	octave

All of the above intervals are major intervals except the fourth, fifth, and octave, which are called "perfect." Minor intervals are ½ step smaller than major intervals. They can be represented by a minus sign.

| minor | minor | perfect | perfect | minor | minor | octave |
| second | third | fourth | fifth | sixth | seventh | |

Two people working together on a study of intervals can take turns at the piano or bells, one playing intervals which the other is asked to identify, thus making something of a game of this drill. (When a minor interval or a perfect interval is made a half-step smaller, it is called a *diminished* interval. When a major interval or a perfect interval is made a half-step larger, it is called an *augmented* interval.)

Chord tones

The practice of piano chording is of great help in ear training because the player can both see and hear what he does. When the learner is well grounded in piano chording, melodies written in notation become much more understandable. A simple example of this is the song *Bow Belinda*. The person who knows piano chording sees almost instantly that the melody is based on I and V chords in root (1-3-5) position, and that it ends with a scale line.

BOW BELINDA

Bow, bow, bow, Be-lin-da, bow, bow, bow, Be-lin - da,

Bow, bow, bow, Be-lin-da, Won't you be my dar-ling?

The student of ear training should analyze melodies in terms of chords, scales, and intervals. (See Things To Do, No. 10, Chapter Three.) He should write melodies to sing and to play that are based on his piano chording and on his awareness of scale lines of notes. Singing chord progressions is another important way to increase one's skill in ear training.

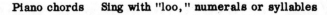

Piano chords   Sing with "loo," numerals or syllables

With this introduction, the learner can write his own chord progressions in the three positions in various keys and practice singing them. Progressions employing minor chords or both major and minor chords can be written and sung after the major chords are well learned. Tone "7" of the V_7 chord can also be added when desired.

Thoughtful drill on the above suggestions and application of the concepts involved should help make the melody lines of the songs children create become more and more readily identifiable.

INDEXES

Index of Songs

Index